LATIN AMERICA IN WORLD POLITICS

LATIN AMERICA IN WORLD POLITICS

NORMAN A. BAILEY

FOREWORD BY / RONALD M. SCHNEIDER

 WALKER AND COMPANY
NEW YORK

This book is dedicated, with gratitude,
to my teacher, Professor Frank Tannenbaum

FOREWORD

A decade ago the literature on Latin America affairs outside the field of history was sparse and, with a few notable exceptions, unsystematic. Since that time a large volume of books treating a wide range of topics have been published in the United States, including a score of studies whose quality and sophistication have earned recognition for their authors. Now a new generation of young economists, sociologists, and political scientists is rapidly building upon the foundations established since 1957 by scholars such as Robert Alexander, Federico Gil, Wendell Gordon, Albert Hirschman, John Johnson, Edwin Lieuwen, Kalman Silvert, and Robert Scott.[1] In the area of comparative politics this enrichment of the academic literature has been significant from year to year. In addition to a variety of monographs, symposia, and texts newly available each time a course on Latin American politics is to be offered, sufficient articles of value have appeared during recent years to provide the basis for several books of readings.

In the field of international relations, however, the situation is much less satisfactory: indeed, relatively less so than two decades ago. A half dozen books have been published on the inter-American system, most of which focus on the formal institutions and juridical problems of the Organization of American States. While the more analytical of these (such as John Dreier's little volume for the Council on Foreign Relations or Gordon Connell-Smith's Royal Institute of International Affairs study), along with J. L. Mecham's historical survey of relations between the United States and Latin American countries, do provide textbook material for narrowly defined introductory courses, the broader aspects of inter-American politics have been all but ignored. Only in the works of Bryce Wood on the decade and a half preceding 1943, and sketchily in Edwin Lieuwen's brief policy paper on contemporary problems, do they receive adequate treatment.[2] Otherwise the international relations of the Latin American republics, and particularly their role in the world arena rather than just in hemispheric affairs, have received very little serious attention, a situation which is reflected in the almost complete neglect of the area in general texts and analyses of international politics.

This unsatisfactory situation has increasingly concerned teachers of international relations, but Norman Bailey was the first to respond with a determination to act. Having specialized in international politics during the course of his doctoral studies at Columbia University and having an abiding interest in Latin America, Professor Bailey developed the basic

[1] For a comprehensive discussion of the state of scholarship in this field through 1963, see Charles Wagley (ed.), *Social Science Research on Latin America*, Columbia University Press, 1964.
[2] See particularly Professor Wood's *The Making of the Good Neighbor Policy*, Columbia University Press, 1959, and Lieuwen's *The Challenge to Security in Latin America*, The Ohio State University Pamphlet Series Number 4, 1966.

scheme of this book in the crucible of his teaching experience at Queens College of the City University of New York.

Conceived as an effort to deal with Latin American reality in the context of atomic age world politics, his text seeks to integrate the study of Latin America's international role and behavior with a systematic framework for the analysis of international politics as that discipline has developed in the post-war period. This is an ambitious undertaking, particularly in light of the overall weakness and manifest flaws in the infrastructure of monographic studies upon which such a broad synthesis must rest. Hence it is far more to the author's credit that he has substantially completed this undertaking than he is to be faulted for the gaps in our knowledge and understanding which may still exist after a reading of his work. Bailey's own subsequent work will help bridge some of the crevices, and this far-ranging volume with its firm opinions and provocative interpretations will certainly help prepare future scholars to carry out the systematic research necessary to amplify our understanding of the role of a developing Latin America in the life of a changing world. It should also enable the lay reader concerned, as we all should be, with questions of foreign affairs to gain a far more adequate appreciation of Latin America's problems and position. And this it appears to me is more of a contribution than can normally be expected from a college textbook, even one which so well reflects the industry and intelligence of its author. Thus, while not in full agreement personally or perhaps politically with many of Norman Bailey's viewpoints and interpretations, professionally I can and do recommend his study to anyone seeking information and clarification on this relatively neglected, though increasingly important, subject of *Latin America in World Politics*.

Ronald M. Schneider
Rio de Janeiro, Brazil
October, 1966

PREFACE

The purpose of this volume is to analyze the role of Latin America in world politics, both for the general reader and for the student. It is structured so as to be usable as a text in courses on the subject; however (as will immediately become apparent), it is not a mere compendium of facts or historical data, but rather seeks to put the international behavior of the Latin American states in an analytical framework of explanatory and predictive power.

In the analysis of the role played in international politics by any single country, group of countries, or region, there are two interdependent variables: the unchanging, or only very slowly changing, nature of the international system as such on the one hand, and the internal political and social structure of the country or region under study on the other. This internal, or domestic, structure, ranging from geographic location to mass and individual psychology, conditions, and to some extent determines, the interaction of the unit actor under analysis with the other unit actors in international society, limited by the imperatives of the system itself.

For this reason, it is impossible to properly understand the role of a given region in international politics without having a basic knowledge or understanding of the dynamics both of the international system and of the region. All specific issues and situations are the result of their interaction. For this reason, PART I of this book will be devoted to an overview, necessarily brief, of the setting of world politics (the society of the sovereign state) and an equally brief overview of those aspects of the domestic situation of Latin America that most directly bear upon international politics.* PART II will demonstrate in what ways these elements interact to produce those challenges to Latin America that arise from the international configuration. PART III will analyze the various ways Latin America has tried to meet those challenges.

For the purposes of our analysis, the term "Latin America" will be used to signify all the externally sovereign states of the Western Hemisphere south of the United States, with the exception of Jamaica, Trinidad, and Guyana. It is not yet clear whether these former British colonies will eventually form part of Latin America or some other partial international system. If they eventually join the Organization of American States, they will be subject to the same challenges as the Latin American states, and their patterns of response, most probably, will be similar.

Professors Frank Tannenbaum, Ronald M. Schneider, and Harry J. Psomiades, as well as Mrs. Edith Lipiner, took the time to read this work in manuscript form and give me the benefit of their invaluable comments and observations. Where their suggestions have not been followed a

---

* Those who already have a substantial theoretical knowledge of international politics may wish to skip Chapter 1; those with a substantial knowledge of Latin America may wish to skip Chapter 2.

poorer book has very probably resulted. The responsibility for any remaining factual errors is, of course, entirely mine.

Thanks are also due to Mrs. Lipiner for bibliographical assistance.

The Center for Strategic Studies of Georgetown University kindly gave its permission to reprint Chapter 2, a slightly different version of which appeared in *Latin America: Politics, Economics, and Hemispheric Security* (New York: Praeger, 1965).

NORMAN A. BAILEY
NEW YORK, NEW YORK
JUNE, 1966

TABLE OF CONTENTS

INTRODUCTORY NOTE

A / POLITICAL SCIENCE

Even a brief discussion of the nature of international politics cannot deal
with that specialized subject only. *International politics* is not an isolated
phenomenon—it is a specialized form of *politics,* and exhibits all the
characteristics of the political act whenever, however, and wherever performed, merely supplementing those characteristics with additional, unique
aspects. Thus, a discussion of international politics must be prefaced by
an outline of the phenomenon of politics and the science that studies it.

Political science, as a science, is in its infancy. Although rare individuals attempted the scientific study of politics earlier, extensive systematic analysis of the political process does not antedate World War II.
One need only consider the controversies that still rage, and the basic
discoveries still being made, in the physical and biological sciences, as
well as the still-precarious state of economics, the oldest of the scientifically-
studied social sciences, to realize how far political science has to go.
Even in the most elementary requirements of a scientific discipline, definition and measurement, political science has barely begun its development.
As a consequence, the statements and conclusions of this note and
Chapter 1 must be taken as indicative and suggestive only.

They are, in fact, part of a theory of international politics, the
hypotheses of which have been only incompletely tested. Nevertheless,
they represent (as does any theory) a way of structuring our perception
of reality so that it makes logical and empirical sense. This is the way,
given the present state of political analysis, that the author finds explains
the most, and does the least violence to international society as it exists
in reality.

This is, perhaps, the place to say a word about the role of value-
judgments in any scientific study. It is not correct to say that scientists
are, or should be, value-free. All scientists have their own values based
on whatever ethical or moral system they subscribe to, and they exercise
value-judgments in choosing their discipline and in deciding what problems to study within that discipline. In the study of the problems they
choose, they must, at least in the social sciences, take into account the
value-systems and judgments of the people and societies they are analyzing.
Since all conscious human beings have values and act upon them, any
analysis ignoring this fact will be partial and, thus, at least to some
extent, invalid. The process of analysis itself, however, must be value-
free to the extent that the investigating scientist can possibly make it.
The terms, good and bad, right and wrong, can properly refer in science
only to the greater or lesser effectiveness of a proposed method in the
achievement of a stated goal. It is in the choosing of goals that ethical

and moral judgments must be applied, and these are outside the scope of science.

B / THE POLITICAL PROCESS

For our purposes here, "political science" may be defined as the study of social power. "Power," in turn, may be defined as the ability to do, and "social power" as the ability to effect or prevent change in the societal relationships of men, using the adjective "societal" in the broadest sense, to include all human interaction. All human action is goal-oriented. Human beings have only two means available to them for the achievement of their goals: the expenditure of wealth, and the exertion of power (studied by economics and political science, respectively). Wealth is expended, and power exerted, by human beings individually and in groups (studied by psychology and sociology, respectively). All the social sciences are, thus, inextricably interrelated, and any attempt to study political man divorced from economic man is doomed to failure, as is any attempt to study man in groups divorced from man as an individual, or vice versa. Still, without ignoring the other factors involved, our study will be principally concerned with power. As social power consists of the influencing of the behavior of others toward the achievement of our ends, it inevitably involves conflict, since if there is no opposing force (even if only inertia) no power is exerted.

All human action relating to other human beings may be thought of as taking place at some point on a cooperation–coercion continuum. The modal points of absolute cooperation and absolute coercion probably do not exist in reality. That is, every act has some element in it of both cooperation and coercion, although the extremes can be approached.

COOPERATION————————COERCION

A hypothetical act of pure cooperation would be an economic exchange, into which the element of persuasion, or influence, enters not at all. This is, in its purest form, the basis of the subject-matter of economics. Coercion, in its purest form, would consist of an act of force, causing another person to do something, without his even having the possibility of preventing it by committing suicide. Political science studies the element of coercion present in every case of human interaction, again, without forgetting the element of cooperation also present. A word of caution here. The terms "power," "conflict," and "coercion" do not necessarily imply the presence of physical force or violence. Violence is merely one way (and, by no means, always the most effective way) to exert power. Persuasion, pressure, threats, display of latent power, and many other means may also be appropriately used, and, generally, involve lower costs and risks than violence. The political process, then, is the exertion of social power for the purpose of the achievement of human goals.

C / POLITICAL ORGANIZATION

An organization is a group of human beings with a common goal, or goals (and not merely individual goals held in common), with a role structure designed to help attain those goals. This role structure is, in the vast majority of cases, hierarchical. Organizations vastly enhance the individual's ability to achieve his goals through the use of pooled wealth and power. As a result, most meaningful acts of social power take place through organizations. The role of the individual may be most important, and even crucial; but even so, that individual usually attempts to achieve his goals by making use of an existing organization, or by creating a new one.

In most societies, there is a multiplicity of organizations, each exerting power against the others, forming coalitions and alliances for particular purposes, and with their own sources and uses of wealth. There are many ways to categorize, or classify, such organizations, a common one being according to the area of their concern, such as economic, professional, cultural, political, and so forth. The political process within a society is precisely the process of the power interaction between and among these groups, generally taking place within the parameters of the rules of the society involved, although occasionally spilling out beyond those parameters (illegal behavior, fraud, rebellion, etc.). Each such organization has a governing, or directing, group, which during the time of its tenure is responsible for the setting of the goals of that organization, and the methods to be used to try to attain them. It also has a bureaucracy of some kind, responsible for the day-to-day continuity of the organization, and for the implementation of the policies as set forth by the governing group. In very small organizations, the governing group and the bureaucracy may be identical.

One such organization, present in most societies, is the state. The governing group within the state is the government, and there is always a state bureaucracy as well. In some societies, the armed forces form part of the state bureaucracy, and in others, they form a separate group or groups within society, pressuring, from outside the state, in the manner of other pressure groups. The state has certain functions and goals within society, as do all organizations, the scope and nature of those functions varying with each society, but almost always including the maintenance of internal tranquillity, the adjudication of domestic disputes, and the protection of the society from attack by other societies. In order to effectively perform these functions, the state attempts to monopolize the use of physical violence in society, although it is never entirely successful.

The struggle among the various organizations in a pluralistic society takes place through a wide range of formal and informal means, and the process is essentially the same in both democratic and authoritarian societies. The difference between the two societal forms results from the individual and group distrust of the state among other elements in society, as the single organization most dangerous to the others, because of its attempted monopoly of violence. As a result of this fear, the democratic societal form was developed, whereby the government (the governing group within the state that decides its policies and methods) was chosen from outside the state by means of some form of election, thereby supposedly serving the ends of the electorate (singly or as organized in groups), rather than ends of its own.

In a totalitarian society, however, the political organization known as the "party" attempts to destroy pluralism, and create a monistic society, identifying the government with the party, the state with the government, and the society with the state, so that private organizations are transformed into state organs (see Fig. 1). The totalitarian monistic ideal has been approximated, but never fully attained, and from the limited experience we have had with totalitarian societies, we may tentatively conclude that they are unlikely to last in their monistic form, but rather evolve into authoritarianism, because of the use they must make of modern techniques of economic and political control—this very technological complexity, perhaps, exerting irresistible pressure toward pluralism.

Any group may be said to have authority if it combines power and legitimacy. A group may have legitimacy, but no power, such as an exile government. It does not exercise authority. A group may have power without legitimacy, as with a usurping band seizing power by fraud against the will of the bulk of the politically conscious members of society. Such a group is *in power,* but does not have *authority,* and will, thus, have to use maximum violence in order to maintain itself, and, if it does not successfully act to gain legitimacy, it is unlikely to remain in power long. Legitimacy, quite simply, is the acceptance of a particular group as governing group by the bulk of the politically conscious population. It is, thus, the people, in any form of society, who confer legitimacy (and, therefore, authority) on any government. The more legitimacy a government has, the less violence it needs to practice on other groups within society and on the populace at large.

Law is the codification of the power structure of a given society at a given period of history. As with any form of codification, law has a tendency to lag behind changes in the power structure, and, thus, is always slightly out-of-date in any rapidly changing society. Whatever constellation of power forces is in the ascendancy at any given moment, however, will change the legal code to conform to its interests and to its value-system, in such a way as to assist it to gain authority and to attain its goals. Although, for their own purposes, the groups in power in a society at a

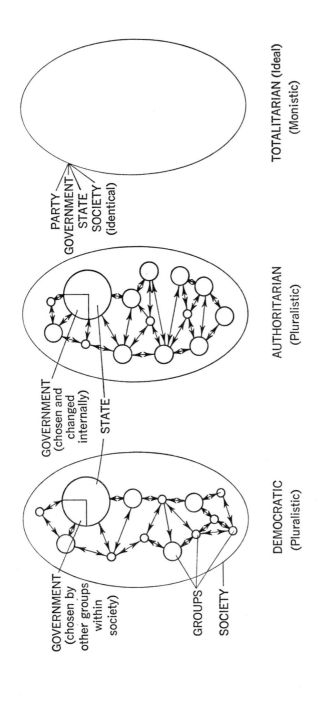

Fig. 1 — Societal Forms

given time may present their legal system as being of divine, or natural, origin, law is a human artifact applied by human beings. For purposes of scientific analysis, the term "justice" can have no other meaning than the impartial and expeditious application of the laws, whatever they are.

One of the most common ways in which a government attempts to gain legitimacy, and, thus, authority, in both the domestic and international political fields of action, is through the replacement of ethnic nationalism with state patriotism as the primary psychological motivating element in the political behavior of its citizens. An ethnic nation is a group of human beings exhibiting a certain cultural identity, usually expressed in language, religion, costume, music, habit, custom, and so forth. A particular society may include several nations, as in the case of the Italians, French, and Germans in Switzerland; a nation may spread out over several societies, as with the French nation, found in France, Belgium, Luxembourg, Switzerland, and Canada, or a society and a nation may coincide, as with The Netherlands. A nation is not, as such, an organization, and, thus, only if organized on the basis of its ethnic nationalism, will it exert power, as with the Zionist Jews prior to the establishment of Israel. The governments of those societies consisting largely of a single ethnic nation obviously have an initial advantage in attempting to develop legitimacy and authority through state loyalty.

Part One / **THE SETTING**

1 / THE SOCIETY OF THE SOVEREIGN STATE

Although the astronomers cannot control the movements of the stars, they have discovered systematic regularities in their movements. The crux of the matter is whether regularities can be discovered which permit the organization of the materials of international politics within a simple framework of reasonable explanatory or predictive power.

MORTON A. KAPLAN
*System and Process in
International Politics*

A / INTERNATIONAL POLITICS

International politics takes place in a quasi-anarchic framework. It is anarchic because there is no overall structure encompassing international society as such, but rather competing societies, operating in accordance with few generally recognized rules of conduct, and within no functioning legal system. It is not fully anarchic because some order is provided by formal and informal arrangements between and among states, entered into for their own purposes, to be sure, but providing some degree of structure, nevertheless.

International politics is the study of the political interaction of states. As such, it is a misnomer, since it is not the study of the political interaction of nations, although national politics, as any form of domestic politics, may (and often does) affect international politics. The study and phenomenon should, therefore, both be called *interstate* politics, but the term "international" is too commonly used and widely accepted to attempt to change it now. Ordinarily, international politics does not study the relations among non-state organizations from different societies, again, unless, and to the extent that, their activities affect interstate relations.

Politics within a quasi-anarchic society does not, by any means, take place without pattern or design. If it did, it could not be studied in a scientific fashion, nor could foreign policy be made in a rational manner. The very absence of universally accepted, or enforced, parameters of action, such as exist in domestic societies, paradoxically makes for a

3

greater uniformity of action and response than in domestic society. Within the societal parameters, narrow or broad, domestic politics has great freedom of maneuver. In international society, in contrast, act and response are more narrowly bounded by the fact that every action will evoke a limited number of responses by the other acting units, thereby limiting the scope of further action.

Certain African tribes, notably the Nuer of the southern Sudan, also lack a state structure, and the study of the political process within these societies can be highly suggestive, with reference to international politics. Jural institutions in such societies rest on the principles of self-help and compensation, and "neutral" areas are provided, where warring clans can meet and negotiate. "Stability is maintained by an equilibrium at every line of cleavage and every point of divergent interests in the social structure." [1] "The whole process of fusion and fission of the segments depends, then, upon conflict. If conflict from outside the segment's parts threatens, the parts unite and the segment takes on an active role in the prosecution of the conflict. . . . Thus segments take on and discard their role only by virtue of the conflict which threatens from outside the segment's parts." [2] The relatively narrow limits of action, and the governing role of conflict, are two of the most important characteristics of international politics.

The bounding limits of international action, and the difference in demonstrated power among the various units therein, lead to the role structuring of these units in a series of hierarchical constructs, organized either completely informally through the realities of power relationships, or formally through treaties, alliances, and international regional organizations. Within this hierarchical structure, the paramounts are those states which are not, themselves, dominated as to foreign policy formulation by any other, not because of their geographic position, or because of the balance of power at any given historical moment, but because of their own ability to maintain autonomous action. The paramounts almost always have under them a hierarchical structure of states, which, to a greater or lesser extent, follow their foreign policy initiatives, although that structure may be very rudimentary, as was the case with Austria–Hungary before World War I. A given paramount may have a very complex hierarchical structure subject to its influence, in which case the structure is likely to be compartmentalized into various sub-hierarchies, subject to sub-paramounts, which direct them, subject, in turn, to the general direction of the paramount. Below the paramounts and sub-paramounts are the clients, who follow the more-or-less detailed foreign policy directives of the paramounts. Paramount dominance may extend to the domestic politics of a client, although this is not essential (and may be damaging) to the relationship. In its loosest form, the paramount merely sets forth

[1] M. Fortes and E. E. Evans-Pritchard, *African Political Systems* (London, 1940), p. 14.
[2] Henry Ross, "Inter-State Society and Nuer Society: Variations of Ordered Anarchy," unpublished manuscript. See also E. E. Evans-Pritchard, *The Nuer* (London, 1940).

parameters of international action, beyond which the client may not stray without the risk of enforcement action (reprisal) by the paramount. The paramounts supply their clients with protection and assistance, and the clients supply the paramounts with foreign policy support.

There are normally states which, for the time being, do not form part of any hierarchical system. These may be termed "floaters." A floater is usually able to maintain its status because its geographic position enables it to preserve a precarious balance among two or more paramounts, all of which covet it as a client. Sometimes this arrangement is formalized, as with the creation of "buffers" and "neutralized" states. The formal arrangements are not necessarily longer-lasting than the informal, however.

It has already been stated that conflict plays the governing role in international relations. International conflict may be categorized with reference to its structure, in terms of the likely intensity (of escalation possibility) of a conflict among its units:

a. *A client versus another client of the same paramount.* This is the least intense form of international conflict, because it can usually be controlled and kept within bounds by the paramount in question. The danger of an increase in intensity comes from the possible attempt by another paramount to take advantage of the conflict to detach one of the clients from its hierarchical structure. (This case also applies to conflicts between clients and sub-paramounts of the same paramount.)

b. *A floater versus a floater.* This is a conflict of greater potential intensity, because of the temptation of the paramounts to take sides, in order (hopefully) to absorb one of the contending parties as a client.

c. *A floater versus a client.* The paramount will support its client, leading to offers of support for the floater by other paramounts, in the hope of absorbing it.

d. *A client of one paramount versus a client of another paramount.* The dangers of an increase in intensity are obvious here, with both paramounts supporting their respective clients.

e. *A paramount versus a floater.* Since the floater has been able to remain so only by playing off one or more of the paramounts against the others, such a conflict is a direct challenge by one of the paramounts against one or more of the others.

f. *A client versus its own paramount.* This takes two forms. In one, the client is trying to establish itself as a paramount in its own right. In itself, this is likely to be an intense struggle, and other paramounts may be drawn in. In the other form, a client attempts to detach itself from the hierarchical system of its paramount. This is often done with the goading and promises of help of another paramount, and, even if not, another paramount is likely to step in, once the conflict has begun. A simple dispute between a client and its paramount, perhaps over interference in domestic politics, may provide another paramount with detachment opportunities. As we have already noted, there is no such thing as power without opposition, and, thus, a state can establish itself as a paramount only by successfully challenging one or more of the already-existing paramounts, as Japan did in the Russo–Japanese War of 1904–5.

g. *A client of one paramount versus another paramount.* If the paramount supports its client, it will come into direct conflict with another paramount. If it does not, it risks losing its client.

h. *A paramount versus another paramount.* This is the most intense form of international conflict, and may lead, as in the World Wars, to the involvement of all the paramounts and most of their clients.

A state, like an individual, may subscribe to a system of values beyond survival and self-defense. Adherence to such an ideology will undoubtedly condition, to some extent, its international behavior, and this must be taken into account, both in the analysis of that behavior and in the policy decisions of other states. Again, however, because of the very nature of international society, scope for value-directed action is more circumscribed than in domestic society, even in those domestic societies with a semi-totalitarian structure. It is a factor that cannot be ignored, however, without risk of gross error in analysis. The same may be said for the role of irrational behavior in international relations. "Irrational behavior" may be defined as the pursuance of an impossible goal, or pursuance of a tenable goal by completely inappropriate means. Since the state is an organization without life of its own, but rather, impelled by a group of men (the government), to the extent that those men are irrational, the behavior of the state will be irrational. This is obviously a greater danger the smaller the governing group, and reaches its most intense form in tightly controlled dictatorships, where the aberrations of a single man, or a very small group of men, may condition the actions of the state in the international arena. Ignoring the element of possible irrationality may also result in gross errors of analysis and gross policy errors. Both ideology and irrationality, however, can be provided for in analysis and in policy-making.

In a domestic society, the weaker units generally attempt to defend themselves against the stronger through organization and through use of the parameter-rules of that society—that is, through law. A weaker unit may also, of course, try to defend itself by seeking the protection of the strong, or by playing strong units off against each other. This type of behavior is the more likely to occur, the more anarchic the domestic society in question. Since there is no state structure in international society, the weaker units can best protect themselves from disappearance or injury by becoming the clients of a paramount (it may very well be unavoidable, in any case). There are obvious risks and dangers in this, of course. The paramount may decide, at some point, to absorb the client, either by physical incorporation into its own society, or by reducing the client to the position of a will-less puppet or satellite. If its geographic position is of a certain type, and if it can bargain effectively within the power organization of international society at a given time, a weaker state may be able to defend itself without the necessity of becoming a client. This is a highly precarious position, however, and subject to any

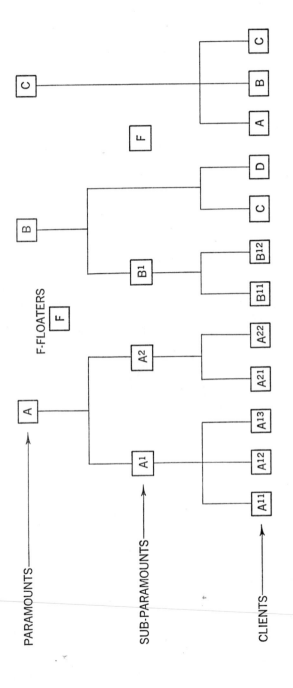

Fig. 2 — The State System

major change in the international situation. Generally, maintaining a high level of military strength will also help a state remain a floater. The time has passed when a state could remain a floater indefinitely, simply by being so isolated and inaccessible that no paramount was interested in dominating it.

Since law is the codification of the power structure of a given society at a given moment, international law plays only a minor role in international politics, except at those times, and with reference to those issues, where the paramounts agree to uphold certain rules of conduct. There was such a time between the Treaty of Westphalia in 1648 and the outbreak of World War I in 1914. If a weaker state violated an agreed-upon tenet of international law, it would be punished by one or more of the paramounts, with the acquiescence of the others. Since 1914, there has been no such agreement among the paramounts, and, since 1945, most of the newly independent states have also refused to accept many of the rules of nineteenth-century international law. As a result, international law in the twentieth century has been an unimportant element in international politics. Even as a propaganda device, it has been of limited usefulness, since an appeal to a principle that is not believed in can be of little effect. At present, states follow the rules of international law (where any such are discernible) when and if doing so is in their own best interests. As in Nuer society, the rules of international society can be reduced to two: self-help and compensation—a state defends itself if it can, and pays compensation if it must, or if it feels that, in doing so, it will attain a more-desired goal.

Organization takes place in international society through the voluntary or coerced association of states for the attainment of mutual goals. These organizations take many forms, some of which are purely informal, but not less effective for that. When formal, that is, when set forth in a treaty, such an association is termed an alliance. When informal, a bloc. When the association is among equals in the international hierarchy, it is entered into voluntarily by the parties involved. When among states of different rank in the hierarchy, it is forced, either directly by the paramount involved, or indirectly through particular circumstance. Two conditions are necessary for a lasting alliance, among individuals, groups, or states—complementarity of resources and similarity of goals. As long as these conditions last (whether spontaneous or induced), the alliance is likely to last. If they disappear, the alliance is in trouble. Since conflict is the governing factor in international society, strong and durable alliances are ordinarily formed either through the medium of an outside threat or in order to pool power for a revisionist international policy.

There is a tendency in twentieth-century international society toward the formation of regional groupings of states, some of them tending toward political union. This is a natural tendency, since the necessary instruments and symbols of international power can today be acquired in sufficient number only by resource aggregates of considerable size. Regional international organizations fall into one of four categories:

a. *Ordinary alliances dressed up as regional organizations.* NATO, SEATO, CENTO, and the Warsaw Pact are examples of this. Such "regional organizations" differ in no analytically important way from any other alliance.

b. *Hierarchical structures, of the ordinary kind, structured as regional organizations for the purpose of more effective control.* The Organization of American States is the best example of this. The British Commonwealth, at one time (when Great Britain was a paramount), was an example of this also, but is no longer. COMECON, though ostensibly economic, is actually such an organization.

c. *Groupings of more or less equal states, on an ethnic or other non-power basis.* The Arab League and the Organization of African Unity are examples of this. Because they lack leadership, and because their basis of membership is basically irrelevant to international politics, these regional organizations are relatively ineffective.

d. *Economic groupings to increase the wealth, and, thus, also, the power resources, of the member states.* The European Economic Community, the Central American Common Market, the European Free Trade Area, and the Latin American Free Trade Association are examples of this. Such a grouping may, of course, be changed into Type b, if one member gains ascendancy. It may also change into a political union, with the member states submerging their individual sovereignties. This is unlikely to happen with any of the other forms of regional organization, except in Type b, through absorption by the paramount.

Besides these regional organizations, there are two forms of "universal" international organization, the functional and the political. The functional, such as the Universal Postal Union, the World Health Organization, the International Labour Organization, and others, provide services to members that they would be able to provide less effectively separately. Because they serve the self-interest of their members without threatening their power position, such organizations are, generally, rather successful. There have been two formal, "universal" organizations of the political type: the League of Nations, which was actually far from universal in membership, and the United Nations, which has come closer to the ideal of having as members all the externally sovereign states of the world. In discussing these organizations, it is necessary to consider the role of authority in international society. No single state in history has been able to dominate the entire world by force, and then attempt to begin the process of creating legitimacy, and thereby, authority. Thus, no single organization has ever been able to claim that it is accorded legitimacy by the bulk of the politically conscious peoples of the world. Therefore, only the individual states have, to varying degrees, legitimacy and authority. For this reason, international political organizations, such as the League and the United Nations, can provide a sort of "neutral" ground for meeting and negotiation (as do the huts of the "leopard-skin chiefs" in Nuer society); they can operate effectively in the economic and social fields, in the same way as the functional organizations; they can serve as a propaganda forum; and they can operate effectively in the political field when the paramount members agree on a particular action, and impose that action on clients and floaters. This, however, is the limit of their effectiveness. They are instruments that the member states use for their own purposes, and to further their own goals within the limitations of the society in which they interact.

B / FOREIGN POLICY

All states have a foreign policy, and the overall foreign policy of any given state is always one of two basic types: revision or stasis. Those states are revisionist that are generally dissatisfied with the current structuring of international society. They, thus, desire to change or revise it. Stasis states, on the other hand, desire to maintain the structure of international society more or less as it is. The most important requirement that a paramount makes on a client is that, with reference to the larger issues of the moment, the client follow the general foreign-policy orientation of the paramount, and be either a revisionist or stasis power, according to the policy of the paramount.

There are two basic responses that a stasis power may have to the actions of revisionist powers. It may appease them, by withdrawing from some portion of its international position, such as giving up territory, surrendering clients, withdrawing military forces from foreign bases, paying an indemnity, etc. The response of appeasement is effective only if the state using it has correctly ascertained that the revisionist state is appeasable, and that what is given up will, in fact, appease it. A classic case of successful appeasement was the withdrawal of Great Britain, during the Venezuelan crisis of 1895–96, from its position as paramount in Latin America. The other basic response to a policy of revision is containment. This may be passive, responding only to initiatives of the revisionist state, or dynamic, attempting to maintain the general balance by probing at the positions of the adversary.

Foreign policy, as domestic state policy, is determined by the governing group within the state—the government. Foreign policy, however, is implemented by the choice, or mix, of strategies employed, and, in their choice as well as in their carrying-out, the state bureaucracy has a principal role. Since the success or failure of any realistic policy is dependent on the strategies employed in its implementation, this gives the state bureaucracy a great deal of influence on the course of international politics. This is, obviously, especially true of those elements of the bureaucracy directly concerned with international affairs, particularly, the foreign office and diplomatic corps, the intelligence agency, the propaganda agency, and the armed forces. For this reason, efficient coordination among these several bureaucratic agencies is of the utmost importance for the successful pursuit of foreign policy, and this is particularly difficult in those societies where the armed forces are, in fact, an autonomous group within society. The conduct of foreign policy is often rendered difficult in democratic societies, for effective implementation of strategy requires continuity of policy. This can be achieved by withdrawing foreign policy from the public political arena, as was done in nineteenth-century Great Britain. If this is not done, because the fullest possible democratic control over policy is considered a more important value, it must be recognized that the choice has its cost in lessened international effectiveness.

Strategies employed to implement foreign policy fall within six general categories. The first, and most common, is *diplomacy*. Diplomacy, the process of international political negotiation, must, to be effective, involve elements of all, or some, of the other strategies. Nevertheless, it is not merely a synonym for strategy itself—other elements must be employed as inducements or threats, but, if the diplomatic negotiation is successful, they may never actually be employed. In short, diplomacy is the art of trying to achieve the ends of the state in the international sphere without the necessity of employing other, more costly and dangerous, strategies.

Propaganda is closely allied with diplomacy, and is often used in conjunction with it, to try to create the conditions necessary for successful negotiation. There are two principal goals that propaganda may be directed toward—creating the impression that the position of the state using it is right and inevitable, or that the other state's position is morally wrong, or dangerous to its own "best" interests or those of other states. Thus, the various techniques of propaganda in international politics may be directed toward the influencing of mass, or elite, opinion in the society using it, in the opposing society, or in societies not directly concerned with the dispute, but which can influence the outcome.

Economic strategies may be employed toward the strengthening of the employing state and its allies, toward the gaining of new allies, or the weakening of an adversary. Obviously, economic strategy is most effective when used by a state which has substantial surplus wealth which it can employ in foreign affairs to further its goals without weakening its own internal structure.

Military display is a strategy that was more common in the nineteenth and early twentieth centuries, but is still used today. Again, it is most effective when least obvious and costly. The mere presence of a powerful army on the borders of a society may be enough to secure the client-status of that society. Military display is the implicit, or explicit, threat of armed violence, and, to be credible and useful, it must be backed by the willingness of a state to actually employ armed violence, if necessary.

Subversion is a strategy directed toward the destruction of the government or state apparatus of another society in order to further the goals of the state employing it. If subversion is successful, its usefulness is obvious. A society in the throes of political chaos will, probably, be unable effectively to counter the foreign policy aims of its enemies.

War is the ultimate strategy in international politics. Physical violence, when directed against an enemy of approximately equal strength, or one which can call upon the aid of powerful allies, is the costliest and most dangerous of international strategies. On the other hand, if employed against a weak and isolated adversary, war may be the quickest and simplest means of attaining state goals.

All of these strategies, employed for the implementation of foreign policy, are, in turn, implemented by a series of tactics. Whereas continuity is important in foreign policy, and strategies are ordinarily changed only when their failure is apparent, tactics are generally most successful when constantly varied, in order to keep the adversary off guard. Each strategy may be implemented through a whole series of interrelated tactics, such as the use of the forum of international agencies, radio and television broadcasting, and sympathetic stooges in propaganda; embargo, economic blocs, blockade, and pre-emptive buying in economic strategy, and so forth. A full exposition of tactical methods is beyond the scope of this chapter.

Strategies and tactics can be effectively and efficiently employed, so as to yield the greatest possible return with the lowest possible expenditure of wealth, time, and human energy and lives, only to the extent that they are based upon complete and accurate information. For this reason, the intelligence activities of states, ranging from spying and foreign informants in key positions to the analysis of foreign publications, are of the highest importance.[3]

[3] The terminology that is used throughout the book to describe the processes of world politics is intended to be precise and descriptive and as devoid as possible of emotional connotation (for example, the terms "great power" and "small power" cannot be substituted for "paramount" and "client"; the United States is a great power vis-à-vis Hungary, but it is not Hungary's paramount). Nothing pejorative is intended in the use of any of the terms. The imperatives involved in the power relationships within a quasi-anarchic society weigh as heavily (or more heavily) on paramounts as they do on clients. A paramount has responsibilities, as well as privileges, and the fulfillment of these responsibilities may entail vast and painful expenditures of wealth and lives, and may involve the paramount in actions which earn it the opprobrium and hatred of other states.

Paramounts need their clients for support, as much as the clients need their paramount for protection. Thus clients exert power, because they have value and are valued. As many examples of clients influencing the foreign policies of paramounts may be adduced from the record of international politics as of paramounts influencing their clients.

Finally, it should be pointed out that the analysis in this volume primarily concerns international politics, not the domestic foreign policy-making processes of the states involved. Thus, the effect that individuals may have on the course of world politics is discussed, by and large, only in its results as manifested in the behavior of states. For example, it may well be true (though impossible to prove) that, if someone other than Franklin D. Roosevelt had been President of the United States in 1938, the United States would have intervened forcibly to prevent the expropriation of the American oil companies in Mexico. Saying this, however, is merely saying that those in charge of American foreign policy, at that time, decided that the possible gains from such intervention were not worth the probable costs and risks involved in intervening, so they decided not to. Their decision did not change, one way or the other, the basic power relationship of the states involved.

In other words, our endeavor throughout the work is to avoid the type of thing John Ruskin meant when he wrote: "There are masked words abroad, I say, which nobody understands, but which everybody uses, and most people will also fight for, live for, or even die for, fancying that they mean this, or that, or the other, of things dear to them."

Selected Bibliography

The bibliographies following each chapter have two purposes: to indicate those works which have been most influential in molding the author's positions concerning the various topics covered, to the extent that those positions have been molded by secondary sources, rather than by personal contacts and experiences; and secondly, to allow the reader, by following the bibliography, to gain a deeper and more thorough understanding of Latin America in world politics. Consequently, an effort has been made to list the bibliographical items in some sort of meaningful order, rather than merely alphabetically. For the same reason, all items have been listed in their English versions, where such are available, and no work has been cited merely because it has gained popular, or scholarly, renown. That is, the author has listed only those works that he is convinced will add substantially to the reader's general knowledge of the subject, either because the work is provocative and controversial or because it is a competent and complete survey of a particular topic. The bibliographies for Chapters 1 and 2 will obviously be more general in nature than those for the remaining chapters.

It is impossible (and undesirable) to attempt a full bibliography here on the methodology of political science, and on the nature of politics, in general. For those unfamiliar with these topics, however, Abraham Kaplan's volume, *The Conduct of Inquiry* (San Francisco, 1963), is an excellent introduction to the application of the scientific method to the social sciences, and Eugene J. Meehan has written a similar work confined to political science, *The Theory and Method of Political Analysis* (Homewood, 1965). *Systematic Politics: Elementa Politica et Sociologica* by George E. G. Catlin (Toronto, 1962) is a compendious and provocative attempt to systematize that which is already known about political behavior.

Michael Lindsay, in *Scientific Method and International Affairs* (Canberra, 1955), provides a discussion of the application of the scientific method to the particular branch of political science under consideration. A short, conceptual framework for the study of international politics is provided by Charles O. Lerche, Jr., and Abdul A. Said in *Concepts of International Politics* (Englewood Cliffs, 1963). Hans Morgenthau's classic, *Politics Among Nations* (3rd ed., New York, 1960), is also conceptual in the main, though marred by an unwarranted and untenable conclusion. The following works set forth theories of international politics, or discuss those theories: Stanley Hoffmann, *Contemporary Theory in International Relations* (Englewood Cliffs, 1960); Klaus Knorr and Sidney Verba, *The International System: Theoretical Essays* (Princeton, 1961); Morton A. Kaplan, *System and Process in International Politics* (New York, 1957); George Liska, *International Equilibrium: A Theoretical Essay on the Politics and Organization of Security* (Cambridge, Mass., 1957); Richard N. Rosecrance, *Action and Reaction in World Politics: International Systems in Perspective* (Boston, 1963), and William T. R. Fox and Thornton Rickert, eds., *Theoretical Aspects of International Relations* (Notre Dame, 1959).

The governing role of conflict in international relations is explored in Thomas C. Schelling, *The Strategy of Conflict* (Cambridge, Mass., 1960) and Roger D. Fisher, *International Conflict and Behavioral Science: The Craigville Papers* (New York, 1964).

The part that personal and mass psychology, including irrationality and ideological commitment, play in international politics is analyzed in Otto Klineberg, *The Human Dimension in International Relations* (New York, 1964); J. David Singer, *Human Behavior and International Politics: Contributions from the Social-Psychological Sciences* (Chicago, 1965), and Herbert C. Kelman, ed., *International Behavior* (New York, 1965).

One of the most realistic assessments of the role and function of international law is still Gerhart Niemeyer, *Law Without Force: The Function of Politics in International Law* (Princeton, 1941). More recent attempts to analyze (or, perhaps, discover) the function of international law are Morton A. Kaplan and Nicholas de

B. Katzenbach, *The Political Foundations of International Law* (New York, 1961), and Urban G. Whitaker, *Politics and Power: A Text in International Law* (New York, 1964). A complete and excellently organized casebook of international law is Herbert W. Briggs' *The Law of Nations* (New York, 1952).

Alliances in general are discussed in William H. Riker, *The Theory of Political Coalition* (New Haven, 1962), and international alliances in George Liska, *Nations in Alliance: The Limits of Interdependence* (Baltimore, 1962). There is little in the way of realistic assesssments of international organization in general, or of specific organizations in particular, but Ruth Lawson, ed., provides in *International Regional Organizations* (New York, 1962) a useful compilation of the charters of various regional organizations, and Leland M. Goodrich's *The United Nations* (New York, 1959), effectively presents the structure and formal functioning of that organization. John G. Stoessinger's *The Superpowers and the United Nations* (New York, 1965), is an excellent and realistic study of the role of the U. N.

The general problem of the formulation of foreign policy is examined in Richard C. Snyder, H. W. Bruch, and B. Sapin, eds., *Foreign Policy Decision Making: An Approach to the Study of International Politics* (New York, 1962); James N. Rosenau, *National Leadership and Foreign Policy: A Case Study in the Mobilization of Public Support* (Princeton, 1963), and Kurt London, *How Foreign Policy Is Made* (New York, 1949). The foreign policies of various countries, including some in Latin America, are surveyed in Roy C. Macridis, ed., *Foreign Policy in World Politics* (Englewood Cliffs, 1958), and Joseph E. Black and Kenneth W. Thompson, eds., *Foreign Policies in a World of Change* (New York, 1963).

The foreign policies of the United States are analyzed from various standpoints in William R. Kintner and Stefan T. Possony, *A Forward Strategy for America* (New York, 1961), and David M. Abshire and Richard Allen, eds., *National Security* (New York, 1963). The machinery of foreign policy formulation in the American Government is described in *Foreign Policy in American Government* (Boston, 1965) by Bernard C. Cohen.

Fred Charles Iklé, in *How Nations Negotiate* (New York, 1964), and Sir Harold Nicolson, in *Diplomacy* (New York, 1964), describe the processes of political negotiation in the interstate sphere. Propaganda as a strategy is surveyed in Urban G. Whitaker, Jr., ed., *Propaganda and International Relations* (San Francisco, 1962). The international uses of nationalism as a strategy are brilliantly analyzed by Alfred Cobban in *National Self-Determination* (Chicago, 1951). Economic strategies in international politics are surveyed in Yuan-li Wu, *Economic Warfare* (Englewood Cliffs, 1952); George Liska, *The New Statecraft: Foreign Aid in American Foreign Policy* (Chicago, 1960), and Robert A. Goldwin, ed., *Why Foreign Aid?* (Chicago, 1963). A most provocative discussion of subversion as a strategy is found in James N. Rosenau, ed., *International Aspects of Civil Strife* (Princeton, 1964). There are many studies of naval and military strategy. A very useful introduction to the subject is André Beaufre, *An Introduction to Strategy* (New York, 1965). The epochal analyses of Karl von Clausewitz are still very much to the point. A good recent translation and condensation is *War, Politics and Power* (Chicago, 1962). Some of the strategic implications of the development of nuclear weapons are spelled out by Herman Kahn, in *On Thermonuclear War* (Princeton, 1960) and Pierre Gallois, *The Balance of Terror* (Boston, 1961).

Journals published in the United States specializing in international politics include *World Politics, Orbis, The Journal of International Affairs,* and *Foreign Affairs.*

2 / *LATIN AMERICA*

Todo es inmenso . . . , todo,
menos el hombre.
Everything is huge . . . , every-
thing, except man.

ALCIDES ARGÜEDAS
Pueblo Enfermo

The part that is played by Latin America in international politics can only be understood through the combining of two elements—Latin America it-self, and the quasi-anarchic society of the sovereign state. The one plays upon and modifies the other, and which is framework and which content depends upon the vantage-point of the observer. It is therefore of great importance to attempt to describe the position of Latin America in international society, not necessarily in order to place *ourselves* at that vantage-point, and see the world with a different distortion, but rather to use that vantage-point in combination with our own in order to widen our field of vision.

It is customary to begin a discussion of Latin America with an apologetic statement that there is no such thing. It is true that we are dealing with twenty different independent states, and the internal reality of Argentina is very different from that of, say, Nicaragua. Nevertheless, with reference to those factors most directly affecting world politics, the common elements shared by the Latin American republics outweigh in importance the factors of divergence. In other words, each Latin American country behaves internationally in such a way as to demonstrate greater general similarity to its neighbors than to any country or group of coun-tries in any other region of the world. It is for this reason that one can speak of the role of *Latin America* in international society, and it is of these common elements that we must first speak.[1]

---

[1] It should be noted that, aside from these basic factors, the countries of Latin America have a profound demonstration-effect upon each other, even when they are not openly meddling in the internal affairs of their neighbors.

Latin America is a hemispheric island in immediate proximity to one of the great powers of the world. This is the geographic and strategic reality common to all of the sub-continent. That influence historically has been greater in the northern regions of the hemispheric island and less in the southern. The difference is small, however, and has tended today to disappear.

The entire region shares an indigenous heritage and a Mediterranean culture-origin. The first provides a symbolic unity, and the second, a system of ethics, a religion, a social structure, and a tradition. The history of Latin America is far more uniform than diverse. Argentina differs from Nicaragua in geography, economy, politics, and race; but it is substantially similar in myth, ethic, history, and tradition.

All the countries of Latin America are classified as economically under-developed, if, by that highly nebulous term, we mean that they have not fully adopted the technical, economic, *social,* and *political* implications of the industrialized, complex societies of the United States, Western Europe, and the other countries of the world generally thought of as being "developed." In some cases, this is through present inability. In others, it may be due to an unwillingess to accept those implications in full. This, again, is as true of Argentina as of Nicaragua.

The countries of Latin America are now, and have always been, client-states, members of a sub-hierarchical structure within the overall international hierarchy. All this means is that they are relatively weak vis-à-vis the paramount powers of the world. It should at once be noted that, in saying this, we have said no more than would be also said of Belgium, Australia, or Japan, or, in fact, the overwhelming majority of the countries of the world.

Finally, the countries of Latin America are "Western." Within the very wide degree of latitude that that term allows, there can be little doubt that the ethical, moral, political, and economic orientation of Latin America is "Western." (So, of course, is that of the Soviet Union—we are not speaking here of the popular division of the world into "East" and "West," but of the quite divergent world-view found from Afghanistan to Japan contrasted with that of the rest of the world.) The Indian heritage of Latin America does not greatly affect this fact.

A / THE PHYSICAL REALITY

There is one overwhelming fact concerning the geographic configuration of the Latin American hemispheric island: it is unfavorable to man. In his attempt to struggle with it, his adaptive responses have, in turn, been unfavorable to political liberty and economic development.

There are five great geographic regions in Latin America. Of the five only one, and that one a part of only four of the Latin American countries, is benign *ab initio,* without the forcible restructuring of nature through the determined application of great quantities of energy and capital—both commodities in short supply in the region. The mountains, the highlands, the deserts, and the swamps *can* be made to flourish. There is, in fact, a higher percentage of *potentially* arable land in Latin America than in some other of the world's regions, but it cannot *cheaply* and *rapidly* be made productive. Only the plains of northern Argentina, southern Paraguay, Uruguay, southern and western Brazil, and several small intermont basins in other countries lend themselves relatively easily to human habitation and cultivation. What man has actually *done* with the plains is another matter, but at least he was not half-defeated before he even began (see Table I).

TABLE I—LAND USE IN LATIN AMERICA

Continent and Country	Period of Survey	Total Area	Land Area	Arable Land & Land Under Permanent Crops	Permanent Meadows and Pastures	Forested Land	Unused but Potentially Productive	Built-on Area, Wasteland, etc.
		1	2	3	4	5	6	7
NORTH AND CENTRAL AMERICA				1 000 hectares				
Costa Rica	1955	5 090	N.A.	281	722	676	N.A.	3 411
Cuba	1946	11 452	N.A.	1 970	3 897	1 300	25	4 260
Dom. Republic	1946	4 873	N.A.	680	580	3 440	N.A.	173
El Salvador	1950	2 139	N.A.	544	704	275	N.A.	616
Guatemala	1950	10 889	N.A.	1 473	582	4 832	N.A.	4 002
Haiti	1950	2 775	2 700	370	500	700	700	505
Honduras	1960	11 209	N.A.	997	2 800	4 816	N.A.	2 596
Mexico	1950	196 927	N.A.	19 928	75 156	38 836	N.A.	63 007
Nicaragua	1960	14 800	13 700	1 793	N.A.	6 450	1 639	4 918
Panama	1961	7 565	N.A.	564	831	5 270	N.A.	900
Panama Canal Zone	1951	143	94	1	11	56	N.A.	75
Puerto Rico	1960	890	886	313	303	125	N.A.	149
SOUTH AMERICA								
Argentina	1957	277 841	274 821	30 000	113 151	99 400	N.A.	35 290
Bolivia	1950	109 858	N.A.	3 091	11 323	47 000	N.A.	48 444
Brazil	1957	851 384	846 989	19 095	107 633	517 936	34 311	172 409
Guyana	1961	21 497	19 684	1 388	N.A.	16 561	1 735	1 813
Chile	1956	74 177	73 300	5 514	454	16 361	7 691	44 157
Colombia	1960	113 834	N.A.	5 062	14 638	69 400	N.A.	24 734
Ecuador	1961	27 067	N.A.	2 081	2 200	14 845	N.A.	7 941
French Guiana	1960	9 100	8 800	3	50	8 544	100	403
Paraguay	1954	40 675	N.A.	517	705	20 906	550	17 997
Peru	1961	128 522	N.A.	1 956	12 000	70 000	N.A.	44 566
Surinam	1961	14 282	13 882	35	6	6 000	N.A.	8 241
Uruguay	1957	18 693	N.A.	2 552	12 038	434	1 651	2 018
Venezuela	1956	91 205	88 205	5 220	17 800	19 000	N.A.	49 185
TOTAL		2046 887		105 428	378 084	973 163	48 402*	541 810
PERCENTAGE		100		5.1	18.4	47.5	2.4	26.4

Source—FAO. *Production Yearbook. 1962,* pp. 4,8.

* Note that there exist statistical estimates of unused but potentially productive land for only nine of the Latin American political units. Much of the land in forest and used for pasture could be productively used for the raising of crops, but estimates are not available.
  This table was prepared by Mario Paz y Miño.

Latin America is an area of isolated communities, isolated originally because of geographic features, and eventually because of traditional rivalries, cultural provincialism, and political hatreds, all of which reinforced geographic isolation. Transportation and communication are perhaps more difficult in Latin America than in any other moderately well-populated region of the world, and the psychological effects of this isolation are difficult for a North American or European to visualize. *There is no part of Latin America with a continental perspective.* Each coastal city looks to the sea and that which is beyond. Each interior city huddled in its intermont basin looks only as far as the surrounding wall of mountains. Buenos Aires could have developed differently, but historical accident decreed that Buenos Aires should look outward to Europe, acting not as a nourisher, but as a drainer, of the Pampas. The various regions of Latin America are closed societies, somewhat hostile to, and suspicious of, the outside world, even the outside world within the same state boundaries. Particularism, regionalism, and provincialism are rife—separatism and secession are constant threats, and have provided much of the excuse needed by centralizing dictatorships. Indeed, had it not been for some of the more bloody dictators of the nineteenth century, there would not be twenty countries now, but many more—and, only for the lack of sufficiently ruthless centralizing strongmen, there would now be twelve countries, instead of twenty, in Latin America.

Nature, the most popular mythopoeic term for geography, is the central fact in the life of all Latin Americans, and even the most hardened urbanite in the largest city is constantly aware of its overwhelming influence. Nature is the real hero and/or villain of practically all of the best literature written by Latin Americans or about Latin America. Usually it is both: hero because it triumphs, villain because it defeats. And the force which it triumphs over and defeats is man. The Latin American lives in constant remembrance of his insignificance, not only because of the grandeur and terror of nature, but also because of the high incidence of natural disaster—flood, volcano, earthquake, hurricane—in the region. Whether he resigns himself, as a result, to defeatist fatalism or overcompensates through fanatic self-assertion, his adaptive responses are equally damaging to the development of consensual government and an economy of free exchange.

B / MAN AND HIS INSTITUTIONS

The population structure of Latin America is built upon a base of the Indian. The exceptions to this statement are extremely few, consisting of the country of Haiti and the cities of southern Brazil, as well as Buenos

Aires and Montevideo.[2] Even in these southern South American cities, although actual Indian blood is largely missing, the tradition of the Indian is strong, through the culture-institution of the "gaucho," who was a mestizo.

Upon this Indian base has been built a layered structure of races and nationalities (see Fig. 3), the most important elements of which have been the Iberian (himself a combination of Latin, Germanic, and Moorish), the Negro; the Mediterranean, Central and Eastern European; the Arab, and the Oriental. The Indian has generally remained at the bottom of the

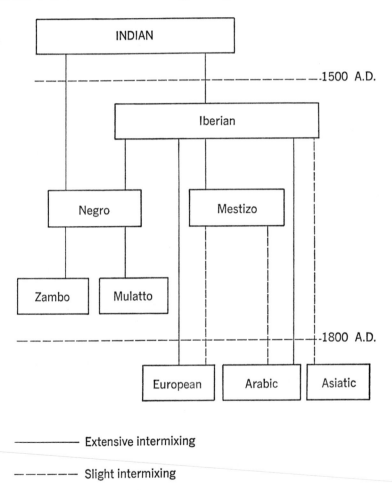

Fig. 3 — Racial and National Structure of Latin America

[2] The contention on the part of some Argentines and Uruguayans that there is practically no Indian blood-mixture in those two countries is demonstrably false to anyone traveling in the interior.

structure; and in most places (including the revolutionary countries) his best (and at times only) chance of rising is through admixture of blood. The great bulk of the Indians, however, remains outside national social, political, and economic life, and this fact, added to the clustering of population due to geographic and cultural features, contributes to the natural fragmentation of Latin American society. It is often said that racial prejudice does not exist in Latin America to the extent that it does, for example, in the United States. The statement is incorrect for Argentina and Uruguay, but in the rest of Latin America it is true if the accent is put on the word "racial." Although purely racial prejudice is neither widespread nor virulent, there is a great deal of prejudice on combined racial, economic, and cultural grounds. The Indians of Peru, for example, were not considered citizens unless they adopted Western dress and spoke Spanish.[3] Nevertheless, this form of prejudice is more favorable to the lower caste-groups, because unlike race, culture and economic status are factors that *can* be changed, no matter how difficult it actually may be to try to do so. It should be noted, in this regard also, that practice varies from Argentina, which has the same racial (and religious and national) prejudices as are found in the United States, Europe, and elsewhere, through Peru, where the Indian and the mestizo can better themselves, although with great difficulty, to Mexico, where, as early as the middle of the nineteenth century, two full-blooded Indians became President of the Republic, and where the mestizos have always taken part in the political and economic process.

One of the most startling things about Latin American history is the continuity of cultural traits from the pre-Columbian period, through the colonial regimes, to and through the period of independence, in some cases until the present, and in all until very recently.[4] One of the fundamental (but least studied) problems with agrarian reform, for example, is the fact that the essentially feudal land structure found in certain areas dates not only from the five-and-a-half centuries of colonial government and independence, but antedates the arrival of the Iberians in the hemisphere. Few of the civilized Indians of the New World knew a widespread system of small private land holdings—the vast majority were organized either on communal farms (which may have been the "property" of the community, as in central Mexico, or of the state, as in the Inca Empire) or, as serfs, on the estates of the nobility or the priesthood. Great political, economic, and social centralization was practiced by the Indian governments wherever possible, and constant warfare, hatred of one's neighbors, exploitation, and tribute were the common conditions of life.[5] The Spaniards stepped into a society that was in many ways very familiar to

---

[3] It should be noted in this connection that the communal Indian did not consider himself a member of Peruvian society either.

[4] Haiti is the exception here. The Haitian social revolution was practically coterminous with Haitian independence (1804).

[5] That there were also differences is shown by the greater initiative that the central Mexican Indian has always shown when compared with the descendants of the other great Indian civilizations.

them, and, in fact, they could (and did) take pride in their having stopped some of the "barbarous" habits of the Indians, such as human sacrifice, polygamy, and cannibalism. The shock of the conquest, which was carried out with ridiculous ease, insofar as the Indian civilizations were concerned (and with great difficulty with respect to nature and the uncivilized, tribal Indians), resulted in a definitive culture submergence on the part of the Indians, without, however, complete culture destruction; so that, in effect, an arrested culture exists at the side of a dynamic one, acting as a brake upon economic and political development.

The most important culture-trait that has been carried through from the Indian civilizations in the New World, and at the same time brought over from Spain and Portugal by the conquerors, is the *patrón-peón* mentality. An essentially feudal colonial structure was imposed upon an already essentially feudal society, so that the only important changes had to do with the greater or lesser efficiency and humanity with which the structure was manipulated. A choice between the native Indian rulers and the Spaniards with respect to these two criteria is not as simple as it may seem at first, and any judgment has to be made in the light of the different goals that were sought.

The Spanish conquest of America was financed, in large part, by South German banking houses. The gold and silver that was found, and later mined, there, eventually (and rapidly) found its way to the counting houses of England and, to a lesser degree, France, helping substantially to finance the industrial revolution—which not by chance coincided with the decadence of Spain and Portugal. A stubborn belief in a false economic theory, then as now, proved disastrous to Latin America, as well as to the parent states. The theory of mercantilism held that true wealth consists of gold and silver, that there was only a certain stock of wealth in the world, and thus to get more you had to steal (conquer) it, or beg it, from others, and that one way to do so was to run a constant trade surplus, and thus, beggar your neighbors. Despite the immense quantities of gold, silver, and other commodities which Spain and Portugal extracted from the New World, they succeeded only in beggaring themselves through constant price inflation and the destruction of the nascent Iberian industries. The specie of the New World was, however, put to good use by those who realized that wealth can be *created* as well as stolen or begged.

In theory, Latin America during the colonial period consisted of a series of feudal fiefs of the Spanish and Portuguese crowns, and, thus, were not "colonies" in the modern sense of the term. They had duties and obligations toward their feudal superiors, but the latter, in turn, had duties and obligations toward them, which Spain and Portugal dutifully attempted to discharge through a series of very complex governmental structures and laws, all of which were quite unsuccessful, insofar as they attempted to protect the Indians from the conquerors. Paternalism was strengthened through encouragement, not only on the spot, but from the home countries, which demanded and exercised an astounding degree of centralized control considering the difficulties of time and space with which they had to contend. Censorship was rigorous, and its effects are still visible in the rather deplorable state of the libraries of Latin America, and the still-prevalent tendency to try to prevent others from coming into contact with ideas considered "unsuitable." The already existing Mediterranean ethic was reinforced, and came to dominate the entire region, in compatible combination with the Indian culture. Manufacturing and commerce, due to the policies of the home countries, became stunted, inward-looking, and niggardly. On the other hand, following the general cynical philosophy of *"Obedezco, pero no cumplo,"* [6] smuggling and contraband flourished then (as they do now), and have during the entire history of colonial and independent Latin America. Contempt for the government as such, coupled with reverence for individual governors, is one of the bitter fruits of this corrupt tree.

The wars for independence in Latin America, with the exception of Haiti, came about because of the expulsion from Spain and Portugal of the Spanish and Portuguese royal families by Napoleon.[7] The revolutions, in fact, for the most part, began as expressions of *loyalty* to the legitimate royal family and of rejection of the Napoleonic usurper. Later, the idea of independence began to beguile some of the Creoles and the wars commenced. Nevertheless, it took sixteen years for Spain to be definitively defeated, despite the facts that it was already in the last stages of economic and political decay, had just fought a naval war with England and a land war with France, a bitter guerrilla battle with the French invaders, had experienced an invasion by the English under Wellington, the restoration of the monarch, a fanatical struggle between the Royalists and the Republicans, and finally, another French invasion in 1823.

During the period of early independence, the Conservative parties throughout the hemispheric island supported a continuation of the colonial social system in practically all of its aspects, except for the absence of a feudal superior above the local state. The Liberals, even when they sincerely espoused nineteenth-century liberalism, merely succeeded in further entrenching the feudal land system by confiscating the lands of the church and the Indian communities—ostensibly to develop a class of small proprietors. In effect, however, practically all of this land went to increase the estates of the great landowners. At least the Liberals did provide a more favorable atmosphere, while they were in power, for the development of education, the spread of ideas, and some commercial growth. The overwhelming fragmentation of nature and man resulted in the collapse of several of the new countries and their division into smaller segments. Even where this did not happen, the forces of separatism and regionalism were among the most important causes of constant warfare and centralizing despotism. The price of this despotism, even where successful, was the surrender of the provinces of the country involved to the tender mercies of local political bosses, who were more

---

[6] I obey, but I will not comply.
[7] The Spanish royal family was imprisoned in France. The Portuguese royal family escaped to Brazil.

often than not, also the most powerful local landowners. The feudal structure produced goods for local subsistence or for export, and in the latter sector the more commercially-minded landowners combined with foreign interests to produce cysts within the economic structure, siphoning off the cream of the national revenues and turning it over in the importation of luxury goods, obviously also destined for the top. Little or no effort was made to develop internal markets or domestic industry. Toward the end of the century substantial immigration was bringing both labor and potential entrepreneurs to Latin America, but they did not enter quickly into the rigid regional power structure, so that they created, for a time, simply another economic cyst within society.

Capitalism and revolution have dominated the twentieth century in Latin America (in most places still operating within the feudal framework), sometimes together, sometimes separately. Both have their weaknesses, but both are decisively undermining traditional society. That this will not, however, necessarily result in its rapid destruction throughout the sub-continent should be clear from the recent history of the much older Mediterranean states of Europe. Perhaps also, fragmentation of traditional society must become even more pronounced before it can be permanently submerged—that is, those sores presently covered with rags or brocades must be exposed to be lanced. The paradoxical record of the 1952 Bolivian revolution is particularly instructive in this respect. Perhaps no place in the sub-continent have nature and man so combined to make progress difficult; indeed, progress has been halting and partial in Bolivia since 1952. But progressive change *is* occurring, as the Indians leave the *Altiplano* and move into the *Oriente,* there to abandon their tradition, language, dress, and customs, to have enough to eat and a surplus for market—in short, to become Bolivians.

C / RESOURCES, ECONOMIC GROWTH, AND ECONOMIC THEORY

For centuries there has been a myth rampant, in both Latin America itself and abroad, which pictures that region as a sort of immensely rich cornucopia, which needs only the enterprising hand of (usually North American or European) man to begin to flow inexhaustively. According to this myth, nature has been lavish—what is lacking is the will to make it flourish. More recently, this myth, although still quite prevalent in its pristine state, has given rise to a counter-myth, according to which nature has been quite astoundingly niggardly to Latin America, and that man can do very little about it given our present level of technical knowledge. Actually, Latin America, like all other regions of the world, is rich in certain resources and poor in others. It is rich, for example, in potentially arable land, but poor in land immediately cultivable with a minimum of effort and capital and a maximum of yield. It is rich in minerals of many kinds, but extremely poor in that one mineral which is still the cornerstone of industrial society—coal.

Many of Latin America's deficiencies are aggravated by her social system and by her system of myths. There are productive myths and counter-productive myths. An example of an economically productive myth is the notion that all that is needed for human happiness is the will to work hard, and carve out a place for oneself in the world. This is not true (thus a myth), but such a myth, if widely believed in, is highly productive for a society as a whole, at least in terms of material wealth. Much of rural Latin America is still burdened with a semi-feudal agrarian structure, and even more of Latin America is governed by a feudal mentality. The feudal social reality and the feudal myth aggravate the material lacks of the region, rather than compensating for them. The myth that the Indian wouldn't move from his miserable habitations into fertile lowland areas persisted (and was assiduously copied by one author from another), until the Bolivian Government cut a path into the *Oriente,* and found that the "immobile" peasants were impeding construction by following the machinery down the road as it was built. Lack of a Homestead Act bids fair to render useless the whole idea of Brasília, and the half a billion dollars that went into its construction. The original idea was to bring settlers into Brazil's enormous, and moderately fertile, interior plains, and it might have worked had not speculators bought up huge tracts of the best land before anyone had a chance to move.

All of this causes a resultant structural imbalance and, at times, a tragic misallocation of resources. The imbalance and the misallocation are, in turn, aggravated by inappropriate economic theorizing, mostly Marxist, pseudo-Keynesian (inflationary), or inspired by the United Nations' Economic Commission for Latin America. A high rate of saving and investment, and thereby, of capital formation, is thus impeded, and misguided super-nationalism, sincere or demagogical, has further slowed economic growth by discouraging an inflow of capital from other regions. Agriculture has been largely neglected in favor of heavy investment in industry (especially the prestige iron and steel industry), resulting in a severe and damaging imbalance in economic growth and, in some cases, a ludicrous dependence on the importance of foodstuffs to keep the inhabitants alive. The desire of the feudal elements to maintain their grasp on the rural structure, coupled with the vague feeling that investment in heavy industry is somehow more "grown-up," has resulted in a grave loss of precious time and capital.

Nevertheless, the very factor which is often cited to show that Latin America is regressing, instead of progressing (that is, the rapid increase in population), demonstrates, rather, that considerable economic progress *has* been made. The dependence upon highly questionable per capita income statistics, the ignoring of factors of progress that cannot be statistically measured, the lack in any case of reliable statistics, and the curious procedure whereby a higher rate of survival of calves is a contribution to economic development, whereas a higher rate of survival of human children is a detriment, have all led to the belief that growth is now practically nil.[8] There can be no doubt that growth in measurable items has at times been slowed (and in some countries reversed), largely due to the discarding of at least partially suitable development policies, and their substitution by policies largely unrealistic and counter-productive. There is, however, no reason to believe that if more suitable policies are re-introduced, rapid growth cannot be resumed, particularly if coupled with successful efforts to destroy the dead hand of feudalism on the land market as part of a general freeing of the energies and initiatives of the people of these countries. A rapid increase in population, far from being a retarding influence, is, in countries as underpopulated as are all the countries of Latin America with the exceptions of Haiti and El Salvador, a necessary concomitant of economic and industrial development—a process most strikingly demonstrated by Europe during the nineteenth century. It is true that modern industrial processes do not require the same quantity of workers as did the industries of nineteenth-century Europe, but, on the other hand, the service, or tertiary, industries require many more. As a result, perhaps the most productive investment that can at present be made in Latin America is that in technical, scientific, managerial, and commercial education, sadly neglected fields—neglected because of culture traits and ethical systems which elevate a professional education, even if useless, above highly useful technical training, in the value structure of society.

Some of the most advanced countries in Latin America are now economically stagnant. The "take-offs" to prosperity, to use Rostow's term, have not occurred. Worse, stagnation is often coupled with inflation, sometimes the cause of the stagnation, but, more often, another result of the same system of societal factors and circumstances—more particularly, the effort to graft an industrial society onto a feudal base, an effort not only pregnant with potential disaster, but also highly inefficient in fulfilling the goals and expectations of *either* form of societal organization. Nevertheless, it should be noted that stagnation can also arise from the revolutionary application of inappropriate development criteria, as is the case today in Cuba, and, to some extent, in Bolivia. Should there be any doubt of this, it is only necessary to point to the case of Haiti, where the hemisphere's first social revolution, which completely destroyed the feudal structure which had been imposed on the island by the French, has led, nevertheless, to the hemisphere's most stagnant economy. It should be obvious by now that revolution is not *per se* a panacea, leading eventually to rapid economic growth.

[8] See, *inter alia,* Harry Stark, *Infirmities of Per Capita National Income Estimates When Employed to Compare Levels of Living Between Developed and Retarded Areas* (Coral Gables, 1961), and Peter T. Bauer, "El Círculo Vicioso de la Pobreza," *Orientación Económica,* No. 9, July, 1963.

D / THE HUMAN PROCESS IN LATIN AMERICA

More important than geography, resources, or economic or revolutionary theories, is man. It has been said that Latin America has only two problems: nature and man. The first offers immense difficulties. The second even more.

Since the early years of the nineteenth century, Latin Americans have lacked a symbol of authority on the national level toward which they could direct an impersonal reverence, leaving their political and economic energies free for the task of economic development and the structuring of consensual government within a class, but not a caste, society. The resulting severe dislocation of personal and group identity and dynamism is only too evident in countries such as Argentina and Uruguay, which, having reached a certain level of economic and political development, proceeded to retrogress in a social morass that only by kindness can be called stagnation. A refusal to leave the fate of society to the forces of the market and to the political interplay of competing groups (which, of course, results in a system short of perfection) has long been a characteristic of Latin America. Utopianism and violence have been the hallmarks of the social process in Latin America (the one leading to the other inexorably), a violence which has been done not only to human beings, but also to institutions and to the tender shoots of a budding impersonalistic ethic.

For consensual government to develop and survive, there must be a large measure of basic conservatism in society at large, a conservatism which has nothing to do with political labels, but one which is simply the agreement on the preferability of operating within structured norms, the rule of law, and a known framework of authority. There must also be a willingness and a possibility of compromise, because only by compromise can consensual government operate. France and Italy today exemplify countries where the ability exists, but the willingness is deficient. In a country where large numbers of the inhabitants have little or nothing, there can be, by definition, no compromise between them and other groups within that society. It is for this reason that the diffusion of property and power must be one of the most pressing goals in a country bent upon prosperity with liberty.

In Latin America, political and social processes have been very different, and diffusion of property has begun only recently and only imperfectly. As a result, *personalismo, caudillismo,* messianism, fanaticism, rigidity, violence, and institution-replacement have been the common fate. Arbitration by the sword and the "compromise of surrender" have been common elements in the Latin American scene. It will be some time before the mentality that gave rise to the admonition, not to throw ". . . the baby out with the bathwater," replaces the fanatic mentality of those to whom the word "compromise" signifies something ignoble and demeaning.

The lack of a symbolic focus of legitimacy and authority has inevitably led to the substitution of purely individual authority based upon charisma and skillful manipulation of the relatively limited number of key power-groups within most Latin American societies (the more limited, of course, the more structurally simple the country involved.) It is generally a combination of both characteristics, although sometimes the charisma can be largely dispensed with by a particularly able politician or military leader. This is rare, however, and generally the manipulative talent who is not at the same time *"simpático"* must operate behind the scenes. The same conditions that give rise to *personalismo* and *caudillismo* have resulted also in habitual political, social, and economic institution-replacement. Perhaps the most obvious manifestation of this symptomatic behavior is the penchant for constitution-writing, whenever a new government comes into power. The process of institution superimposition (which may, of course, eventually lead to the original institution or forms becoming merely façades or empty shells) has not taken deep root in the Latin American countries; although, in those which have created some form of symbolic authority (such as the "Revolution" in Mexico), that process may be beginning to dominate. Another reason for the predominance of institution-replacement is the fact that Latin American institutions, particularly political institutions, tend to be empty shells at their very inception.

Spontaneous Latin American philosophical and theoretical systems have been rare; indeed, almost nonexistent.[9] Philosophies and ideologies have traditionally been imported from abroad and applied whole-cloth to the domestic social reality, sometimes with disastrous results. Some attempts at original formulations have been made, but they have been intellectually unsatisfying and unsuccessful in their attempts at proselytism. The pedantic indigenism of the Peruvian *Apristas* and their followers has found no great response, and in any case, represented a monstrous grafting of imported ideas onto the unprotesting back of the Indian mass in the Andean countries. Perón's Justicialism and Vargas' *Estado Novo* added little to fascist and socialist-communist thought, unless the Justicialist fourfold division of human group life is considered an important contribution.[10] The ideologies or philosophical systems which have had the greatest influence in Latin America have been those of Rousseau, the positivists, the anarchists, Karl Marx, and the fascists (especially Italian Fascist thought, Portuguese Corporativism and Falangism). (See Fig. 4.) Except in constitution-making, North American democratic theory has had very little influence since the earliest years of independence—even then, the ideas of the French revolution were more influential. The Communist or semi-Communist regimes in Guatemala (1951–54) and Cuba (1959–Present) have added nothing to Marxist theory (even Ché Guevara's famous book on guerrilla warfare is largely cribbed from Mao Tse-tung and Giap).

[9] See Risieri Frondizi, "Is there an Ibero-American Philosophy?," *Philosophy and Phenomenological Research,* vol IX, no. 3 (March, 1949).
[10] According to Justicialist theory, the ills of the world can be traced to an incorrect balancing or co-ordination of the demands of idealism, materialism, individualism, and collectivism.

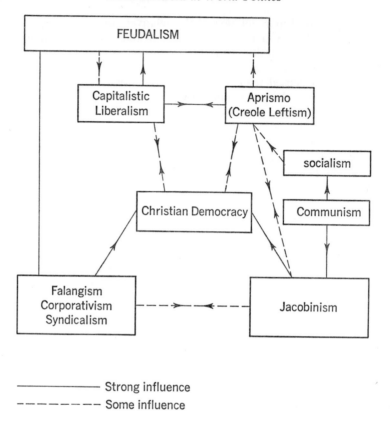

Strong influence
Some influence

Fig. 4 — Ideological Structure of Non-Revolutionary Latin America

More important, perhaps, than imported or domestic theory has been the superimposition of the Freudian ethic in recent years upon the basic Mediterranean ethic of the various Latin American societies. The former (in the oversimplified terms in which it is applied in Latin America), with its emphasis upon the basically irrational character of human behavior, and the seemingly natural corollary that human effort along ordered, goal-oriented, and rational lines is something less than highly effective, reinforces various aspects of the latter—particularly the view that work is a punishment visited upon man by supernatural forces (irrationality can be considered a form of supernatural phenomenon, even when considered the "natural" state of man), and also the feeling (reinforced by the physical geographic reality of Latin America) that man is basically helpless in the hands of forces beyond his control, whether they be earthquakes, volcanoes, floods, hurricanes, God, devils, or the irrational behavior of himself and his fellow men.[11] The Freudian ethic has also enabled the Latin American intellectual to feel "modern" while at the same time maintaining his original instinctual beliefs, in much the same way that Corporativist, Falangist, and Syndicalist theories can give an aura of "modernity" to what is essentially an *apologia* for the semi-feudal society still dominant in parts of Latin America. As industrialization and economic development attempt to wrench open the closed societies of Latin America, the Puritan ethic (with its emphasis on work, rationality, and the efficacy of logical, goal-oriented effort) is also gaining adherents,[12] thereby adding a basic ethical fragmentation to the many other factors already contributing to the division of Latin American society. New, dynamic, identity and status structures are imposing themselves upon the entrenched, accumulated status of whole groups of Latin Americans. The difficulty of this transition must be appreciated against a background of the absence of any widely accepted authority symbol other than the personal-*cum*-traditional one of individual paternalism (the *patrón-peón* mentality). In short, the individual Latin American is being asked, *not* to adopt relatively minor changes in already functioning institutions, or to adapt himself to deviations in his accepted behavior patterns, but rather, to abandon his only link with legitimacy and strike out into unknown territory, beset with new and highly disagreeable terrors. Some of the most seemingly thoroughgoing changes in Latin American societies have foundered upon this fear, and have resulted, not in a basic restructuring of society, but in a mere reshuffling of the *patrón-peón* roles within what is basically the same ethical-moral system. This can be said of the Vargas upheaval in Brazil, Peronism in Argentina, and Communism in Guatemala and Cuba.

In contrast, those revolutions seemingly more chaotic, and perhaps, for that reason, necessarily more gradual, such as those of Mexico (1910) and Bolivia (1952), are resulting in a genuine, if frictioned, reorganization of mental attitudes, and not merely outward forms. (In this regard, it is significant that Mexico is one of the very few countries in Latin America which has achieved a fairly powerful symbolic authority—the revolution itself, which according to official doctrine, still continues, now "institutionalized".)

All of the above factors have brought about a division of politically conscious Latin Americans into four basic social universes, which are

[11] Arturo Uslar Pietri notes that the principal theme of 3,149 entries in the *Life en Español* short story contest was "Man's insignificance before fate or nature." *Prize Winning Stories from Latin America* (New York, 1964), p. ix. Contrast this with "The shape of things to come depends on us: our moral decision, our wisdom, our vision, and our will." (Quoted from Russell Davenport, *U.S.A.: The Permanent Revolution*, by L. B. Worthington in "The Business of America," pamphlet, U. S. Steel Corporation, 1964, p. 16.)

[12] In some areas of Latin America, such as Costa Rica, Monterrey, Antioquia, and São Paulo, the Puritan ethic has always been strong. Conjectures vary as to the reasons for this. See E. E. Hagen, *On the Theory of Social Change—How Economic Growth Begins* (Homewood, 1962), chapter 15.

fundamentally split on the two great issues of economic development and consensual government.[13]

The feudal elite and a portion of the political elite [14] constitute practically all of the Traditional Right in Latin America. These are the people with the accumulated, accepted status, a status that is not by any means dead or dying, although it is under severe attack and has been for some time. The more modern segments of the Traditional Right have adopted Corporate, Falangist, or Syndicalist philosophies; all of them, in effect, attempts to adapt a medievally-structured society to the modern world. The Traditional Right attempts (so far, quite successfully, in many cases) to contain the forces of industrial and commercial expansion—so destructive to traditional society—within "safe" limits. The Traditional Right has no basic commitment to either economic development or consensual government. It rightly considers the former the greatest single threat to its position, and the latter as contrary to human nature—the idea itself the cause of all, or most of, the ills of modern civilization. Consequently, the Traditional Right is virulently anti-United States and anti-capitalist, besides being, obviously, anti-Communist. It will often ally itself, however, with the opportunistic Jacobin Left against all of these groups, as well as against the Democratic Left.

The Democratic Left consists of those groups, formed mostly during the decades of the 1920's and 1930's, which at that time posited a revolutionary program of the destruction of feudal society, and its substitution by a vague and poorly structured system combining elements of Marxism, indigenism, Fabianism, and Liberalism. Since that time the movements and parties of the Democratic Left have moved steadily toward a center position, abandoning in the process many of their original beliefs, including widespread nationalization of industry. As a result, split-offs have occurred in practically all of these parties, the dissidents usually forming or joining movements of the Jacobin Left. The Democratic Left has lost some of its dynamism; its leadership, coming almost completely from the political elite, is old and shopworn. The Democratic Left is committed to both economic development and consensual government, and has thus long been the implacable enemy of the Traditional Right, as it is now of the Jacobin Left.[15]

The Jacobin Left emerged as a discernible universe during the 1940's and 1950's primarily, although the first of the Jacobin Left regimes, that of Getúlio Vargas, dates from 1930[16] The Jacobin Left, formed primarily by split-offs from the Democratic Left, but also from the "modern" ele-

---

[13] "Consensual government" is used in this chapter rather than "democracy," because the latter term is now practically devoid of meaning.

[14] There is in Latin America a quite distinct political elite, whose power and influence is based almost completely on having, or potentially having, political-bureaucratic position.

[15] The best-known Democratic Left parties are the APRA of Peru, the AD of Venezuela, *Liberación Nacional* of Costa Rica, and the MNR of Bolivia. Major leaders of the Democratic Left are Víctor Raúl Haya de la Torre, Rómulo Betancourt, José Figueres, Víctor Paz Estenssoro, and Luis Muñoz Marín.

[16] Vargas took power in that year, but the "Estado Novo" did not begin to develop until about 1937.

ments of the Traditional Right, has no commitment to either consensual government or to economic development. Indeed, judging from Latin America's experiences thus far with Jacobin Left governments, the universe seems to have a positive predilection for decapitalization. It will use consensual government to gain power and will support the concept verbally, or attack it, whichever seems the more useful in gaining (or keeping) power. The Jacobin Left is essentially opportunistic and has no established set of principles.[17] As a result, Jacobin governments are often easy marks for the Communists, with their complete ideology and vastly superior organizational techniques. This happened with Jacobin governments in Guatemala and Cuba. For expediency, the Jacobin Left will often make alliances with the Traditional Right, since their immediate goals, despite all outward appearances, are very similar.[18]

The newest of the politico-economic universes in Latin America is that of Neoliberalism, which developed into a coherent group only after 1960.[19] Since then, however, it has grown with remarkable rapidity, until there are formal Neoliberal organizations in all of the Latin American countries except Haiti and Cuba. The Neoliberal universe is composed of industrialists and businessmen, and their allies in the professions and in the middle sectors of society. The leadership comes mostly from the industrial elite, but also, partially, from the political elite. The Neoliberals are, of course, committed to economic development, and also to consensual government, because of their need for stability within an atmosphere of, at least economic, freedom. The late emergence of Neoliberalism as a politico-economic universe is probably due to the fact that many early members of the industrial elite came from feudal elite families (in contrast to Europe, where most of the early capitalists came from the traditional merchant and banker families), that much of Latin American industry is foreign-controlled, and that a good deal of what isn't was founded by individuals who migrated to Latin America fairly recently, and thus were not, for some time, accepted as forming part of the general elite pattern. Although it is still too early to be sure, the Neoliberals seem to be tending toward an alliance with the Democratic Left, an alliance that would appear to make sense, considering their quite similar basic goals and complementary resources.

In the briefest possible form, we have tried to present the domestic variables affecting the international behavior of the Latin American states. (See Fig. 5.). In summary, Latin American society is a frag-

---

[17] "His (Perón's) primary objective—and the primary objective of the people in his entourage—is the retention of power." George I. Blanksten, *Perón's Argentina* (Chicago, 1953), p. 234.

[18] "Some analysts have even come to regard Perón as a champion of the interests of the country's *estancieros,* or major landowners." (*Ibid.,* p. 249.) Some of the major past and present Jacobin Left leaders are Getúlio Vargas, Juan Domingo Perón, Jacobo Arbenz, Fidel Castro, João Goulart, Salvador Allende, and Lázaro Cárdenas.

[19] See Norman A. Bailey, "Organization and Operation of Neoliberalism in Latin America," *Latin America: Politics, Economics, and Hemispheric Security* (New York, 1965), ed. Bailey; and Bailey, "The Colombian Black Hand: A Case Study of Neoliberalism in Latin America," *The Review of Politics,* vol. 27, no. 4, October, 1965.

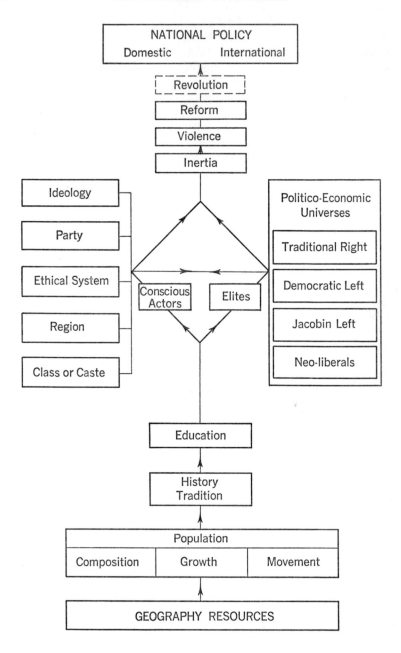

Fig. 5 — Spontaneous Features Affecting National Policy in Latin America (read up)

mented society, fragmented geographically, regionally, racially, socially, economically, politically, and ideologically. Due largely to this fragmentation, Latin America is underdeveloped economically, and it is weak politically and militarily due partially to its economic deficiencies. It is strategically important, a repository of large quantities of raw materials, and Western in its ethical, moral, and social structure.

Selected Bibliography

The only general surveys of Latin America which can be recommended are *Ibero-América, Su Evolución Política, Socio-Económica, Cultural e Internacional,* by José de Galíndez (New York, 1954), and Frank Tannenbaum, *Ten Keys to Latin America* (New York, 1962). They should be read in conjunction with one of the most penetrating and thorough analyses of a single Latin American society ever written, *Pueblo Enfermo,* by Alcídes Argüedas (3rd ed., Santiago, 1937), and with an excellent example of an integrative regional analysis, Miguel Covarrubias' *Mexico South* (New York, 1954). Two other works, which should be read together, give a vivid impression of the way educated Latin Americans like to think of themselves, coupled with the brutal vision of an imaginative outsider: José Enrique Rodó's *Ariel* (many editions, including Mexico, 1957) and Ramón del Valle-Inclán's *Tirano Banderas* (many editions, including Buenos Aires, 1937).

In the field of the physical reality of Latin America, it is really necessary to cite only one work, one of the best written about any aspect of Latin America, Preston James' *Latin America* (3rd. ed., New York, 1959); a magnificent imaginative evocation of the geography of Latin America as well as its effects on the sub-continent's inhabitants is set forth in *La Vorágine,* by the Colombian novelist José Eustasio Rivera (available in English translation, New York 1935).

Resources and economic organization and development in Latin America is a field in which it is hard to make recommendations. The reader should probably start with works not specifically centered on the sub-continent, such as Erich W. Zimmermann, *World Resources and Industries* (New York, 1951) and Peter T. Bauer and Basil S. Yamey, *The Economics of Under-developed Countries* (Chicago, 1957). A competent general survey of the Latin American economic situation can be found in Simon G. Hanson, *Economic Development in Latin America* (Washington, 1951) and the concepts touched upon can be deepened with Howard S. Ellis (ed.), *Economic Development for Latin America* (London, 1962); then questioned and reformulated in *Journeys Toward Progress,* by Albert O. Hirschman (New York, 1963); *Economia, Planejamento e Nacionalismo,* by Roberto de Oliveira Campos (Rio de Janeiro, 1963), and *El Sentido Común en la Economía Colombiana,* by Hernán Echavarría Olózaga (3rd ed., Cali, 1962).

There is no satisfactory general history of Latin America, but Alfred B. Thomas, *Latin America, a History* (New York, 1956), has a good bibliography. The pre-Columbian and colonial periods are very thoroughly covered, and here the embarrassment comes only from having to make choices. For the pre-Columbian period, see Sylvanus G. Morley, *The Ancient Maya* (2nd ed., Stanford, 1947), G. C.

Vaillant, *The Aztecs of Mexico* (New York, 1944), and J. Alden Mason, *The Ancient Civilizations of Peru* (Hammondsworth, 1957). A highly provocative, controversial, and interesting interpretation of the Inca Empire is found in Louis Baudin's *A Socialist Empire—The Incas of Peru* (New York, 1962). The period of Iberian exploration in the Western Hemisphere is thoroughly covered in chapters I through XIII of E. Gaylord Bourne's *Spain in America, 1460–1580* (New York, 1906). The finest accounts of the conquests of Mexico and Peru are still found in W. H. Prescott's *The Conquest of Mexico* (New York, 1843) and *The Conquest of Peru* (New York, 1908). These should be read in conjunction with one of the few readable, accurate, and fairly objective eye-witness accounts, *The Discovery and Conquest of Mexico, 1517–1521,* by Bernal Díaz del Castillo (New York, 1956). A truly fine task of compilation, selection, and analysis has been done by Bailey W. Diffie in his *Latin American Civilization—Colonial Period* (Harrisburg, 1945), and C. H. Haring has gone into even greater detail (for Spanish America only) in *The Spanish Empire in America* (New York, 1947). The reader will have a better understanding of what these authors are writing about if he also reads *Broad and Alien Is the World,* by Ciro Alegría (New York, 1941) and *The Masters and The Slaves,* by Gilberto Freyre (New York, 1946).

In the field of the general social structure of Latin America the reader perhaps should start with J. Lloyd Mecham's *Church and State In Latin America* (Chapel Hill, 1934), and go on to Lyman Bryson *et. al., Social Change in Latin America Today* (New York, 1960), and Frank Tannenbaum, *Mexico, The Struggle for Peace and Bread* (New York, 1950). The traumatic violence produced by this social structure is well described by Mons. Germán Guzmán, *et al.* in *La Violencia en Colombia* (Bogotá, 1962). A brilliant analysis of the effect of modernization on an essentially feudal substructure is *Raíz y Futuro de la Revolución* (Bogotá, 1963) by Fernando Guillén Martínez.

The illusory gulf between sociology and political science can be bridged through reading K. H. Silvert's *The Conflict Society, Reaction and Revolution in Latin America* (New Orleans, 1961). Two books can be recommended as general introductions to Latin American politics and government: *Latin American Politics,* by William S. Stokes (New York, 1959), and *The Government and Politics of Latin America,* Harold E. Davis, ed., (New York, 1958). The most minutely detailed studies of single Latin American governments available are Jesús de Galíndez, *La Era de Trujillo* (Santiago, 1956), William S. Stokes, *Honduras, an Area Study in Government* (Madison, 1950), and K. H. Silvert, *A Study in Government: Guatemala* (New Orleans, 1954). Frank Brandenburg's *The Making of Modern Mexico* (Englewood Cliffs, 1964) is an excellent analysis of the most stable governmental experiment to date in Latin America, and James Payne, *Labor and Politics in Peru* (New Haven, 1965) is an extremely provocative conceptual analysis of a segment of the political process in a Latin American country.

A fairly good idea of at least the original concepts of the Democratic Left can be gleaned from the writings of two of its greatest leaders. The author suggests *Adónde Va Indoamérica?,* by Víctor Raúl Haya de la Torre (2nd ed., Santiago, 1935), and *Venezuela, Política y Petróleo,* by Rómulo Betancourt (Mexico, 1956). George I. Blanksten's *Peron's Argentina* (Chicago, 1953) is an excellent description of a Jacobin Left government. The closest thing to a spontaneous description of Neoliberal ideas is Joaquín Reig, *et. al., Deliberaciones Sobre la Libertad* (Caracas & Buenos Aires, 1961).

Three periodicals that deal with Latin American affairs are *Inter-American Economic Affairs, Hispanic American Historical Review* and the *Journal of Inter-American Studies.* The *Hispanic American Report,* until it ceased publication in November, 1964, was an invaluable source of current information on the region.

Part Two / **THE CHALLENGE**

3 / LATIN AMERICA AND THE WESTERN HEMISPHERE PARAMOUNT

> . . . the Latin American policy of the United States has reflected constantly the vital necessities of national security and the idealism of the American people. Of these two elements, national security has always been uppermost.
>
> SAMUEL FLAGG BEMIS
> *The Latin American Policy*
> *of the United States*

The interaction of the Latin American states with the Western Hemisphere paramount has taken place within a framework of the imperatives of any client-paramount relationship reinforced by the *patrón-peón* psychology of Latin American society. Any client expects protection from its paramount in return for general foreign policy support. At a maximum, depending on the importance of the client, it can also expect substantial assistance from the paramount, in the technical, military, and financial fields. In the other direction, client status may range from that of a satellite, with little or no real foreign policy autonomy, and sometimes little domestic autonomy either, to a loose arrangement extending only to the foreign policy sphere, and perhaps, even there, only to an agreement not to impede the policy initiatives of the paramount. At the minimum, even the smallest and weakest client represents a market for the goods of the paramount and a piece of territory denied to other paramounts. At the maximum, certain clients may be of such vital strategic importance to a paramount, that to interfere with the relationship is to invite the highest intensity of international conflict.

In the provincial and national political spheres the *patrón* mentality of Latin American economic and social life is carried over into what we may call the *"caudillo"* mentality. As with the local *patrón,* the *caudillo* has not only authority but responsibilities, and is expected to be benevolent in his discharge of those responsibilities, while at the same time being firm and efficient in fulfilling them. "Strong" but benevolent leadership is the ideal of the Latin American in the national sphere. He is not, of

37

course, a masochist, and if the government or *caudillo* attacks his liberties or what he considers his private concerns, he will resist. At the same time, a "weak" government, no matter how benevolent and well-intentioned, is despised and obstructed, especially if it is not, in the individual's opinion, fulfilling its responsibilities.

This psychology is carried over by the Latin American states into the international sphere. They are perfectly aware of their disabilities in the world arena and their military weakness. They expect to be benevolently protected, and will as actively seek such protection as they will fight back against their "protector" if they feel it is interfering with their private, domestic concerns. But, precisely because they are preoccupied with their internal problems, which are manifold, they are not interested in being asked to share meaningfully in the risks and responsibilities of the international *caudillo*.

A / COLONIAL LATIN AMERICA, 1492–1806

From the end of the fifteenth century to about 1806, Latin America was organized into a series of vassal kingdoms under the crowns of Castile and Portugal, as we have seen. As a result of this position, the Latin American viceroyalties were not formal actors in international politics, lacking external sovereignty. They were very definitely objects of international politics, however, and as Spain and Portugal gradually weakened in the seventeenth, eighteenth, and nineteenth centuries, their Western Hemisphere possessions were subjected to raiding by other European powers. At times this raiding was strictly intermittent and limited to attacks on shipping and ports for the purpose of looting. As time went on, however, raiding became more serious and was intended to result in the transfer of territory from Spain and Portugal to either France, Great Britain, or Holland. In practice, the Iberian powers were able, largely through judicious use of the European balance of power, to prevent the physical transfer of important pieces of the hemisphere under their control. Thus the nineteenth century opened with their empires intact, except for the three Guianas, Jamaica, Trinidad, the eastern portion of the island of Santo Domingo and a number of other, smaller, islands in the Caribbean, in large part originally seized as bases for attacks on Spanish shipping. In the meantime, Dutch power had waned, leaving the struggle to replace the Spanish and Portuguese to the French and the British. Both had already staked out a claim to influence the course of events, Britain through the Treaty of 1713 (ending the War of the Spanish Succession), in which Spain pledged not to transfer its possessions to any third power; France through the Bourbon Family Compact, in which the French and Spanish royal families agreed to come to one another's support in case of attack on the home country or any of its possessions.

B / THE INDEPENDENCE OF LATIN AMERICA, 1806–24

The Bourbon Family Compact, however, lapsed between the downfall of Louis XVI in 1792 and the restoration of Louis XVIII in 1814. In the meantime, Napoleon I had forced the Portuguese royal family to flee in 1807 and the Spanish king to abdicate in 1808, placing his brother Joseph on the throne in Madrid. Joseph Bonaparte was accepted as legitimate monarch neither in Spain nor in Spanish America. While Spain was still allied to Napoleon, and their combined fleets were being destroyed by Nelson at Trafalgar (leaving Britain for a century in control of the seas), the British government was laying elaborate plans for detaching all of the Spanish territories from their mother country and annexing them itself. With the Bragança royal family in exile in Brazil, totally dependent upon the British Navy, and allied, in any case, for many centuries with Britain, the plan for directly or indirectly controlling the entire sub-continent seemed an eminently feasible one. Only after the failure of this effort between 1806 and 1808, did Britain change its policy to one of aiding in the independence of the Latin American countries, and then dominating them as Western Hemisphere paramount.

In 1806, Sir Home Popham attacked Buenos Aires, drove out the Viceroy and occupied the city with 1,700 men. But the creole, or native-born, Argentines gathered together an improvised army and drove the British out. In the meantime, General Whitelocke had been dispatched with an army of 11,000 men to secure the Viceroyalty of La Plata for the British. First occupying Montevideo, he launched an attack on Buenos Aires in 1807 and was ignominiously defeated, losing between 3,000 and 4,000 men. In the capitulation agreement, he was forced to evacuate all Spanish territory. When the British expedition poised to attack Mexico was diverted in 1808 to aid the uprising in Spain against Napoleon, British efforts at wholesale territorial aggrandizement in the Western Hemisphere came to an end, never to be revived. From 1808 until the last of the Viceroys was vanquished in 1824, British policy was directed toward covertly assisting the Latin American countries to emancipate themselves from Spain, and overtly preventing France from taking advantage of the situation for its own imperial purposes.

Many Englishmen and Irishmen fought in the armies and navies of the incipient states, including some of high rank, notably the famous admiral, Lord Cochrane, commander successively of the Chilean and Brazilian navies. British agents and diplomats constantly attempted (without success) to convince the restored Bourbon ruler Ferdinand VII to recognize the independence, or at least the autonomy, of his former possessions. The French, meanwhile, attempted to use the anti-republican league that had been formed in Europe following Napoleon's downfall, the Holy Alliance, to assist Spain in regaining its territories, which would then, of course, recognize overriding French influence in the area. Prussia, Austria, and Russia, all countries with little or no naval strength, were willing to fall in with French plans in the name of the restoration of monarchical legitimacy, but the British, for obvious reasons, refused to have anything to do with them. In 1823, the French, acting in the name of the Holy Alliance, marched into Spain to put down a temporarily successful republican-liberal rebellion against Ferdinand VII. With Ferdinand their virtual prisoner, and in any case utterly dependent upon French arms, the French Government hatched one last scheme for dispatching the Spanish *infantes,* or princes, to the American territories with a French-allied army, and placing them on the thrones of a series of semi-independent states allied in a family compact with Spain (and, of course, France). The British Foreign Minister, George Canning, apprised of this plan, approached the American Minister in London, Richard Rush, with the proposal that the two countries declare openly their opposition to the projected expedition. Canning expressed his belief that, by itself, Spain could not recover its possessions, and stated that it was only a matter of time until Britain recognized the new states; that Britain itself did not wish to occupy these territories, but that it would not allow their transfer to a third party. John Quincy Adams, American Secretary of State, when apprised of Canning's approach, correctly concluded that the British, for their own reasons, would not allow the Holy Alliance to invade Latin America under the leadership of France; thus, a joint declaration was unnecessary and would make the United States appear to be acting as a sort of appendage of Britain.

Consequently, he wrote a similar, but unilateral, declaration and persuaded President Monroe to include it in his message to Congress on December 2, 1823. Meanwhile, the French, realizing that their expedition could not succeed if the British opposed it with their navy, renounced the project in a memorandum signed by French Ambassador Polignac in the presence of Canning, almost two months before the date of Monroe's message.

The epoch of the wars for independence in Latin America ended in the year 1824, with the surrender of the Viceroy of Peru. Two years later, Simón Bolívar, liberator of northern South America, called the Congress of Panamá into session, so that the new states could form a league together, the better to prevent any attempts to destroy their newly won independence (see chapter 8). Both the United States and Great Britain were invited to send delegates. It is symbolic of the situation of the hemisphere through most of the rest of the nineteenth century that the American delegates never arrived. The British delegate was there to remind the representatives present of past British favors and present British power, and Canning had instructed delegate Dawkins to make sure they realized that ". . .any project for putting the US of North America at the head of an American confederacy. . .would be highly displeasing to your Govt." Even at the inception of its paramountcy, Great Britain realized from which quarter of the globe its eventual nemesis would probably arise.

C / GREAT BRITAIN AS PARAMOUNT, 1824–96

For more than seventy years following the independence of Latin America, Great Britain exercised paramountcy over the Western Hemisphere. This position was valuable to the British in various ways. The least important of these was the acquisition of territory. In point of fact, the only territory that Britain seized and retained from a Latin American country during this entire period was the Falkland Islands (*Islas Malvinas*), off the southern coast of Argentina, hardly an important acquisition. Possession of the islands was taken by Argentina in 1820, and the Argentine garrison was expelled in 1831 by American whalers, following which, the British occupied the islands in 1833. They are still claimed by Argentina. All other British possessions in the hemisphere had been in British hands before Latin American independence, including British Guiana and British Honduras (*Belice*) on the mainland, and various Caribbean islands.[1] Between 1844 and 1860, Britain exercised a protectorate over the "Mosquito" Coast (roughly the Caribbean coast of Nicaragua), in order the better to dominate the Isthmus of Panama and keep a watch on American filibusterers, but, in 1860, the protectorate was relinquished.

Of much greater importance was the use of the Latin American region for naval-military purposes. The possession of bases and fueling rights enabled Britain effectively to dominate the seas off the hemisphere, and various American and French efforts to break this domination were uniformly unsuccessful. Since British armed interventions were rare, as we shall see, the bases served principally to protect and maintain British trade with Latin America, and the British Caribbean and South Atlantic squadrons were kept at peak efficiency during the period of paramountcy.

Strategically, Latin America has only a peripheral importance to Europe (see accompanying map). From the strategic standpoint, British influence and power were directed toward maintaining an interest in any future interoceanic canal, and in preventing, so far as possible, the spread of American power. From the very beginning of Latin American inpendence, the feeble new state in North America had tried to act as a

---

[1] Although Spain had recognized the right of commercial exploitation of Belice by the British, it had never recognized British sovereignty, laying the basis for the continuing Guatemalan claim to the territory.

Europe-Centered Map, Showing Peripheral Position of Latin America

counter to British influence. As the century advanced, the United States became more and more involved in the Caribbean, under the cover of the Monroe Doctrine, and some have claimed that the United States and Britain enjoyed a sort of condominium paramount status in the Caribbean between 1856 and 1896 (in 1856, Prime Minister Benjamin Disraeli made a speech in the House of Commons recognizing special American interests in the Caribbean). This conclusion is supported neither by a comparison of American and British naval strength in the Caribbean during this time nor by the attitude of the affected Latin American states themselves. The United States was not successfully appealed to against Britain until 1895, and that occasion was precisely the beginning of the end of British paramountcy.

Nevertheless, the British *did* recognize the special interests of the United States in the Caribbean, after failing in their effort to erect an independent Texas as a strategic buffer, and reluctantly signed, in 1850, the Clayton-Bulwer Treaty establishing joint control over any contemplated interoceanic canal. At the same time, Britain assiduously chased filibustering expeditions out of Central America and tried diplomatically to prevent Cuba from falling into American hands. In both these endeavors it was ultimately successful.

All the above goals, however, were themselves directed primarily at the maintenance of Latin America as a source of raw materials and as a prime outlet for British exports, investments, and, to a lesser extent, British emigration and colonization. With the exception of the maintenance of preferential rights in Brazil between 1810 and 1844, this was done solely through the availability of British goods and British tonnage, and the protection and potential threat of the British navy. The extent and importance of British investment can be demonstrated by the fact that, by 1900, these investments totaled £ 540 million, of which £ 312 million were in share capital and £ 228 million in government bonds.[2]

After its initial abortive attempts to seize Latin America from the feeble grasp of Spain and Portugal, Great Britain was, from the Latin American standpoint, an excellent international *caudillo,* protecting Latin America *in its own self-interest* from the other European powers, with a policy at once effective and highly predictable. Except as their policies might touch on the interests of British investors, property, or persons, the British Government interfered hardly at all in the internal governmental arrangements of the Latin American countries. Even in the protection of property and persons, such intervention as was indulged in was often looked upon by the investors themselves as highly inadequate.[3]

More important than the bits and pieces which Britain seized, and occasional armed intervention for the collection of debts, was the British willingness, on occasion, to indulge in these interventions in concert with other European powers, in Argentina, Mexico, and elsewhere. In one case, such willingness led to the establishment of the short-lived empire of Maximilian in Mexico under the very noses of the British, who had originally entered Mexico with the French and the Spanish to force the payment of debts.

Despite these temporary aberrations and failures, however, the British–Latin American association during the nineteenth century was largely a peaceful and successful one on both sides. The British effectively monopolized Latin American trade, allowing only such competition as they wished, and extensive investments were made in the region, yielding high returns at least to the promoters. In return, an area in constant turmoil and chaos, with little capability of defending itself, sailed through the era of maximum European colonization with scarcely a scratch, and with no territorial loss whatsoever to any European country other than Britain itself.

[2] This was the equivalent of over $2,500,000,000, an enormous sum for the day.
[3] See the following articles, all by D. C. M. Platt: "British Bondholders in Nineteenth Century Latin America—Injury and Remedy," *Inter-American Economic Affairs,* vol. xiv, no. 3, Winter, 1960; "Business Influence in the Anglo-Mexican Reconciliation of 1884," same journal, vol. xv, no. 2, Autumn, 1961; "The Allied Coercion of Venezuela, 1902–3—A Reassessment," same journal, vol. xv, no. 4, Spring, 1962.

D / THE UNITED STATES SEIZES PARAMOUNTCY, 1896–1904

An obscure boundary dispute between Venezuela and Great Britain (over the boundary with British Guiana) led to the actual changeover of paramounts in the Western Hemisphere. By 1895, British power was heavily engaged throughout the world, and its strategic position was being challenged everywhere. The United States, in contrast, was just beginning to flex its muscles, and was about to embark on a new extra-continental period of imperialism, relying principally on naval power. For the first time, a Latin American state called upon the United States to protect it against the English, and the United States responded. President Cleveland demanded that Britain arbitrate its boundary dispute, and British Foreign Secretary Lord Salisbury refused. As a result, on July 20, 1895, Secretary of State Olney issued his famous and flamboyant declaration:

> Today the United States is practically sovereign on this continent, and its fiat is law upon the subjects to which it confines its interposition.[4]

This could not have been a more perfect *pronunciamiento* had it been proclaimed by any of the great Latin American *caudillos,* and was a fitting answer, sixty-nine years later, to Canning's instructions to Dawkins. For the next half-century, the only dispute concerning it would revolve about the questions of to *what* subjects the United States would and should properly confine its "interposition." After considerable hesitation, and the possibility of war, the British yielded in 1896, and the United States replaced Britain as *caudillo* of the Western Hemisphere. "In the Caribbean, Britain's surrender of 1896 proved to be only the beginning of a process which within a decade converted that hitherto British-dominated sea into a primary defense zone of the United States." [5]

The process of paramount-replacement begun in 1895 continued with the Spanish-American War of 1898, when the United States took Cuba and Puerto Rico; and, rather than resist, Great Britain in the same year withdrew its fleet from the Caribbean. In 1901, the Hay-Pauncefote Treaty replaced Clayton-Bulwer and gave the United States full control over any future interoceanic canal. In 1902, before establishing a blockade of Venezuela to assure redress of various grievances, Great Britain, Germany, and Italy obtained the permission of the United States, and American naval units under Admiral Dewey maintained surveillance of the blockading fleets. In 1903, Britain dismantled its naval bases in the Caribbean, and, in the same year, acquiesced in the detachment of Panama from Colombia under the aegis of the United States. The changeover was complete by 1904, when American investment funds began to flow into Latin America, soon to overshadow the British stake.

[4] *Foreign Relations of the United States,* 1895, p. 558. Olney to Bayard, July 20, 1895.
[5] Arthur P. Whitaker, *The United States and Latin America—The Northern Republics,* (Cambridge, Mass., 1948), p. 160.

E / THE UNITED STATES AS PARAMOUNT, 1904–54

In the half-century following 1904, the United States extended and consolidated its hegemony over the Western Hemisphere, first through liquidating the vestiges of French and British influence and meeting the new, but essentially feeble, challenge of Imperial Germany, and then, free of all challenge, replacing a policy of aggressive assertion of paramountcy with one emphasizing benevolence toward the client-system.

American interest in Latin America did not, of course, begin in 1896, and certain American statesmen, from the turn of the nineteenth century on, assumed that someday the United States would become paramount over the hemisphere in which it existed. The quite sincere belief that the Americas represented liberty and purity in the face of despotism and corruption in the Old World added a convenient and powerful mystique to strategic and commercial interest. The natural sympathy of a people which only a few years before had broken its colonial ties with its European homeland added an element of emotion to the policy-mix that was not without influence.

As early as 1811, the United States Congress had evinced an interest in the rebellions that were beginning to spread throughout Latin America, by passing a resolution that, whereas the United States had no objection to Spain's retaining its possessions in the hemisphere, any transfer of possessions bordering the United States to a third party would be looked upon with disfavor. The War of 1812, however, sealed off the possibility of a strong American challenge to British commercial dominance for many decades, and the very promising incipient United States–Latin American trade declined.

From the time of the No-Transfer Resolution until 1822, American policy toward Latin America was one of benevolent neutrality in the colonial war that was raging. Although recognition was not extended to the struggling local governments, little impediment was placed in the way of their recruiting and fund-raising activities in this country.[6] Although certain American statesmen, such as Henry Clay, pressed for recognition during this period, principally on sentimental grounds, recognition was withheld by a cautious government in Washington, principally for two reasons. At least until 1820, it was far from clear that the independence movements in Latin America would succeed in throwing off the tutelage of Spain (it should be remembered that the Viceroy of Peru did not finally surrender until 1824), and secondly, the United States was negotiating with Spain for the acquisition of Florida. Recognition of the rebel governments would almost certainly have resulted in Spain's breaking off these negotiations. Signature of the Adam-Onís Treaty in 1819, and its ratification in 1821, left the way clear, and by 1822, it was obvious that

---

[6] This informal policy has been maintained until very recent times, as witness the unhampered activities of Fidel Castro and his associates in the United States prior to their re-entry into Cuba in December, 1956.

at least some of the new governments were going to be able to maintain their independence. Gran Colombia was recognized in June of 1822, and by 1826, with the recognition of Peru, the process was complete, with reference to the Latin American states then existing.[7]

The history of the relations between the United States and Latin America from 1823 until the present can be considered as the history of the Monroe Doctrine, proclaimed in December of 1823. The original announcement of the Doctrine was in direct response to the overtures of Canning to Rush during the previous summer. Secretary of State John Quincy Adams seized upon the evidence that Britain would back up the Doctrine, in its own self-interest (as well as an attempt on the part of the Russian Government to extend its territories in the Western Hemisphere by fiat), to justify the issuance of a unilateral declaration by means of a Presidential message to Congress.

The Monroe Doctrine makes two points. One is a restatement of the No-Transfer Resolution, now extended to all of rebellious Latin America. This is part of what Canning wanted in a joint resolution. The other point of the Monroe Doctrine is that the United States would consider any attempt on the part of the European powers to impose *their political system* upon this hemisphere as "endangering our peace and happiness" and could not view any such attempt in any form "with indifference."[8]

It is obvious that had such an attempt taken place at any time in the years immediately following the issuance of the Monroe Doctrine, there was little that the United States could have done about it, except, perhaps, for an attack on Cuba or Mexico. That this fact was well appreciated in Washington, and that the Monroe Doctrine was issued solely in the national interests of the United States, is attested to by the refusal of the United States Government to entertain the possibility of signing any treaties of mutual aid and assistance with the various Latin American governments, some of which proposed such treaties in the light of Monroe's statements. In effect, in issuing the Doctrine, and for some years afterward, due to the power imperatives brought sadly home in the War of 1812, the United States acted as sub-paramount to Great Britain in North America. With reference to South America, Great Britain simply ignored the Doctrine, seizing the Falkland Islands and intervening freely in the regional disputes of the South American states. France also ignored the Doctrine, not only blockading the port of Buenos Aires twice (once in concert with Great Britain), but blockading Mexico in 1838 and seizing the port of Vera Cruz (in the so-called "Pastry War," waged for the recovery of damages to the property of French citizens). Both disputes were settled through British mediation, without reference to the United States.

[7] With the exception of Haiti, which, because of slave-holding opposition in the United States, was not recognized until 1862.
[8] See Appendix A for the texts of the No-Transfer Resolution, the Monroe Doctrine, and all subsequent modifying corollaries and doctrines.

After the proclamation of the Monroe Doctrine, and until 1836, the United States entered upon a period of quiescence in its foreign policy toward the rest of the hemisphere, devoting its energy and attention to the exploitation of the vast virgin territories acquired from Britain in 1783 and France in 1803.

From the outbreak of the Texas rebellion against Mexico in 1836 to 1860, when the impending Civil War blotted all else out of the public consciousness of the United States, American policy toward Latin America was dominated by two themes—the continental expansion of this country to the west, and the earliest challenges to the British position of paramountcy in the Caribbean. Relations with the South American countries remained of minor importance. We have already mentioned that Britain and France attempted to use the new Texas Republic to stem the westward expansion of the United States, trying to erect it as a buffer between the United States and Mexico. Oddly, this effort was seconded for political reasons by one of the two great parties in the United States, the Whigs. With the accession of Democrat James Polk to the Presidency in 1845, the United States finally annexed Texas by Joint Resolution of Congress, and this act, later ratified by Texas, led, in 1846, to the advance of American troops across the Nueces River to the Rio Grande, precipitating war with Mexico, which, in less than two years, resulted in the loss to that Latin American country of its entire, sparsely populated, northern half. Although the only actual further territorial expansion of the United States at the expense of Latin America was the Gadsden Purchase in 1853, it was far from clear at the time that much more extensive incursions would not take place, and there was a great deal of agitation in the United States, particularly from slave-owning interests, for further seizure of territory.

Much of this agitation was directed toward Cuba. As far back as the Jefferson Administration, interest had been shown in the eventual acquisition of Cuba, and various filibustering expeditions to the island originated in the United States. Several offers were made to the Spanish Government for purchase of the island, and in 1854, the American Ministers in London, Paris, and Madrid met at Ostend and issued a manifesto declaring that if Spain refused to sell, the United States should seize Cuba. Spain continued to be adamant, however, and the Ostend Manifesto was repudiated by Washington. In the meantime (1845 and 1848), President Polk had proclaimed the so-called Polk Corollary to the Monroe Doctrine, in which he expressed America's special interest in the Caribbean, and extended the No-Transfer Doctrine to include the takeover of independent territories in the hemisphere by extra-continental powers. Filibustering increased during the 1850's, with expeditions to Mexico and Central America, and this put the United States in direct conflict with Great Britain for influence in the "American Mediterranean." In 1846, the Bidlack Treaty was signed with Colombia, offering that country the protection of the United States and the integrity of the Isthmus of Panama, in return for the right of transit across the Isthmus. In 1850, the Clayton-Bulwer Treaty was signed with Great Britain, providing for joint U.S.–

British control over any canal, and binding both parties not to fortify the Isthmus or exercise exclusive control. American sub-paramountcy in the Caribbean was formally recognized by the British, by means of Prime Minister Disraeli's speech in the House of Commons in 1856.

The outbreak of the Civil War in the United States provided the cover for two important violations of the Monroe Doctrine, which the United States was powerless to counteract. Outwitting the British under the cover of a joint expedition, the French invaded Mexico in 1861 and installed Austrian Archduke Maximilian as puppet Emperor. Upon invitation of the Dominican Government, Spain retook possession of the eastern half of Santo Domingo in the same year, the British apparently preferring a weak Spain in control in preference to constant chaos inviting stronger intervention. The United States protested both incursions diplomatically, however, and upon the termination of the Civil War pressured both European governments to withdraw, moving troops to the Rio Grande. Spain retired from Santo Domingo in 1865, and Napoleon III, faced with European complications, abandoned Maximilian in early 1867, which was followed shortly by the puppet Emperor's capture and execution by Mexican patriot forces. These incidents marked the first enforcement of the No-Transfer portion of the Monroe Doctrine, as well as reasserting the prohibition on the introduction of European doctrines.

These triumphs were not followed up, however, and during the period 1867–89, preoccupied with reconstruction and industrialization, the United States again held its Latin American policy in abeyance. During these twenty-two years, only the abortive annexation request by the Dominican Republic in 1871, and Secretary of State James G. Blaine's equally abortive attempt to call a continental conference in 1881 are worthy of note.[9]

The holding of the first Inter-American Conference in 1889–90 (see Chapter 4) heralded the opening of the final spurt leading to the establishment of American paramountcy during the 1896–1904 period, already traced. Further evidence of the impending change was the issuance of the Hayes Corollary in 1889, stating that the United States should have sole control of any interoceanic canal.

Between 1904 and 1928, the United States successfully consolidated its newly gained paramountcy through the employment of three interrelated strategies. The first was the "protection" of Latin America from further nineteenth-century-style interventions by the European countries. The only, even mildly, plausible threat during this time was the informal German offer to Mexico to help it regain its lost territories if it came into World War I on the German side in case of American entry. The case is principally interesting as an example of German diplomatic naïveté. Under cover of this "protection," the United States itself intervened extensively in the Caribbean region, both informally and in accordance with written protectorate agreements with Cuba, Panama, and Nicaragua.

---

[9] An annexation treaty was actually signed with the Dominican Republic, but rejected by the U.S. Senate. The Yucatán Peninsula of Mexico had earlier applied for admission to the United States in the 1840's.

Formal expression of these policies was given by President Theodore Roosevelt in 1904, in the Roosevelt Corollary to the Monroe Doctrine. In his message to Congress in December of that year, he proclaimed the right of the United States to exercise ". . . an international police power" in the Western Hemisphere for the protection of the states involved, and to prevent chaos. In accordance with the Roosevelt Corollary, the United States took over the administration of the Dominican customhouses in 1904, to ensure payment of debts to European countries. In 1906, Cuba was intervened, under the formal terms of the Platt Amendment to the Cuban Independence Act. In 1907, the United States actively pressured for the adoption of a Central American treaty which it hoped would pro- vide a tranquil environment for the Panama Canal it was already digging. American troops intervened in Panama itself in 1908, 1912, and 1918. In 1912, the United States established a virtual protectorate over Nicara- gua, maintaining a sizable garrison of Marines. In 1914, American Marines occupied Vera Cruz in an attempt to topple the government of Victoriano Huerta in Mexico. In 1916, General Pershing invaded Mexico in an unsuccessful effort to capture and punish the bandit-revolutionary Pancho Villa, who had sacked an American border town.

Meanwhile, in 1915, in response to conditions of continuous chaos, the United States occupied Haiti, later signing a protectorate agreement. Having evacuated Cuba in 1909, American troops returned in 1916, leaving again in 1920. In 1917, the United States purchased the Virgin Islands from Denmark, to prevent their falling into the hands of any other power. In 1916, the Marines occupied the Dominican Republic, remain- ing until 1924. In 1926, Nicaragua was occupied. In 1923, another Central American treaty was signed with the prodding of the United States, the institutional arrangements of the 1907 treaty having in the meantime collapsed.

Meanwhile, in 1912, an attempt by a private Japanese company to lease a Mexican port for fishing purposes, led to the issuance of the Lodge Corollary to the Monroe Doctrine, to be resurrected a half-century later in Cuba (see Chapter 5). This corollary, proclaimed in a speech by Senator Henry Cabot Lodge, declares that the United States will oppose any moves by extra-continental powers which might lead to the establish- ment of military or naval bases in this hemisphere. The declaration was directed as much toward Germany as Japan, Admiral von Tirpitz having eyed the Dutch possessions in the Caribbean, and heavily German- populated southern Brazil, as possible sources of bases and extensions of German influence.

The third prong of American policy was the extension of trade and investment, in order to replace Britain as the principal economic influence on Latin America. By 1930, American investors had over five billion dollars in Latin America, in direct investments and government bonds, exceeding the British stake by, perhaps, a billion dollars. The value of American trade with Latin America had passed the British by 1913, and in 1917, under the influence of World War I, the United States accounted

TABLE II—PRIVATE INVESTMENTS IN LATIN AMERICA, 1897–1958
(IN MILLIONS OF DOLLARS)

Country	1897	1929	1946	1958
United States				
Direct Investments	308	3,705	3,000	8,730
Portfolio Investments	—	1,724	672	1,039
Total	308	5,429	3,672	9,769
Great Britain	2,060	4,500*	3,575	2,547****
France	628	454**	307	N.A.
Germany	—	700***	—	160

Source: United States Senate, *United States Business and Labor in Latin America,*
(A Study Prepared at the Request of the Subcommittee on American Republics
Affairs of the Committee on Foreign Relations by the University of Chicago Research Center in Economic Development and Cultural Change), January 22, 1960.
    * 1929 figures not available. $4,865 in 1913 and $4,542 in 1940.
  ** 1929 not available. $454 in 1940.
 *** 1929 not available $677 in 1918 and $969 in 1940.
**** 1958 not available. $2,547 in 1950.

for over forty percent of both the imports and the exports of Latin
America.

American interventions in the period 1904–28 quite naturally aroused
intense resentment in Latin America. In asserting its hegemony, the new
paramount was proving far too obstreperous. Conveniently forgetting the
long-distant invasions of Buenos Aires in 1806–07 and the British Mexican plans of 1808, the Latin Americans compared the Yankees unfavor-
ably with the British as paramounts. A wave of anti-Americanism swept
Latin America, and was reflected in polemics such as the following:

> Wilson and Roosevelt have torn the glorious flag; they flaunt the
> insolent rag over the affliction of the Latin race of America, which
> they dream of exterminating, in the savage ferocity of their barbarous
> souls! English imperialism makes for civilization. Proof of this may
> be seen in great and prosperous India, in Egypt, in Australia, and
> in Canada. . . . Wherever the Englishman goes, a village is born,
> wherever the Yankee goes, a race dies.[10]

Anti-Americanism was even reflected in folk art, as in the following
romance composed in Mexico at the time of the Pershing expedition:

> Mother of mine of Guadalupe
> Bless this soldier of your nation,
> Tomorrow I march to war,
> The war against intervention.
>
> Oh beautiful Guadalupe,
> Sacred and belovéd Virgin.
> You must not let the gringoes
> Consume the blood of your children.[11]

[10] Vargas Villa, quoted in A. Curtis Wilgus, ed., *Readings in Latin American Civilization* (New York, 1946), p. 354.
[11] Quoted in *Ibid.,* p. 313.

In World War I, only eight Latin American countries followed the United States in declaring war on the Central Powers. Of these, seven were tiny Caribbean and Central American states. Only Brazil, among the larger powers, declared war. Five states broke relations with the Central Powers, including Peru. Seven countries remained completely neutral, including such strategically located countries as Mexico, Colombia, and Venezuela.

The end of the period of assertive paramountcy, and the beginning of the period of benevolent paramountcy (from 1928 to 1954) was, as always, signaled by an addition to the Monroe Doctrine. In 1928, Under Secretary of State J. Reuben Clark presented a memorandum on the Doctrine to the Hoover Administration. The Clark Memorandum, published in 1930, was a revision of the Roosevelt Corollary, and, in effect, stated that the Monroe Doctrine, directed against Europe, did not by itself justify United States intervention in the internal affairs of the Latin American countries.

By 1928–30, the United States was secure in its paramount position in the Western Hemisphere. Having repulsed all real and imaginary extra-continental threats and having demonstrated graphically its overwhelming power, it could afford to reduce the element of power in its client relationships and stress the element of legitimacy, largely through use of the Western Hemisphere mystique already mentioned. In accordance with this basic change in strategy, Secretary of State Cordell Hull journeyed to Montevideo in 1933 and signed a nonintervention pledge, with a reservation maintaining the rights of the United States under general international law (see Chapter 6). In the same year, the Marines left Nicaragua. In 1934, Haiti was evacuated and the United States gave up its protectorate over Cuba. In 1936, the right to intervene in Haiti and Panama was relinquished, and at a conference in Buenos Aires, an absolute nonintervention pledge was signed, this time without reservations. The mystique of the "Good Neighbor" was propagandized throughout the hemisphere to create still further legitimacy. The Good Neighbor Policy was given its first severe test when Bolivia nationalized foreign oil companies in 1937. The United States did not intervene, but confined itself to expressing hope for a just settlement, thereby adopting the policy generally followed by Britain in the nineteenth century, when faced with financial claims of its citizens (basically a policy that investors must accept the risks of their investments). A graver test came in 1938, with the Mexican nationalization of oil. Despite heavy internal pressures to intervene forcibly, the administration did not do so. Finally, in 1940, United States inspectors withdrew from the Dominican customhouses, fittingly ending the period of withdrawal by evacuating those bits of Latin American territory, the occupation of which had begun the period of intervention.

For a decade-and-a-half following this final withdrawal, it appeared that the United States had been successful in replacing power, to a large extent, with legitimacy in maintaining its authority in Latin America. In World War II, Latin American cooperation was forthcoming in large measure, with all countries eventually declaring war on the Axis (Chile and Argentina very late and reluctantly—these being the two countries farthest from United States influence, and with large German and Italian populations). Extensive Nazi efforts to influence Latin America by means of investment and trade (largely barter agreements and loans), and the manipulation of local Germans, under the terms of the Stuttgart Decrees of 1937 (demanding absolute obedience of overseas Germans to the German Government under the threat of reprisals to relatives at home), were successfully counteracted, in most cases with the support of the governments involved. Bases and raw materials were supplied to the United States under advantageous terms, and Mexico and Brazil supplied military forces as well.

Following the end of the war, between 1945 and 1948, in a series of conferences in Mexico City, Rio de Janeiro, and Bogotá, the inter-American system was strengthened and perfected (see Chapter 4). The paramountcy of the United States appeared to be absolutely secure and to be based on a large element of legitimacy. Nineteen forty-eight was the high-water mark of this legitimacy. Between that year and the emergence, in 1954, of a new and infinitely more powerful threat to American hegemony than the Germans had ever posed, the United States rested on its laurels in the Western Hemisphere, and became politically, militarily, and economically involved throughout the world (as it had to, as one of the only two remaining international paramounts after Great Britain abdicated that position in 1947). Latin America was neglected while the processes of modernization and industrialization (in other words, social change) created discontents ignored by the paramount (which during this period granted more economic assistance to Yugoslavia alone than to all of Latin America). As a result, legitimacy declined and a vacuum was created, which the Soviet Union sought to fill. The new era of international politics in the Western Hemisphere began as usual with an interpretation of the Monroe Doctrine, this time the Dulles Doctrine, and in a most unlikely spot, the tiny Central American republic of Guatemala. The Soviet challenge has been, by far, the principal element in United States–Latin American relations since 1954, and will be analyzed in Chapter 5.

As is natural, the reign of the *Pax Americana* in Latin America has led to important cultural and social influences, as well as to political and economic ones. Although we do not have the space to go into these developments in detail, it should be noted that cultural and social influences can be very important in international politics, especially in the effort of a paramount or sub-paramount to develop legitimacy in its client system. In this respect, the United States suffers from the fact that it is not Latin. Latin American resistance to American cultural penetration is symbolized by the polemic *Ariel,* published in 1900, at the very dawn of the American century. Written by Uruguayan José Enrique Rodó, *Ariel* contrasts the spiritually oriented Latins with the crass, materialistic, Anglo-Saxons, to the detriment of the latter. Despite intellectual resistance, however, the Americanization of Latin American cultural and social life continues apace, and seems destined to continue until another power becomes dominant in the hemisphere.

How, then, may we characterize American paramountcy during the half-century of its virtually unchallenged sway over Latin America? It must first be said that there is no area of the world more strategically important to the United States than the Caribbean, if that term is used to include Colombia and Venezuela, as well as Mexico, Central America, and the islands. In the strategic sense, the boundary between North and South America is the Amazon Basin, and between 1904 and 1954, the Caribbean was a "closed sea." South America, in contrast, is strategically important mainly because of its possible demonstration, or spread-effect, on the Caribbean countries. Thus a less strict client relationship may be maintained with the South American countries (". . . the temperate zone of the southern continent lies too far away from the center of our power to be easily intimidated by measures short of war.")[12] As we shall see in the next section of this chapter this looser tutelage has enabled the countries of southern South America to wage a struggle for sub-paramountcy.

For an ideal relationship, from the standpoint of the clients involved, the United States is, perhaps, a little too close for comfort, and its power, perhaps, too overwhelming. Certainly, it has seemed much too willing to interfere in the domestic affairs of its clients, rather than confining itself to defending its own international interests as Great Britain did, by and large (after 1808). More important than either of these, perhaps, is the unpredictability of United States policy, seemingly eternally vacillating between direct intervention and absolute indifference, between power politics and idealism.[13] Material assistance and military protection against outside threat are acceptable elements coming through the paramount-client pipeline, as far as the clients are concerned. Marines and indifference are not, unless clearly motivated by the unquestionable national interest of the paramount, and then only temporarily.

> . . . it is useful to keep in mind the tolerance Latin Americans have shown to infractions of the (nonintervention) doctrine when they were convinced that such deviations were prompted by generous motives.[14]

[12] N. S. Spykman, *America's Strategy in World Politics* (New York, 1942), p. 62.
[13] It should be noted that the Latin American policy of the United States has not really been quite as unpredictable as it often seems to the Latin Americans. Generally, non-interference predominates when the United States feels its hegemony secure, while forcible intervention takes place when that hegemony seems to be threatened. The period of the Good Neighbor Policy, perhaps, saw a policy-combination most like the earlier British paramountcy: noninterference in the internal affairs of the Latin American countries, solicitude with reference to regional disputes, coupled with vigorous defense of more narrowly defined national interests than in earlier periods. It must be added, however, that all of this took place at a time when United States hegemony seemed unchallengeable, and, also, that Latin America is more strategically important to the United States than it was to Great Britain.
[14] George Wythe, *The United States and Inter-American Relations* (Gainesville, 1964), p. 230.

United States-Centered Map, Showing Position of Latin America

TABLE III—SCHEMATIC HISTORY OF THE MONROE DOCTRINE

Year	Statement	Meaning
1811	No-Transfer Resolution	No transfer of bordering lands from Spain
1823	Monroe Doctrine	No transfer of any of Spain's territories No introduction of alien political doctrines
1845 & 1848	Polk Corollaries	U.S. interest in Caribbean No transfer of independent lands
1889	Hayes Corollary	U.S. control of any canal
1895	Olney Declaration	U.S. paramountcy
1904	Roosevelt Corollary	International police power
1914	Lodge Corollary	No foreign bases
1928	Clark Memorandum	Revokes Roosevelt Corollary
1954	Dulles Doctrine	Restates no introduction of alien political doctrines.

F / THE STRUGGLE FOR SUB-PARAMOUNTCY IN LATIN AMERICA

The struggle for hemispheric sub-paramountcy among the various more powerful Latin American countries has gone through three phases. In the first, between 1821 and 1883, because of the immense distances involved, and the limited and relatively primitive means of transportation and communications available, no single Latin American country attempted to establish sub-paramountcy over the whole hemispheric island. Rather, Brazil and Argentina disputed hegemony over Atlantic South America, Chile succeeded in controlling Pacific South America, and, as we have seen, the United States became *de facto* sub-paramount in the Caribbean after the collapse of Gran Colombia and the defeat of Mexico—all under the general hemispheric paramountcy of Great Britain.

Under the Emperor Iturbide, Mexico annexed Central America in 1821, only to lose it again in 1823 upon Iturbide's downfall. Plans to invade Spain's island possessions and reunite the Viceroyalty of New Spain (with the exception of the Philippines) came to nothing, and shortly thereafter, internal chaos forced Mexico's attention inward. Mexico was not even successful in maintaining the integrity of its own territory, and the Mexican War with the United States effectively put an end to any possibility of sub-paramountcy for Mexico in the Caribbean. Nevertheless, the strategic position of Mexico is such, that it seemed the logical base to Napoleon III for his ill-fated attempt to build a Latin Empire in the New World to challenge the British and American hegemony. As we shall see later, Mexico's interest in the Caribbean has more recently revived. Gran Colombia remained as a power contender in the Caribbean for even a shorter time than Mexico. Following Colombia's lead in calling the Panama Congress of 1826, internal political conditions rapidly disintegrated, leading to the breakup of the country into its constituent parts of Venezuela, Colombia, and Ecuador in 1831. No one of the parts had sufficient inherent weight to aspire to a position of regional hegemony.

From the earliest years of its independence, Chile strove to control South America's Pacific coast. In this temporarily successful effort, it used three strategies: the sponsorship of regional conferences during the nineteenth century (see Chapter 8), the maintenance of regional naval supremacy, and war. In 1835, General Andrés Santa Cruz, dictator of Bolivia, united that country to Peru. Sensing in this a direct challenge to its pretensions to regional dominance, the Chileans declared war in 1836, by 1839 defeating the combined forces of the confederacy and forcing separation of the recently united countries. Argentina, also, took a minor part in the war against the Confederation. Between 1840 and 1878, Chile continued to build up its naval forces, and, in the latter year, attacked Bolivia under the pretext of an increase in Bolivian taxation of Chilean nitrate companies operating in the then Bolivian portion of the Atacama Desert. Peru entered the war on the side of Bolivia, and Chile handily defeated both countries, seizing the entire desert region from Bolivia and Peru in negotiations subsequent to the end of the war in 1883, leaving

Bolivia without a seacoast, and both countries without nitrate resources. The Chilean Navy, at this time, was powerful enough to discourage United States attempts at mediation, and following the war, Chile was undisputed sub-paramount over Pacific South America. This was, in fact, the apogee of Chilean regional influence, never to be maintained or exceeded in subsequent years.[15]

Throughout the nineteenth century, Brazil and Argentina disputed sub-paramountcy over Atlantic South America, without reaching a clear-cut conclusion. In 1777, Portugal had recognized Spain's right to the *Banda Oriental,* the territory to the east of the Uruguay River, with its capital at Montevideo. In 1817, however, following the independence of Argentina, Portuguese troops seized the region, annexing it to the territory of Brazil. In 1822, it passed to the independent Empire of Brazil. In 1825, a local uprising against the Brazilians began, and was immediately supported by Argentine troops. By 1828, the Brazilians were driven out of the *Banda,* and the two countries agreed to establish an independent republic of Uruguay as a buffer between them. This result was brought about through British mediation, the British regularly supporting Brazilian pretensions against Argentina during this period. Internal fighting between the Colorado and Blanco factions in Uruguay gave both Argentina and Brazil a new excuse to intervene, and, between 1836 and 1852, the so-called Long War raged in Uruguay, with the Argentines supporting the Blancos and the Brazilians supporting the Colorados. In 1845, France and Great Britain actively intervened against Argentina, breaking the Argentine blockade of Montevideo and establishing their own blockade of Buenos Aires. The downfall of dictator Juan Manuel de Rosas, in 1852, resulted in the withdrawal of Argentina from the struggle, and assured the continued independence of Uruguay as a buffer. In 1864, the Paraguayan dictator Francisco Solano López entered the South American power struggle against both Argentina and Brazil, again under the pretext of supporting one of the political factions in Uruguay. Attacking first Brazil and then Argentina, he was faced with a triple alliance of Brazil, Argentina, and Uruguay against him, and after six years of bloody warfare and the annihilation of some eighty per cent of the Paraguayan male population, the war concluded with the defeat of Paraguay. Brazil and Argentina both took portions of Paraguayan territory, leaving a rump state as another buffer between them. For the rest of the nineteenth century, the power struggle between Argentina and Brazil remained inconclusive, both staying aloof from the Latin American conferences of the period (see Chapter 8), in order to avoid compromising their claims to leadership. Between 1851 and 1907, however, Brazil succeeded through war and extremely able diplomacy in extending its territory at the expense of Uruguay, Paraguay, Argentina, Bolivia, Ecuador, Venezuela, and Colombia, or, in other words, all of its neighbors except for Peru and the Guianas. Brazil was unable to match the Argentine record of moderniza-

---

[15] Chile and Peru still maintain a 5:3 naval ratio in the Pacific.

Territory from Uruguay, 1851
Territory from Venezuela, Treaties of 1859 and 1905
Territory from Bolivia, Treaty of 1867
Territory from Paraguay, Treaty of 1872
Territory from Argentina, Arbitral Award of 1895
Territory from Bolivia, Treaty of 1903
Territory from Ecuador, Treaty of 1904
Territory from Colombia, Treaty of 1907

Map of Brazil Showing Territorial Expansion, 1851-1907

tion and phenomenal economic development in the second half of the nineteenth century, and had to extend itself to keep up with Argentine military growth. International prestige is attained through a combination of fear and admiration. By 1883 (the end of the Second War of the Pacific), regional prestige in Latin America was about equally shared among Argentina, Brazil, and Chile, the so-called ABC powers.

The period of ABC sub-paramount condominium, between 1883 and 1924, coincided with the changeover of paramounts, from Great Britain to the United States. The resulting confusion enabled the ABC powers to play a more flexible role than would otherwise have been the case. Two factors created an opposite tendency, however. Jealousy among the three powers prevented joint action in many cases, and the imposition of the *Pax Americana* by the end of the first decade of the twentieth century drastically reduced any likelihood of changing the *status quo* by direct action. ABC intervention in intra-regional politics, formalized by the Tripartite Treaty of 1915, was thus limited to offers of mediation and diplomatic intercession, as in the Tacna-Arica dispute between Peru and Chile, and the Leticia dispute between Colombia and Peru. As the period drew to its close, however, it became clear that Chile would not be able to continue in the race for sub-paramountcy because of its inherent limitations of location, population, and resources. The last gasp of Chilean participation in the conflict was the abortive Valparaíso naval limitation conference of 1923, and, even there, Chile's role was largely limited to that of cat's paw between Brazil and Argentina. As American power grew, it became clear that, in any case, a condominium approach to sub-paramountcy could not be successful, and the last gasp of the ABC concept was the joint mediation of the powers, along with the United States, in the only formal Latin American war of the twentieth century, the Chaco War between Paraguay and Bolivia (1928–38). By the time of the Ecuador-Peru dispute of 1941–42, mediation was supplied principally by Brazil, acting as American sub-paramount.[16] During this same period, the long-term dictatorship of Porfirio Díaz in Mexico had enabled that country again to take an interest in the affairs of the Caribbean, and that country actively participated along with the United States in imposing the 1907 treaty on Central America. The Mexican Revolution of 1910, however,

---

[16] It should be noted that the Peru–Ecuador boundary dispute, as well as the earlier Leticia dispute between Colombia and Peru (1932–35) erupted into large-scale military operations, although there were no formal declarations of war. United States interests were not directly involved in the Leticia and Chaco disputes, which the paramount allowed to rage with only mediatory efforts until stalemate resulted, at which point the United States was instrumental in securing final settlement (see Chapter 7). The Ecuador–Peru boundary "war" took place between July, 1941 and January, 1942, however; before, during, and after Pearl Harbor. The United States refused to countenance armed conflict in Latin America at a time of a crisis of such magnitude, and particularly armed conflict that could, perhaps, be exploited by the Japanese. Thus, a very unfavorable settlement was imposed upon Ecuador, which has never ceased to protest against it, whereas the settlements achieved in the Leticia and Chaco disputes appear to be accepted by all sides. It is true that Ecuador was militarily helpless, and Peru's legal claim to the disputed area was better, but it is also true that Ecuador was the victim of unprovoked military aggression on the part of Peru.

again plunged the country into chaos, and again, Mexico withdrew into itself, in the task of reconstruction and consolidation.

Despite indications in the 1960's of a renewed interest in regional influence on the part of Mexico and Chile, the story of the struggle for sub-paramountcy since 1924 has been that of Brazil *vs.* Argentina. The two South American powers have generally adopted diametrically opposed strategies in attempting to attain their goal. Brazil has, by and large, supported the United States in its international policies, while Argentina has rather consistently opposed the hemispheric paramount. Argentina has thus directed its search for legitimacy toward playing upon the innate resentment of clients toward their paramount, while Brazil has aimed its search for legitimacy upward, claiming, as a result, to be able to "do more" for the Latin American client system because of its special relationship with the paramount. The struggle between the two powers has been indecisive, largely because of internal developments. Between 1924 and the end of World War II, Brazil was generally more successful than Argentina in the competition for influence, although there was, by no means, any clear-cut decision. With the advent of dictator Juan Perón in Argentina, however, Argentine efforts at dominance were redoubled. The original manifesto of the *Grupo de Oficiales Unidos* (GOU) (the military clique that ousted the civilian government in the 1943 *coup* leading to Perón's rise to power) recognized that Brazil was the only other claimant to leadership in South America. The manifesto proposed neutralizing Brazilian influence through successive Argentine dominance of Paraguay, Bolivia, Chile, and Uruguay, presenting Brazil with no choice but to go along with Argentine initiatives. Perón spent billions of dollars in the attempt to gain the fear and admiration of the other Latin American states, through his purchase of foreign utilities and railroads, the formation of a regional labor confederation (ATLAS), the *Agencia Latina* news agency, a disastrously expensive attempt to create an atomic capability, attempts to disrupt the functioning of the inter-American system, and the building up of the Argentine armed forces. By 1951, the Argentine bid for hegemony reached its apogee. ATLAS had been moderately successful. The Paraguayan government was an Argentina puppet. Diplomatic initiatives in Uruguay, Bolivia, and Chile, while not as successful as in Paraguay, were not effectively countered by Brazil. Temporary success, however, had been bought at the cost of the long-term health of the Argentine economy. As this fact became clear, Perón was forced to turn for help to the United States, thus undercutting his entire strategy. After his downfall in 1955, the Argentine economy continued its decline, for the time being putting Argentina firmly in the position of a direct and needy client of the United States. Only by mid-1960, provided a breathing-spell by the relative stability of the colorless Illia Administration, was the Argentine foreign office able to take a few timid steps toward the reassertion of influence, signing an economic agreement with Chile and threatening to walk out of a meeting of the Latin American Free Trade Association over the issue of the formation of a permanent commission that might someday exercise supranational authority. (Brazil also opposed this, of course.)

Taking over where Argentina left off, the Kubitschek Administration in Brazil, riding on a wave of economic growth and national euphoria (symbolized by the building of Brasília), made a strong bid for sub-paramountcy in terms of its own strategy, reinforcing the inter-American system and acting as friendly spokesman for Latin America to the United States. The proclamation by President Kubitschek of "Operation Pan America" in 1958 coincided with Vice-President Nixon's disastrous trip around Latin America the same year, which marked the beginning of American realization of the cost of its policy of neglect of Latin America during the preceding decade. Unfortunately, the United States undercut the Brazilian initiative, relegating its ally to a subordinate position in the formation of the Inter-American Development Bank and the signing of the Act of Bogotá in 1960, the Charter of Punta del Este in 1961, and the Alliance for Progress. The succeeding Quadros Administration responded by reversing traditional Brazilian policy and asserting independence of the United States in rather adolescent ways, such as decorating Ernesto "Ché" Guevara, Argentine co-leader of the Cuban revolution. Maintenance of Brazilian economic momentum, coupled with the skill of the splendid Brazilian diplomatic service and foreign office, might well have overcome these temporary disappointments, however, and impelled Brazil into undisputed sub-paramountcy over the sub-continent. The Brazilian economy was no more able than the Argentine to withstand the strain, however, and galloping inflation debilitated the country. President Goulart (August, 1961–April, 1964) attempted to continue the independent policies of his short-term predecessor (Quadros resigned after only a few months in office), but the economic decline rendered his policies inoperative. Following the rebellion of April, 1964, the new government of Marshal Castelo Branco has returned to a foreign policy of support for the United States, but internal dissension and continued economic weakness prevented an immediate resurgence of Brazilian influence.

As of the mid-1960's there was no effective claimant to Latin American sub-paramountcy. The weakness of the two logical candidates, Argentina and Brazil, has enabled Chile and Mexico to seize the initiative on various occasions. Nevertheless, Chile is too weak, and Mexico, despite the prestige of its successful revolution, present stability, and independent foreign policy, is perhaps, too close to the United States to be truly effective. Thus, the race remains between Brazil and Argentina, and the likelihood is that whichever of the two succeeds in putting its domestic house in order will eventually succeed.

Recently an acute observer of Latin American politics noted that recent intra-regional trends have been ". . . towards a strengthening of the solidarity of the Latin American group and a weakening of the group's ties with the United States." [17] This has been attempted largely through economic strategies, and will be examined in Chapter 8.

[17] A. P. Whitaker, *Nationalism in Latin America* (Gainesville, 1962), p. 72.

Selected Bibliography

Inter-cultural psychology is a sorely-neglected field, and its international implications even more so. Thus Lloyd A. Free's *Some International Implications of the Political Psychology of Brazilians* (Princeton, 1961) is mentioned, not because it is particularly exhaustive or enlightening, but because it is almost unique. António Austregesilo has a rather weak chapter on Brazil in George Kisker, ed., *World Tension: The Psychopathology of International Relations* (New York, 1951). See also the very suggestive chapter by Fernando Guillén Martínez in Norman A. Bailey, ed., *Latin America: Politics, Economics, and Hemispheric Security* (New York, 1965). Other works on the general subject of psychology and international politics are mentioned in the Selected Bibliography for Chapter 1. The British, French, and Dutch efforts to detach parts of Spanish and Portuguese America prior to independence are described and discussed in many works on colonial Latin America, including the ones mentioned in the Selected Bibliography for Chapter 2.

Highly recommended as a stimulating attempt to construct a theory of international politics and the role of underdeveloped countries in international society is Gustavo Lagos' *International Stratification and Underdeveloped Countries* (Chapel Hill, 1963). Lagos, who is Chilean, illustrates his hypotheses with many Latin American examples. He sees the action of underdeveloped countries as ". . . systems of action oriented to enhance the real status of the nation in a stratified world, dominated by the values of wealth, power and prestige." (p. x) For many years, Professor J. Fred Rippy has been the outstanding student of the role of Latin America in international politics, and his works, *Latin America in World Politics* (3rd. ed., New York, 1938), *South America and Hemisphere Defense* (Baton Rouge, 1941), and *Globe and Hemisphere* (Chicago, 1958), should be consulted.

For accounts of the maneuvering among Great Britain, France, and the United States during the independence wars in Latin America, see W. W. Kaufman, *British Policy and the Independence of Latin America* (New Haven, 1951); J. Fred Rippy, *Rivalry of the United States and Great Britain Over Latin America, 1808–1830* (Baltimore, 1929); W. S. Robertson, *France and Latin American Independence* (Baltimore, 1939); J. Rydjord, *Foreign Interest in the Independence of New Spain* (Durham, 1935); and H. W. V. Temperley, *The Foreign Policy of Canning, 1822–1827* (London, 1925). C. K. Webster has edited and annotated a volume of documents on the period, *Britain and the Independence of Latin America, 1812–1830* (London, 1944). For the period of British paramountcy, see "Foreign Policies in Latin America," *Current History,* vol. 28, no. 163, March, 1955; W. H. Koebel, *British Exploits in South America* (New York, 1917); A. K. Manchester, *British Preeminence in Brazil* (New York, 1964); and J. Fred Rippy, *British Investments in Latin America, 1822–1949* (Minneapolis, 1959).

There are many general works on United States–Latin American relations, among which the following can be especially recommended: W. S. Robertson, *Hispanic American Relations with the United States* (Washington, 1923); Samuel Flagg Bemis' classic study *The Latin American Policy of the United States* (New York, 1943); Graham H. Stuart's confused, but useful, *Latin America and the United States* (5th ed., New York, 1955); Thomas W. Palmer, Jr., *Search for a Latin American Policy* (Gainesville, 1957); Dexter Perkins, *The United States and Latin America* (Baton Rouge, 1961); George Wythe, *The United States and Inter-American Relations* (Gainesville, 1964) and J. Lloyd Mecham, *A Survey of United States–Latin American Relations* (Boston, 1965). Although it is a general history of United States diplomatic relations, T. A. Bailey's *A Diplomatic History of the American People* (New York, 1955), is still one of the great classic texts. The development of the Western Hemisphere mystique is traced by A. P. Whitaker in *The Western Hemisphere Idea: Its Rise and Decline* (Ithaca, 1954). It is Whitaker's thesis that the "idea" has seen its day and is on its way out. This thesis is disputed by Rippy in *Globe and Hemisphere,* already mentioned. Useful compendia of documents on United States–Latin American relations will be found in J. W. Gantenbein, *The Evolution of Our Latin American Policy: A Documentary Record* (New York, 1950), and Norman W. Graebner, *Ideas and Diplomacy* (New York, 1964).

A sufficiently detailed understanding of the Monroe Doctrine can be obtained by reading Dexter Perkins', *Hands Off: A History of the Monroe Doctrine* (Boston, 1941), without going through the various tomes of which this volume is a condensation. Gaston Nerval [R. Díez de Medina], *Autopsy of the Monroe Doctrine* (New York, 1934), should be read in conjunction with Perkins. The chapter on the Monroe Doctrine by Donald M. Dozer in the book mentioned above edited by the author is excellent.

On specialized topics in the general field of United States–Latin American relations, the choice is not quite so great. Harry Bernstein, in *Origins of Inter-American Interest 1700–1812* (New York, 1945) flows into C. C. Griffin, *The United States and the Disruption of the Spanish Empire 1810–1822* (New York, 1937), and A. P. Whitaker, *The United States and the Independence of Latin America* (Baltimore, 1941). The period of the changeover in paramounts is traced in W. H. Callcott, *The Caribbean Policy of the United States 1890–1920* (Baltimore, 1942). Dana G. Munro provides a detailed historical overview of the period of assertive hegemony in *Intervention and Dollar Diplomacy in the Caribbean 1900–1921* (Princeton, 1964). It is Prof. Munro's thesis that the principal motivation of the United States during this period was political—putting an end to conditions that threatened the independence of various Latin American countries and inviting foreign intervention from Europe, thus posing a potential threat to the security of the United States (see, especially, page 531). The story of the transition into benevolent hegemony is splendidly told in Bryce Wood, *The Making of the Good Neighbor Policy* (New York, 1961). The same author has examined United States involvement in three armed disputes in twentieth-century Latin America: *The United States and Latin American Wars, 1932–1942* (New York, 1966).

Analysis of separate countries or regions is found in A. P. Whitaker, *The United States and South America: The Northern Republics* (Cambridge, Mass., 1948); *idem., The United States and Argentina* (Cambridge, Mass., 1954); and Howard F. Cline, *The United States and Mexico* (Cambridge, Mass., 1953). Some aspects of American cultural influence are explored in René de Visme Williamson, *Culture and Policy: The United States and the Hispanic World* (Knoxville, 1949). There are many works on American world strategy, but a still very pertinent classic that concentrates on the position of Latin America is N. S. Spykman, *America's Strategy in World Politics* (New York, 1942). The effect that rapid social change in Latin America is having on United States policy is analyzed by various authors in Council on Foreign Relations, *Social Change in Latin America Today, Its Implications for United States Policy* (New York, 1960). A more conventional but suggestive analysis will be found in Adolf A. Berle, Jr., *Latin America: Diplomacy and Reality* (New York, 1962).

There is very little in English on the struggle for sub-paramountcy in Latin America. But, see A. P. Whitaker, *Nationalism in Latin America* (Gainesville, 1962), the book by Gustavo Lagos already mentioned, and the chapter by Lewis Tambs in the book edited by the author, already mentioned. A work on the subject by a Latin American, published in English, is the monograph by Víctor Lascano, "Argentine Foreign Policy in Latin America," *University of Miami Hispanic-American Studies,* no. 2, January, 1941. Intra-Latin American conflicts often arise over ill-marked boundaries, as in the Leticia dispute, the Ecuador-Peru clash, the Argentine-Chilean dispute and the Chaco War, all in the twentieth century. The history of these disputes is exhaustively examined in the two volumes by Gordon Ireland, *Boundaries, Possessions and Conflicts in South America* (Cambridge, 1938), and *Boundaries, Possessions and Conflicts in Central and North America and the Caribbean* (Cambridge, 1941). Two of the wars that resulted have been surveyed in David H. Zook, Jr., *The Conduct of the Chaco War* (New York, 1960), and *idem, Zarumilla-Marañón: The Ecuador-Peru Dispute* (New York, 1964).

An excellent expression of Argentine nationalism and anti-Americanism, as well as the search for extra-continental counterbalances for the United States is *La Política Argentina y el Futuro de América* (Buenos Aires, 1944), by Enrique Ruiz-Guiñazú. A more systematic statement of the Argentine position will be found in Lucio M. Moreno Quintana, *Elementos de Política Internacional* (Buenos Aires, 1955). An interesting exposition of traditional peaceful, anti-expansionist sentiment found in segments of the Radical Party in Argentina is *Geopolítica Imperialista y la Nueva Argentina* (Buenos Aires, 1948) by Atilio E. Cattaneo. Hélio Vianna, *Historia da República: Historia Diplomática do Brasil* (2nd ed., São Paulo, [1962?]) is a good general survey, except that the period between the two world wars is ignored completely. On the Brazilian side of the struggle for sub-paramountcy, see also Pedro Calmon, *Brasil e América* (2nd ed., Rio de Janeiro, 1944) and Heitor Lyra, *Historia Diplomática e Política Internacional* (Rio de Janeiro, 1941). Alberto Cruchaga Ossa, in *Estudios de Historia Diplomática Chilena* (Santiago de Chile, 1962) and Alejandro Magnet, in *Nuestros Vecinos Justicialistas* (Santiago de Chile, 1953), present interesting fragments of Chilean participation. The Magnet book is about the 1953 treaty of economic union signed between Argentina and Chile, part of an Argentine plan to dominate its neighbor republic. The death-rattle of the ABC period is described in Angel F. Avalos, *El Proyecto Brasileño De Conferencia Internacional de Valparaíso: Estudio Sobre Política Internacional y Militar del Brasil y la Argentina* (Córdoba, Argentina, 1923).

4 / THE INTER-AMERICAN SYSTEM: INSTITUTIONALIZATION OF THE "PAX AMERICANA"

> *If in the spirit of peace the American Conference [of 1890] agrees upon a rule of arbitration which shall make war in this hemisphere well-nigh impossible, its sessions will prove one of the most important events in the history of the world.*
>
> JOHN GREENLEAF WHITTIER

As the United States, following the Civil War, became aware of the commercial potentialities of Latin America as an outlet for the goods produced by the phenomenal expansion of American industry, as it began to develop a powerful navy and a sense of its future as a world power, and as it thus reaffirmed the Monroe Doctrine and began to assert a claim to hemispheric paramountcy, the emerging North American colossus cast about for a gesture that would publicize its intentions and power and simultaneously initiate the organization of its first client system.

The result, after a decade of domestic political pulling and hauling, was the First Inter-American Conference, held in Washington in January of 1890, some six years before paramountcy passed definitively from Great Britain to the United States. It is significant that, prior to the opening of the Conference, the Latin American delegates were taken on an extended tour of the industrial centers of the United States, to impress them with the industrial and commercial might of the United States, and by extension, with its potential international power.

Since 1890, the Inter-American system has passed through three stages of development. Between 1890 and 1945, the system was loose and informal, gaining effectiveness as the United States became more skillful in diplomatic manipulation, as the possibility of rival claims to paramountcy faded, and as the United States could thus pass from the phase of intervention to that of the Good Neighbor Policy. Capping off this period was the substantial degree of cooperation the United States was able to elicit from Latin America in prosecuting World War II. Between

1945 and 1954, the Inter-American system, apparently headed by a power now unchallengeable and invincible, was codified and formalized; and effectively, efficiently, and rapidly used on several occasions to maintain the *Pax Americana* in the hemisphere. Within a decade, however, a new threat to United States hemispheric paramountcy developed, and the second period was climaxed by the proclamation of the Dulles Doctrine at the Tenth Inter-American Conference, held in Caracas in 1954. The third stage, from 1954 to the present, has been dominated by the adjustment of the United States and the Inter-American system to the challenge of a new paramount, working largely by means of internal subversion within the countries of the system. This process will be analyzed in Chapter 5.

Aside from the Organization of American States (OAS), since 1948 the formal agency used by the United States for maintenance of the hemispheric *Pax Americana,* there is one other political regional organization in the hemisphere worthy of brief mention. At a meeting of the Central American republics in San Salvador in 1951, the Charter of San Salvador was adopted, providing for formation of the Organization of Central American States (ODECA). The Charter provides for mutual consultations on matters of regional importance and for yearly meetings of a Council of Foreign Ministers empowered to make decisions by unanimous vote. ODECA began to function only in 1955, and since then, has been principally important with relation to its role in the achievement of economic unity through the Central American Common Market (CACM— see Chapter 8). ODECA is a manifestation of the constantly frustrated Central American desire for political unity, lost in 1838. In the context of this chapter, the only other comment that needs to be made is that if in the future political unity is once again achieved by Central America, so that its five votes become one in the OAS, it will be more difficult for the United States to muster the two-thirds majority necessary in the OAS on important matters that may be unpopular with other member states. Besides ODECA there was for some years a Caribbean Organization made up of the colonial powers in the Caribbean for coordination of economic and social policies. This organization ceased to exist in the summer of 1965. There is some indication that Puerto Rico is interested in attempting to fill the resulting organizational gap among the smaller islands of the Caribbean. At any rate, in June of 1965, a meeting was held in San Juan, at which ten islands were represented and where they agreed to establish a Caribbean Development Corporation.

A / THE GENESIS OF THE INTER-AMERICAN SYSTEM, 1881–90

In 1881, James G. Blaine became Secretary of State of the United States, under newly-elected President James Garfield. Blaine had always been an advocate of Pan-Americanism, and one of the first acts of the new administration was to send out invitations to all the states of Latin America to attend a general conference to be held in Washington. Blaine was in the forefront of that wing of the Republican Party most interested in pushing the expansion of American foreign trade and challenging the commercial supremacy of Great Britain in Latin America. The United States was also interested in maintenance of peace in the hemisphere, both to avoid excuses for European intervention and to facilitate the peaceful development of trade. Blaine himself expressed his objectives in the following way:

> The foreign policy of President Garfield's administration had two principal objects in view: first, to bring about peace, and prevent future wars in North and South America; second to cultivate such friendly commercial relations with all American countries as would lead to a large increase in the export trade of the United States by supplying those fabrics in which we are abundantly able to compete with the manufacturing nations of Europe.[1]

As a result, the prolonged and bloody Second War of the Pacific between Chile on the one hand, and Peru and Bolivia on the other, was seized upon as the excuse for calling a conference to discuss the establishment of a hemispheric arbitration system. Several of the Latin American states accepted the invitation immediately, and the others would probably have followed suit, but soon after the invitations were sent out, President Garfield was assassinated. His successor, Vice-President Chester A. Arthur, was a political opponent of Blaine's, and as soon as Arthur had eased Blaine out of the cabinet, the invitations were rescinded.

The project, however, had proven popular with Congress, and a number of resolutions were introduced into the House of Representatives and Senate expressing the approval of the legislative branch. When Grover Cleveland became President in March of 1885, another resolution was passed in the House of Representatives requesting the President to invite delegates to an Inter-American Conference. President Cleveland procrastinated, but invitations were finally sent out by Secretary of State Bayard on July 13, 1888. The Republicans won the election of November, 1888, and took office in March of 1889, with Benjamin Harrison as President and Blaine once again as Secretary of State, so that the old campaigner was on hand to open the conference he had so long worked for.

B / DEVELOPMENT OF THE INTER-AMERICAN SYSTEM, 1890–1945

Eight formal Inter-American conferences were held between 1890 and 1945. At these conferences, and at the many specialized conferences held

[1] James G. Blaine, *Political Discussions* (Norwich, Conn., 1887), p. 411.

during the same period (see Table IV), dozens of treaties and conventions were signed and hundreds of resolutions passed, dealing with every imaginable subject of interest to sovereign states in their dealings with one another. The assertion of United States paramountcy was exercised principally through informal mobilization of its Latin American clients, as soon as it became clear that its commercial supremacy could, for the time being, scarcely be challenged. As a result, the Inter-American system developed in an *ad hoc* fashion, with little formalization of procedure or institutions.

1 / Organization of the Clients

At the first conference in 1890, the establishment of an International Union of American Republics was authorized, its sole organ being a Commercial Office of the American Republics, which was given the task of collecting and disseminating information bearing on tariffs and commercial laws in the member countries. This resolution needed, and received, specific acceptance on the part of the American governments, and according to paragraph 16 of the resolution, the plan of the union could be modified at any time by a majority vote of its members. The Commercial Office was established in Washington.

At the second conference (Mexico City, 1901–02), the name of the office was shortened to Office of the American Republics, and it was given an executive council consisting of the diplomatic representatives of the Latin American republics in Washington, plus a special representative of the United States. The conference also voted to regularize its meetings and hold them every five years. At the fourth conference (Buenos Aires, 1910), the name of the organization was changed to Union of American Republics and the name of its secretariat to Pan American Union.

At the sixth conference (Havana, 1928), the name of the organization was changed to Union of American States. Although it still had no political functions, the Council of the Pan American Union was reorganized and given greater administrative autonomy. These changes were incorporated into a convention, the first attempt to give the Pan American system a basic charter. Although the convention was never ratified by a sufficient number of states to bring it into force, its main provisions were followed. At the eighth conference (Lima, 1938), an additional organ was established, the Meeting of Consultation of Foreign Ministers, to handle emergency matters according to the terms of the Convention on Maintenance, Advancement, and Reestablishment of Peace, signed at Buenos Aires in 1936 (see below). At the second Meeting of Consultation of Foreign Ministers (Havana, 1940), the resolution authorizing the establishment of an Inter-American Peace Committee was passed.

Thus, as of 1945, the Pan American Union with its Governing Board, the Inter-American Conferences, and the Meetings of Consultation of Foreign Ministers, were the only organs constituting the Union of American States (the Inter-American Peace Committee held its first meeting in 1948). In addition, certain specialized functional organizations had been established, the most important being the Pan American Sanitary Bureau.

2 / Peaceful Settlement—Assuring the "Pax Americana"

Peaceful settlement of disputes within the hemisphere has been one of the major preoccupations of the United States since it began to assert its paramountcy. We have already noted that peaceful settlement of the Second War of the Pacific was the primary excuse for the original invitations in 1881. At the First Inter-American Conference one resolution was passed condemning wars of conquest, and another suggesting that a general arbitration treaty be signed by the American states. In accordance with this resolution, a treaty was signed by eleven countries after the conference formally adjourned. It never received sufficient ratifications to bring it into force.

Another arbitration treaty was signed at the 1902 conference and was ratified by six states, being thus the oldest of the Inter-American treaties of peaceful settlement in force.

An important step forward was taken with the signing at Santiago de Chile in 1923 of the Treaty to Avoid or Prevent Conflicts between the American States (Gondra Treaty). This treaty, in force among twenty of the twenty-one member states (all except Argentina), provides for the submission to a Commission of Inquiry of all disputes which do not appear to be amenable to settlement through regular diplomatic channels and which involve imminent danger of armed conflict. It established two permanent commissions, with headquarters in Washington and Montevideo, and provided for a maximum delay of eighteen months between submission of a dispute to one of the commissions and the time when the parties would recover full liberty of action should a settlement prove impossible. The Gondra Treaty is the only Inter-American treaty of pacific settlement in force among as many as twenty of the American states.

In 1928–29, a special Conference on Conciliation and Arbitration was held in Washington, and at that conference a General Convention of Inter-American Conciliation and a General Treaty of Inter-American Arbitration were signed. The conciliation convention is in force among eighteen states, and the arbitration treaty among sixteen.

In 1933, the Anti-War Treaty of Non-Aggression and Conciliation (Saavedra-Lamas Treaty) was signed by six states in Rio de Janeiro. All disputes were to be submitted to *ad hoc* conciliation commissions, and eighteen months were to pass before the parties regained their freedom of action. At the Inter-American Conference on the Maintenance of Peace held in Buenos Aires in 1936, the Inter-American Treaty of Good Offices and Mediation was signed, thus completing the pre-World War II cycle of Inter-American peaceful settlement agreements. This treaty has been ratified by fifteen of the American states. At the same conference numerous other conventions, treaties, and resolutions were signed, including the

Table IV—TABLE OF REGULAR AND SPECIAL INTER-AMERICAN CONFERENCES AND MEETINGS OF FOREIGN MINISTERS, 1889–1954

Name	Date	Location	Countries Attending	Major Agenda Items	Outcome
First International Conference of American States	October 2, 1889–April 19, 1890	Washington, D.C., United States	All the American republics then in existence, except the Dominican Republic (18)	Discussion of problems of mutual interest, principally questions of peace, trade, and communications.	Formation of the International Union of American Republics and the "Bureau of American Republics."
Second International Conference of American States	October 22, 1901–January 22, 1902	Mexico City, Mexico	All the American republics then in existence (19)	Discussion of international legal questions; procedures for arbitration of disputes; problems of hemispheric peace.	Protocol of adherence to Hague Convention for Pacific Settlement of International Disputes. Treaty of Arbitration for Pecuniary Claims.
Third International Conference of American States	July 21–August 26, 1906	Rio de Janeiro, Brazil	All the American republics except Haiti and Venezuela (19)	Consideration of problem of forcible collection of debts; discussion of Drago and Calvo doctrines.	Conference decided to take question of forcible collection of debts to Second Hague Conference. Convention on International Law.
Fourth International Conference of American States	July 12–August 30, 1910	Buenos Aires, Argentina	All the American republic except Bolivia (20)	Consideration of various economic and cultural matters.	Decision to change name of international Bureau of American Republics to Pan American Union.

Conference	Date	Place	Participants	Discussion	Result
Fifth International Conference of American States	March 25–May 3, 1923	Santiago, Chile	All the American republics except Bolivia, Mexico, and Peru (18)	Discussion of reorganization of Pan American Union (PAU) for purpose of reducing U.S. dominance; discussion of possible modification of Monroe Doctrine.	Treaty To Avoid or Prevent Conflicts Between American States (Gondra Treaty). Decision to make chairmanship of PAU elective.
Sixth International Conference of American States	January 16–February 29, 1928	Havana, Cuba	All the American republics (21)	Latin American delegates anxious to secure condemnation of U.S. intervention in the Caribbean.	Convention on Duties and Rights of States in the Event of Civil Strife (designed to prevent use of other American countries as bases for launching revolutionary activity).
International Conference of American States on Conciliation and Arbitration	December 10, 1928–January 5, 1929	Washington, D.C., United States	All the American republics except Argentina (20)	Problem of arbitration and conciliation of disputes	General Convention of Inter-American Conciliation. General Treaty of Inter-American Arbitration.
Seventh International Conference of American States	December 3–26, 1933	Montevideo, Uruguay	All the American republics except Costa Rica (20)	Problem of U.S. dominance and intervention.	Convention on Rights and Duties of States; concerned with the principle of nonintervention.

TABLE IV—CONTINUED

Name	Date	Location	Countries Attending	Major Agenda Items	Outcome
Inter-American Conference for the Maintenance of Peace	December 1–23, 1936	Buenos Aires, Argentina	All the American republics (21)	Security of hemisphere in event of war in Europe or Far East; principle of nonintervention.	Declaration of Principles of Inter-American Solidarity and Cooperation; additional protocol relative to nonintervention.
Eighth International Conference of American States	December 9–27, 1938	Lima, Peru	All the American republics (21)	Consideration of the relation of American republics to Europe and possible German and Italian penetration of the hemisphere.	Declaration of the Principles of the Solidarity of America; established the Meeting of Consultation of Foreign Ministers.
Inter-American Conference on Problems of War and Peace	February 21–March 8, 1945	Mexico City, Mexico	All the American republics except Argentina (20)	Consideration of possible postwar problems. Hemispheric relations of Argentina.	Act of Chapultepec; dealt with acts or threats of aggression against any American republic; recommended consideration of a treaty to deal with such acts and measures to take when they occurred.
Inter-American Conference for the Maintenance of Continental Peace and Security	August 15–September 2, 1947	Rio de Janeiro, Brazil	All the American republic except Nicaragua (20)	Consideration of proposals for a treaty of mutual defense of the hemisphere.	Inter-American Treaty of Reciprocal Assistance (Rio Treaty).

Ninth International Conference of American States	March 30–May 2, 1948	Bogotá, Colombia	All the American republics (21)	Discussion of means to strengthen the inter-American system and to promote inter-American economic cooperation; consideration of juridical and political matters, including recognition of governments and colonies.	Charter of the OAS; American Treaty on Pacific Settlement (Pact of Bogotá); American Declaration of the Rights and Duties of Man; Economic Agreement of Bogotá.
Tenth International Conference of American States	March 1–28, 1954	Caracas, Venezuela	All the American republics except Costa Rica (20)	Consideration of hemispheric policy respecting the intervention of Communism in the Americas; discussion of possible economic assistance to Latin America.	Declaration of Solidarity for the Preservation of the Political Integrity of the Americas against the Intervention of International Communism.

Source: U.S. Senate, Committee on Foreign Relations, *United States–Latin American Relations. The Organization of American States* (Washington, D.C.: Government Printing Office, 1959), pp. 8–9.

Meetings of Consultation of Ministers of Foreign Affairs, 1939–1951

Meeting	Location	Date	Major Agenda Items	Outcome
First	Panama City, Panama	September 23–October 3, 1939 (after start of World War II)	Consideration of means for maintenance of the neutrality of the hemisphere.	Declaration of Panama, establishing a hemispheric zone embracing the American republics within which the belligerent nations were to commit no hostile acts; general declaration of neutrality.
Second	Havana, Cuba	July 21–30, 1940 (after fall of France)	Discussion of European possessions in the Americas and the danger of their possible transfer to other non-American powers.	Act of Havana and Convention of Havana, concerning the provisional administration of European colonies and possessions in the Americas. (Resolution XV: Any attempt by a non-American state against sovereignty or independence of an American state to be considered an attack on all.)
Third	Rio de Janeiro, Brazil	January 15–28, 1942 (after Pearl Harbor)	Determination of attitude to be adopted by American republics in face of attack by a non-American power upon an American state and subsequent declaration of war by Germany and Italy.	Resolution: "The American Republics . . . recommend the breaking of their diplomatic relations with Japan, Germany and Italy." Establishment of the Inter-American Defense Board; establishment of the Emergency Advisory Committee for Political Defense.
Fourth	Washington, D.C., United States	March 26–April 7, 1951 (after Korea)	Consideration of problems of Communism and hemispheric security.	Recommendation that each republic examine its resources to determine what steps it could take to contribute to collective defense of continent; recommendation that governments examine their laws with view to adopting changes considered necessary for prevention of subversive activities of Communists.

Convention on the Maintenance, Advancement, and Reestablishment of Peace already mentioned and a resolution suggesting the formation of an Inter-American Court, an idea that has constantly recurred at Inter-American conferences, most recently at the Inter-American Conference at Rio in 1965, where the establishment of a Court of Human Rights was proposed.

Thus, between 1890 and 1945, twelve treaties were signed and dozens of resolutions and declarations were passed by the Inter-American system dealing with good offices, mediation, investigation, conciliation, arbitration, and judicial settlement. Every state in the system was bound by at least one of these treaties[2] and many had ratified several. In addition, provision had been made for a permanent Inter-American Peace Committee.[3] The Inter-American system of peaceful settlement was loose and uncodified and was backed up by no enforcement procedures except unilateral United States pressures. These pressures were, however, quite effective, and since 1890, only one formal war has been fought between Latin American states (the Chaco War between Paraguay and Bolivia, 1932–35). Procedures for dealing with informal armed conflicts and threats to the peace were inadequate, however, as of 1945.

3 / Consultation—Mobilizing the Clients

The concept of Inter-American consultation in case of threats to, or breaches of, the peace in the Western Hemisphere had its inception at the Inter-American Conference for the Consolidation of Peace, held in Buenos Aires in 1936. At this conference, the Convention for the Maintenance, Preservation, and Reestablishment of Peace was signed, providing for mutual consultation in the event of a threat to the peace of the Americas; that in case of war among American states they shall consult immediately to seek a method of peaceful collaboration; and, in the case of external aggression, the American nations shall consult together to coordinate defensive measures. This convention is linked to the Declaration of Principles of Inter-American Solidarity and Cooperation, signed at the same time, which states that ". . . every act susceptible of disturbing the peace of the Americas affects each and every one of them, and justifies the procedure for consultation provided for in the Convention for the Maintenance, Preservation, and Reestablishment of Peace." Related to both of these is the Convention to Coordinate, Extend, and Assure Execution of Existing Treaties and Conventions, Article 2 of which states that one reason for consultation would be to see that states involved in a dispute fulfilled their treaty obligations.[4] Article 3 of the same convention provides that there shall be no war declared for six months while consultation is in progress. Thus, in 1936, the procedures of peaceful settlement, found by the United

---

[2] Argentina had ratified only the Saavedra-Lamas Treaty.
[3] Resolution XIV of the Second Meeting of Consultation of Ministers of Foreign Relations, Havana, 1940.
[4] This provision is the forerunner of the enforcement provisions of the Pact of Bogotá (see below).

States to be inadequate to prevent political conflicts such as the Chaco War, were subordinated ". . . to what might be described as a new summary procedure for the settlement of the disputes which had hitherto been outside the scope of arbitration treaties. . . ."[5]

As yet, however, the procedure of consultation was very imperfect. No organ of the Inter-American system had been designated as the one to hold the consultations, and what the meeting of consultation was supposed to do was not completely clear. At the Eighth Inter-American Conference (Lima, 1938), it was debated whether the Governing Board of the Pan American Union should be the organ of consultation, but it was finally decided not to give the Governing Board political functions. Consequently, the Declaration of Lima was adopted establishing a new organ, the Meeting of Consultation of Ministers of Foreign Affairs. It also provided that such a meeting might be called by any member state, and that it would meet in the capital cities of the Americas in rotation.

The first such Meeting of Consultation took place in Panama in 1939, on the occasion of the beginning of World War II. At the second Meeting of Consultation at Havana in 1940 (following the fall of France), the procedure for calling the meetings was regularized in Resolution XVII. Any government part of the Inter-American system which discerned any situation likely to disturb the peace and security of the American continent was to apply to the Governing Board of the Pan American Union in Washington, which would then send messages to each government, asking if it believed there was sufficient danger to warrant a meeting. If a majority of states concurred, then the Governing Board would issue the call. The Havana Meeting also declared that outside aggression against any American state was aggression against all, and would immediately call into action the procedure of consultation. Under the terms of this provision, the third Meeting of Consultation met in Rio de Janeiro in 1942 (following Pearl Harbor), and extended the scope of the Inter-American security system for the first time to encompass conflicts between American states by means of a resolution condemning Inter-American conflicts.[6]

By 1945, on the eve of the Chapultepec Conference, the Pan-American system consisted of a conglomeration of treaties, conventions, resolutions, permanent and intermittent organs, and a building in Washington. The Latin American states had often resisted formalization of the client organization by signing Inter-American instruments and then neglecting to ratify them. The system had no basic charter, no organic treaty binding all the member states, and no permanent body with political functions. It had, however, served to maintain the *Pax Americana* with few and minor exceptions and it had been useful to the United States in mobilizing support in World War II. With the end of that war and with the position of the United States apparently unchallengeable, the time was felt to be ripe to weld the hemisphere clients into a tight, formal organization.

[5] Charles G. Fenwick, "Inter-American Regional Procedures for the Settlement of Disputes," *International Organization,* vol. x, no. 1, February, 1956, p. 13.
[6] This resolution was inspired by the border war between Peru and Ecuador.

C / CODIFICATION OF THE INTER-AMERICAN SYSTEM, 1945–48

The republics of the Western Hemisphere, except for Argentina, which had not yet declared war on the Axis Powers, met at the Palace of Chapultepec in Mexico City at the Inter-American Conference on Problems of War and Peace during the months of February and March, 1945. Ironically, the principal pressures for strengthening the Inter-American system came from the Latin American states, who feared submergence of their client interests in the incipient world organization (see Chapter 7), and diversion of United States attention. This is, of course, what happened in any case, between 1948 and 1954 (see Chapter 3).

The United States submitted proposals to the Conference, looking toward minor changes in the Inter-American structure, such as the creation of an Economic and Social Council, and an Educational and Cultural Council. Colombia and Uruguay submitted proposals more in accord with the Latin American desire to make the Inter-American system so strong that it could deal with any dispute, without turning to the new world organization. A compromise was reached, much closer to the original Latin American drafts than to the United States' draft; this became Resolution VIII of the Chapultepec Conference, known as the "Act of Chapultepec." The Act of Chapultepec reiterated the juridical equality of all sovereign states, and declared that every attack against the integrity and inviolability of territory of a state shall be considered an act of aggression against the other states signatory to the declaration. There was a partial attempt to define aggression, and in case of its occurrence, the states signatory were to consult together, being empowered to invoke a wide range of sanctions against the aggressor.

The Act of Chapultepec further recommended the conclusion of a treaty establishing procedures, whereby such threats or acts of aggression might be met by use of the sanctions already mentioned. Part III declared that the Act provided for the eventual establishment of a regional arrangement to ensure the maintenance of international peace and security in this hemisphere, but that the arrangement would be consistent with the purposes and principles of the general international organization, when established.

The Act of Chapultepec broke new ground because it was aimed at *any* aggression, whether from with or without the Western Hemisphere, so long as it was directed against an American state; because it included, for the first time in Inter-American history, a list of sanctions to be applied against an aggressor state; and because it foreshadowed the signing of a permanent and binding treaty incorporating genuine collective security, coupled with the Inter-American institution of consultation.

The Chapultepec Conference had other important results. Resolution IX, largely based on the original United States draft, committed the signatory states to the eventual adoption of a basic charter for the Inter-

American system. Resolution XXXIV, which finally resulted in the Pact of Bogotá signed in 1948, recommended the final codification and strengthening of the various pacts of arbitration, mediation, and conciliation signed by the American states since 1890.

In pursuance of the Act of Chapultepec, the Inter-American Conference for the Maintenance of Continental Peace and Security met in Rio de Janeiro during August and September of 1947, and, at this conference, the Inter-American Treaty of Reciprocal Assistance, or Rio Treaty, was signed. The Ninth Inter-American Conference met in the city of Bogotá during March, April, and May of 1948. At this conference, the Inter-American system was finally given a fundamental law with the signing of the Charter of the Organization of American States (OAS), and all previous peaceful settlement treaties and conventions were superseded by the American Treaty of Pacific Settlement (Pact of Bogotá).

1 / The Charter of the Organization of American States

The Charter of the Organization of American States was signed in May of 1948 and came into force on December 13, 1951.[7] The highest deliberative body of the OAS is the Inter-American Conference, comprising all member states of the organization and meeting supposedly every five years. This conference sets policy for the organization, and its directives must be followed by the Council of the OAS. These directives are generally in the form of resolutions or declarations of the conference, and no ratifications are needed.

In case of emergency during the interval between meetings of the conference, a Meeting of Consultation of Foreign Ministers may be called; this is ordinarily limited to dealing with the immediate emergency situation. The executive body of the OAS is the Council, made up of representatives of all the member states. The Council of the OAS is in permanent session in Washington, and thus, available at any time to deal with any dispute or emergency. There is no veto in the Council of the OAS. Procedural matters are decided by a majority vote and substantive matters by a two-thirds vote. The Council has three subsidiary organs: the Economic and Social Council, the Council of Jurists, and the Cultural Council. There are, besides, numerous specialized conferences and specialized organizations affiliated with the OAS, and the Pan American Union, the secretariat of the organization (see Figs. 6 and 7).

The Charter of the OAS proclaims the legal equality of all states, and denies recognition to territorial acquisitions or special advantages obtained by force or other means of coercion. The use of force, in any case, is renounced except in self-defense and Article 15 of the Charter proclaims

---

[7] When the fourteenth ratification, that of Colombia, was deposited. The last country to ratify the Charter, Argentina, did so in January, 1956; the ratification was deposited on April 10th of that year. Many provisions of the Charter were put into effect prior to its formal coming into force, however, and states, such as Argentina, which had not yet ratified the Charter, were allowed almost full participation.

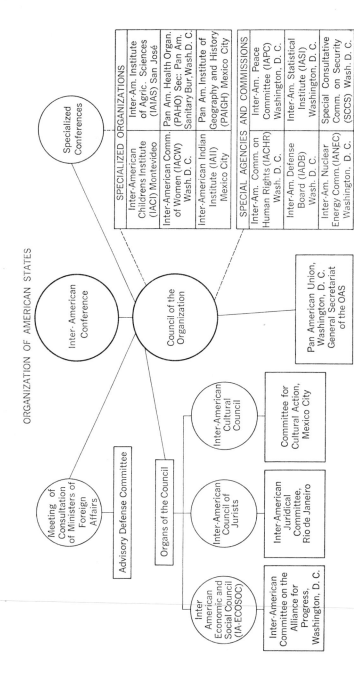

Fig. 6 — Organizational Chart of the Organization of American States as of January, 1967

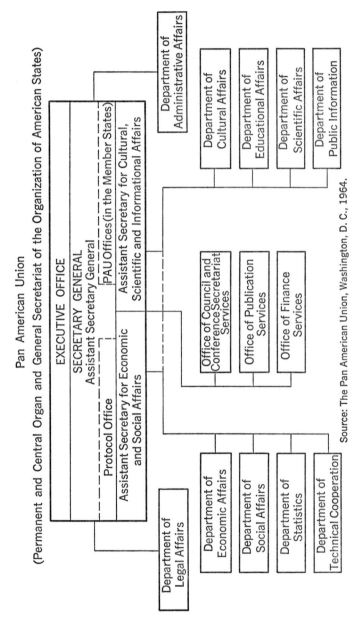

Fig. 7 — Organizational Chart of the Pan American Union

Source: The Pan American Union, Washington, D. C., 1964.

the absolute principle of nonintervention by any state in the internal affairs of any other state. All disputes, according to the Charter, must be settled through the use of good offices, mediation, conciliation, arbitration, or judicial settlement.

Aggression against one member is declared to be aggression against all, and the Charter states that the Meetings of Consultation of Foreign Ministers shall serve as Organ of Consultation in case of threats to, or breaches of, the peace. In case of armed attack, the Chairman of the OAS Council may call a Meeting of Consultation on his own initiative, without waiting for a vote of the Council. An Advisory Defense Committee is established to advise the Organ of Consultation on problems of military cooperation arising due to the application of collective security measures. In case of emergency not allowing for delay, the Council of the OAS may act as provisional Organ of Consultation, pending the Meeting of Foreign Ministers. (See Appendix B for the full text of the Charter of the Organization of American States.)

2 / The Inter-American Treaty of Reciprocal Assistance (Rio Treaty)

The Inter-American Treaty of Reciprocal Assistance, signed at Rio de Janeiro in 1947, constitutes the teeth of the Inter-American system, the means whereby peace is maintained and territorial integrity ensured—by force, if necessary. It is, in short, the cornerstone of the entire client structure. The Rio Treaty entered into force on December 3, 1948, when Costa Rica, the fourteenth country to do so, deposited its ratification with the Pan American Union in Washington. Guatemala was the last country to deposit an acceptable ratification, which it did on April 6, 1955.[8]

The bases of the Rio Treaty are Article 51 of the United Nations Charter and the Act of Chapultepec. The sanctions listed in the Treaty are a combination of Articles 41 and 42 of the United Nations Charter and the Act of Chapultepec. The principle of immediate help to the victim of an attack, should such aid be requested, *before* the Meeting of Consultation, is similar to provisions of the League of Nations Covenant and Article 51 of the United Nations Charter.

The Rio Treaty condemns the use of force or the threat of violence in international relations, and the signatories renounce their use. All contracting parties must come to the aid of the victim of an act of aggression, and, until such time as the Organ of Consultation may meet, any contracting party may individually aid the attacked state or states, upon the latter's request. Any situation, not an armed attack, but endangering the peace of the Americas, or constituting substantive aggression, calls for the immediate convening of the Organ of Consultation. If there is a conflict between two or more *American* states, the Council of the OAS will call for a suspension of hostilities and a return to the *status quo ante bellum.*

---

[8] Guatemala had previously ratified the treaty with a reservation unacceptable to the other contracting parties.

Rejection of this call will be considered in the determination of the aggressor.

The measures of enforcement which may be taken by the Organ of Consultation include recall of chiefs of mission; breaking of diplomatic relations; breaking of consular relations; complete or partial interruption of economic relations, or of rail, sea, air, postal, telegraphic, telephonic, and radio-telegraphic or radio-telephonic communications; and use of armed force. All these measures may be adopted by a two-thirds majority of the OAS Organ of Consultation, and are binding, if adopted, upon all members, with the exception that no state may be forced to use armed force without its express consent.

The Rio Treaty, in Article 9, defines aggression as follows:

> In addition to other acts which the Organ of Consultation may characterize as aggression, the following shall be considered as such: a. Unprovoked armed attack by a State against the territory, the people, or the land, sea or air forces of another State; b. Invasion, by the armed forces of a state, of the territory of an American State, through the trespassing of boundaries demarcated in accordance with a treaty, judicial decision or arbitral award, or, in the absence of frontiers thus demarcated, invasion affecting a region which is under effective jurisdiction of another State.

In summary, the Rio Treaty provides for immediate assistance to the aggrieved party in the case of an armed attack on an American state. It provides for immediate consultation in case of an armed attack outside the zone of security (the Western Hemisphere), or any other fact imperiling the peace of America. In such cases, sanctions may be applied, if approved by the Organ of Consultation (a Meeting of Foreign Ministers or the Council of the OAS acting provisionally). (See Appendix C for the complete text of the Inter-American Treaty of Reciprocal Assistance.)

Since it came into force in 1948, the Rio Treaty has been invoked on several occasions to deal with minor breaches of, or threats to, the peace. Sometimes, the matter was handled by the Council acting as Provisional Organ of Consultation, and sometimes, the Foreign Ministers met. At one time or another, the Treaty has been invoked by, or against, Guatemala, Honduras, Nicaragua, Costa Rica, Panama, Cuba, the Dominican Republic, Haiti, Venezuela, Peru, and Ecuador, or more than half the member states of the OAS. All of these cases were successfully handled by the Inter-American system, except for those involving some aspect of the Cold War (see Chapter 5). In dealing with these disputes and charges of aggression, the OAS, at one time or another, has sent investigating commissions, established neutral zones, sent military and air observers, supplied war materiel to the victim of an aggression (Costa Riva *vs.* Nicaragua in 1955), invoked sanctions of a diplomatic and economic nature (against the Dominican Republic and Cuba) and settled a long-standing boundary dispute that had erupted into armed clashes (Honduras *vs.* Nicaragua in 1957).

3 / The American Treaty of Pacific Settlement (Pact of Bogotá)

The American Treaty of Pacific Settlement completes the structure of the Inter-American system as constructed between 1945 and 1948. The Pact of Bogotá supersedes the Gondra Treaty of 1923, the conciliation and arbitration pacts of 1929, the anti-war treaty of 1933 (Saavedra-Lamas), and the Good Offices and Mediation Treaty of 1936, among others, for those states ratifying it. For those states which do not ratify the Pact of Bogotá, the previous treaties which they *have* ratified remain in force. The Pact of Bogotá has been ratified by, and, thus, is in force among, ten of the twenty-one American states.[9]

Those states which ratify the Pact of Bogotá bind themselves to submit all disputes to methods of peaceful settlement. Such disputes must be submitted to regional peace-keeping procedures before being referred to the United Nations. Although the usual proviso is included exempting matters "within the domestic jurisdiction of the state," if there is controversy over the question of whether a particular matter is, in fact, a domestic one, that question will be submitted to the International Court of Justice on the request of either of the parties to the dispute. The peaceful settlement procedures of good offices, mediation, conciliation, arbitration, and judicial settlement are spelled out in detail, as they are to be applied among members of the Inter-American system, and, with reference to judicial settlement, contracting parties accept the compulsory jurisdiction of the International Court of Justice in all disputes concerning the interpretation of a treaty, any question of international law, the existence of any fact which, if established, would constitute the breach of an international obligation, or the nature or extent of the reparation to be made for the breach of an international obligation.

As to the enforcement of arbitral or judicial decisions, the Pact of Bogotá states:

> If one of the High Contracting Parties should fail to carry out the obligations imposed upon it by a decision of the International Court of Justice or by an arbitral award, the other party or parties concerned *shall,* before resorting to the Security Council of the United Nations, propose a Meeting of Consultation of Ministers of Foreign Affairs to *ensure* the fulfillment of the judicial decision or arbitral award. (Italics added.)

This provision of the Pact of Bogotá relates it to the Rio Treaty and foreshadows coercive enforcement of peaceful settlement procedures. (For excerpts from the Pact of Bogotá, see Appendix D.)

The Inter-American Peace Committee (IAPC) is actually a more important agency of peaceful settlement of disputes within the Inter-American system than the Pact of Bogotá. The latter is incomplete in its

---

[9] Brazil, Mexico, Uruguay, Costa Rica, El Salvador, Haiti, Honduras, Nicaragua, Panama, and the Dominican Republic.

TABLE V—TABLE OF INVOCATIONS OF THE RIO TREATY AND ACTIONS OF THE INTER-AMERICAN PEACE COMMITTEE
1948–54

Invocations of the Rio Treaty, 1948–54

1948:   Costa Rica *vs.* Nicaragua
1949:   Haiti *vs.* the Dominican Republic
1950:   The Dominican Republic *vs.* Haiti, Cuba and Guatemala
1954:   The Guatemalan Case

Actions of the Inter-American Peace Committee, 1948–54

Situation	Date Request for Action Received	Date Action Terminated	Charges by Country Initiating Action on Reasons for Requesting Action	Outcome	Countries Involved in the Situation
1. Dominican Republic —Cuba situation	August 13, 1948	September 9, 1948	Dominican Republic alleged organization of revolutionary forces in Cuba directed against Dominican Republic.	Both sides agreed to continue negotiations.	Dominican Republic, Cuba
2. Haiti–Dominican Republic situation	March 21, 1949	June 9, 1949	Haiti requested Committee's good offices in a dispute with the Dominican Republic. Haiti cited certain acts it claimed could create situation between both countries endangering the peace.	Both governments signed a joint declaration of friendly relations on June 9, 1949.	Haiti, Dominican Republic

3. Cuba-Peru situation	August 3, 1949	(Not applicable)	Cuban Embassy in Lima gave asylum to two Peruvian citizens; on August 14, asylees left embassy and incident was closed.	Cuba withdrew its request that the Committee meet.	Cuba, Peru
4. General Caribbean situation	September 14, 1949	(Not applicable)	U.S. requested the Committee study the general situation in the Caribbean.	Committee declined to take action; said jurisdiction limited to specific matters of controversy.	
5. Cuba–Dominican Republic situation	December 6, 1949	(Not applicable)	Cuba invited the Committee to investigate charges by Dominican Republic that Cuba was permitting movement to exist in its borders directed at Dominican Republic.	Committee declined the invitation; no situation calling for specific measures.	Cuba, Dominican Republic
6. Cuba–Dominican Republic situation	November 26, 1951	December 25, 1951	Cuba alleged that five Cuban sailors on a Guatemalan vessel were seized and imprisoned by the Dominican Republic.	Dominican Republic and Cuba signed a joint declaration of peacefulness and nonintervention.	Cuba, Dominican Republic
7. Colombia-Peru situation	November 18, 1953	January 21, 1954	Colombia called attention to the dispute over presence of Raúl Haya de la Torre, a Peruvian, in Colombian Embassy in Lima.	Committee recommended the resumption of bilateral negotiations.	Colombia, Peru
8. Guatemalan situation	June 19, 1954	June 30, 1954	Guatemala requested Committee meet to consider acts violating her sovereignty. Withdrew request, renewed it on June 26.	Committee sent subcommittee to make study; however, before it reached scene, new government in Guatemala.	Guatemala, Honduras, Nicaragua

coverage of the member states and has never been used, whereas the former has had a long and useful life. Although authorized in 1940, the committee was not actually established until July 31, 1948, when its aid was first invoked during a dispute. At that time, it was made up of representatives of the United States, Brazil, Mexico, Argentina, and Cuba. The committee operated without a constitution, and with the same members, until 1956, when the Council of the OAS adopted statutes for the IAPC. As presently constituted, the members of the IAPC are elected by the Council for five-year terms and may be re-elected. With the exception of the election of its members, the IAPC is an almost completely autonomous agency, theoretically responsible only to the Meetings of Consultation. The IAPC cannot intervene in a dispute, unless it is invited to do so by both parties to the dispute, and even then, the scope of its activities is determined by the parties; whether it is to be mere fact-finding, or whether the IAPC is expected to reach an independent solution. The Council, and the Meeting of Consultation, may also refer matters to the IAPC. In any case, the decisions of the IAPC are not binding. Nevertheless, the IAPC has had an enviable record of achievement in the field of peaceful settlement, when it has not been asked to deal with Cold War matters.

Since 1948, several disputes have been brought before the IAPC, and the committee has been asked to perform a variety of tasks by the Council and the Meetings of Consultation. The committee sometimes suggests solutions, and sometimes only suggests means and methods of settling a dispute. Sometimes, the committee intervenes directly, by sending an investigating commission to the locus of the dispute. In one case, the committee even questioned a law of the Dominican Republic giving the President of that country personal power to declare war. The law was subsequently repealed. Perhaps the IAPC's greatest contribution to hemispheric peace came in 1961–62, when the committee was charged with marking boundaries and moving populations in accordance with an International Court of Justice decision awarding an area in dispute between Honduras and Nicaragua to Honduras.

The Rio Treaty and the IAPC have served well, within the formal structure of the OAS, to keep the *Pax Americana* in the Western Hemisphere with reference to interstate disputes of a local nature. The Rio Treaty and the Charter provide for rapid action, and some invocations of the Rio Treaty have been acted upon within one or two days. The Organ of Consultation has at its command an impressive arsenal of sanctions, but it operates on the principle that the sanctions need not be used, and indeed, should not be used, if the procedures of consultation and investigation by themselves produce a solution to the conflict. The Organ of Consultation generally calls for a return to the *status quo ante bellum,* and an aggressor is seldom formally named, facilitating eventual settlement, with minimum loss of face all around. The Organ of Consultation, for all practical purposes, has ignored the legal fiction that its actions merely constitute collective self-defense, a distinction no longer meaningful in the light of the development of the functions of the OAS in the field of regional peace and security.

The Inter-American system was developed in the years since 1890 to organize the United States' new system of clients in the Western Hemisphere. As such, its principal functions are to facilitate trade and investment, maintain the *Pax Americana,* act as a funnel for paramount assistance, and lend support to the paramount in its international disputes. As should be obvious, such a system functions best when there is no credible challenger to the paramount. This was the case between the end of World War I and 1954, with relations between the paramount and its clients improving as the necessity for armed intervention receded, and then disappeared. The Tenth Inter-American Conference, held in Caracas in 1954, marked the beginning of a new era in Inter-American relations, an era when the hemispheric paramount would again be challenged in its position. At that conference, a reluctant group of Latin American states, upon the application of heavy pressure by the United States, adopted a Declaration of Solidarity for the Preservation of the Political Integrity of the American States against the Intervention of International Communism. The adoption of this Declaration was a milestone in U.S.–Latin American relations, and in the development of the Inter-American system. Latin America, very much against its will, became involved in, and eventually a battleground of, the Cold War.

Selected Bibliography

Much of the material in this chapter has been taken from the author's doctoral dissertation, *The Inter-American Peace and Security System for Dealing with Threats to the Peace and Breaches of the Peace, 1948–1959* (Columbia University, 1962). This is also true, to a lesser extent, of Chapters 5, 7, and 8. A useful introductory handbook, although devoid of meaningful analysis, is O. C. Stoetzer, *The Organization of American States* (New York, 1965). Other good handbooks, published by the Pan American Union itself, are *The Organization of American States: What It Is, How It Works* (Washington, 1965) and *The Inter-American System: Its Evolution and Role Today* (Washington, 1963).

A detailed description and analysis of the Inter-American system is provided in Ann van Wynen Thomas and A. J. Thomas, Jr., *The Organization of American States* (Dallas, 1963), and in Charles G. Fenwick, *The Organization of American States* (Washington, 1963). The Venezuelan Government, on the occasion of the Tenth Inter-American Conference, held in Caracas in 1954, offered two prizes for the best works on the Inter-American system. The two prize-winning volumes, both by eminent Latin American international lawyers, are detailed and scholarly examinations, largely historical: Jesús-María Yepes, *Del Congreso de Panamá a la Conferencia de Caracas, 1826–1954* (Caracas, 1955) and Francisco Cuevas Cancino, same title, city and date. Both works should also be consulted for their relevance to the subject-matter of Chapter 8.

Brazil's special Pan-American problems, as an aspiring hemispheric sub-paramount, are examined in Hélio Lobo, *O Pan-Americanismo e o Brasil* (São Paulo, 1939), and the perennial question of whether Canada should join the organization in the pamphlet by John D. Harbron, *Canada and the Organization of American States* (Washington, 1963). The continuing question of Central American unity or disunity is traced in Thomas Karnes, *Failure of Union—Central America: 1824–1960* (Chapel Hill, 1961). Some mention is made of the Organization of Central American States. Works on Central American economic union are mentioned in the Selected Bibliography to Chapter 8.

The role played by James G. Blaine in the genesis of the Inter-American system is examined in David Saville Muzzey, *James G. Blaine* (New York, 1934) and A. F. Tyler, *The Foreign Policy of James G. Blaine* (Minneapolis, 1927). The same story is traced from the Latin American point of view in Alejandro Alvarez, *L'Histoire Diplomatique des Républiques Américaines* (Paris, 1902). The United States Government *Foreign Relations* series and the *Congressional Record* for the period should be consulted, as well as the record of the first conference itself, *International American Congress,* Report of Committees and Discussions Thereon, 2 vols, (Washington, 1890). There is a useful historical appendix.

The record of the development of the Inter-American system is traced in the three volumes of *Conferencias Internacionales Americanas,* published in Washington in 1938, 1943, and 1956 and covering, respectively, the years 1889–1936, 1938–42 and 1945–54. The developments of the inter-war years are perceptively analyzed in Jesús-María Yepes, *Le Panaméricanisme au Point de Vue Historique, Juridique, et Politique* (Paris, 1936) and in a book published by a Canadian, just as the period of development was coming to a close, John P. Humphrey, *The Inter-American System: A Canadian View* (Toronto, 1942).

Inter-American activities in the field of collective security are detailed in the continually revised Pan American Union publication *Applications of the Inter-American Treaty of Reciprocal Assistance,* in the detailed and perceptive volume by J. Lloyd Mecham, *The United States and Inter-American Security, 1889–1960* (Austin, 1961), and in the pamphlet by Jerome Slater, *A Revaluation of Collective Security: The OAS in Action* (Columbus, 1965). The Mecham book should be carefully examined by anyone interested in the use the United States has made of the Inter-American system in maintaining the *Pax Americana.*

The text of the American Treaty of Pacific Settlement (Pact of Bogotá) is published by the Pan American Union (Washington, 1948), and the following Pan American Union publications should also be consulted, in addition to those mentioned above: The *Actas* of the sessions of the various Organs of Consultation; the *Bulletin of the Pan American Union;* the *Annals of the Organization of American States;* the *Reports* of the Secretary-General of the OAS; the *Minutes* of the meetings of the OAS Council (mimeo); the *Reports* of the Inter-American Peace Committee; the *Status of Pan American Treaties and Conventions:* the *Manual of Inter-American Relations;* the *Regulations* of the Council of the OAS; *Inter-American Peace Treaties and Conventions,* and the recently founded *OAS Chronicle.*

5 / *LATIN AMERICA AND THE COLD WAR*

> *The American nations cannot, must not, and will not permit the establishment of another Communist government in the Western Hemisphere.*
>
> LYNDON B. JOHNSON

As a result of their strategic location and power deficiencies, the international challenge to the Latin American states, as we have seen, stems from their position as clients or potential clients of one or another paramount. This fact has been permanent and unchanging ever since Latin America entered the international political arena. There are, however, two very different situations that this fact can give rise to, and the response of the Latin American states to their challenge will vary accordingly. During periods of dominance by a given paramount, their freedom of international action (not necessarily internal or inter-regional action) is severely limited to those initiatives and responses encouraged or at least tolerated by the paramount. During periods when the Latin American client system is the object of a struggle between two or more competing paramounts, the freedom of international action of the Latin American states is enhanced —temporarily, to be sure, but no less dramatically for that. The period since 1954 has been such a period, and the situational challenge to Latin America and to the Organization of American States as of the 1960's is that of an indecisive struggle between the incumbent paramount, the United States, and the challenging paramount, the Soviet Union, for control of the strategic and economic resources of the Latin American states.

Because of the geographic, military, and strategic situation in the hemispheric island, the strategies that the Soviet Union can bring to bear in attempting to attain this goal are severely limited. Overt military display and the threat of war are ruled out (the more so since the Soviet Union's failure in attempting to use them in 1962). Diplomacy and economic strategies can be and are used, but are of limited effectiveness for a variety of reasons, which will be discussed below. Propaganda and subversion, then, are the strategies available to the Soviet Union that have the maximum likelihood of effectiveness. For this reason the local Communist parties in Latin America are of central importance to Soviet strategy in its Western Hemisphere struggle with the United States. Through them, it engages in propaganda, indoctrination, infiltration, the formation of front groups and mass movements, potential control of movements and parties of the Jacobin Left (see Chapter 2) and of peasant and labor movements. Through these parties, it can support and hopefully control rebellious movements in the towns, the countryside, and even in the armed forces and other elite groups. The Soviet Union did not create the conditions which make possible its challenge in Latin America, but where it has been able to take decisive advantage of them, it has done so through the tactical use of the organizational apparatus of Communism in the area. As a result, this chapter will examine first the history of the development of Communism in Latin America from 1918 to 1966, but only from the standpoint of its use by the Soviet Union (that is, its social, political, and economic causes; its internal struggles and tactics, and similar topics, are outside the scope of this book). Following this examination the response of the United States will be analyzed, from the political-military and economic standpoints. The attemps by the United States to mobilize its clients through the OAS to meet the new threat to its hemispheric hegemony will then be examined, as well as the resistance of the Latin Americans to this mobilization. Finally, within the limitations imposed by the fact that we are now in the midst of this struggle, there will be an attempt to assess its present, and possible future, course.

Through long, laborious years, the United States developed a hemispheric system designed to maintain internal peace and prevent outside aggression. It did so successfully. Then, just as it relaxed and concentrated its attention on extra-hemispheric matters it was challenged, not by regional war nor by invading armies, but by the processes of subversion, infiltration, and guerrilla warfare. The course of that new challenge, and the response of the United States, its clients, and its client organization, is the story of this chapter.

A / COMMUNISM IN LATIN AMERICA, 1918–54

The first Communist party in Latin America was the Argentine, founded on January 6, 1918, barely two months after the triumph of the Bolsheviks in Russia. This was a spontaneous movement breaking away from the old

Argentine socialist party. A Communist party was founded in Mexico in September of 1919, and in Uruguay in October of 1920. This ended the spontaneous process of the development of Communism in Latin America. In 1920, the Comintern sent the Indian Communist M. N. Roy and the Japanese Communist Sen Katayama to Latin America to bring the existing parties into the Comintern and to found new ones in the countries that did not yet have them. From that time until the death of Stalin thirty-three years later, the Latin American Communist parties were slavish, dogmatic puppets of the Soviet Union, with practically no autonomy or flexibility.

Roy and Katayama brought the Mexican, Argentine, and Uruguayan parties into the fold, and they and their successor Comintern agents founded, by 1929, Communist parties in seven additional countries: Chile (where the unions were already under Communist control), Brazil, Guatemala, El Salvador, Cuba, Paraguay, and Honduras. In May of 1929, Communism had gained enough adherents and enough of an apparatus in Latin America to justify the holding of a General Congress in Montevideo. Following the congress, agents fanned out across the sub-continent, and, by 1931, there were Communist parties in Peru, Colombia, Ecuador, Costa Rica, Haiti, and Venezuela. In 1934, a meeting of Latin American Communist leaders was held in Moscow, and certain Brazilian and Argentine Communists attained high positions in the Comintern. Between 1937 and 1942, Communist parties were founded in Nicaragua, Bolivia, and the Dominican Republic, completing at least the skeleton of the Communist hemispheric structure.

In its early years, the Communist movement in Latin America concentrated on gaining control of the urban proletariat, in accordance with its own background and predilections, and with directives from Moscow. Success was achieved in taking over control of the labor movement from the anarcho-syndicalists and socialists in several countries, and, in 1929, the Communist labor confederation *Confederación Sindical Latino Americana* was founded. With the advent of the depression, the Communists attempted to use the resulting unrest, and the position they had gained in the labor movement, to rise in armed insurrection in alliance with other disaffected groups within society. Insurrections were tried in 1931 in Chile, in 1932 in El Salvador, and in 1935 in Brazil. All these attempts were brutally and effectively suppressed by the governments in question, and the respective Communist parties were outlawed.

Throughout the early thirties, the Communists, in accordance with orders from Moscow, tried to work in tandem with other parties and movements in "popular fronts." As part of this tactic, the Communists supported candidates of other leftist parties, and, at times, made alliances with traditional centrist parties. In 1938, the Communist trade union confederation was dissolved, and a new confederation established with the collaboration of non-Communist elements. This was the *Confederación de Trabajadores de la América Latina* (CTAL). After the founding of

CTAL, the Communists gradually took greater and greater control of the confederation, until by 1944–45 it was completely Communist-dominated.

With the signing of the Nazi-Soviet Pact in 1939, the Latin American Communist parties dutifully made a complete turnabout, and began attacking their erstwhile Popular Front allies, and making generally futile overtures to the various fascist movements and parties in the region. When Germany attacked the Soviet Union in June of 1941, the formation of Popular Fronts again became the tactic ordered by Moscow, and, strangely enough, willing collaborators were again found. During the Soviet phase of World War II, an intense propaganda campaign was conducted by the United States directed toward convincing the American people and America's allies that the Soviets were freedom-loving democrats worthy of total support. This campaign was quite successful in Latin America, and from 1942 to 1947, when the Cold War began in earnest, the Communists consolidated their position throughout the hemisphere. As of 1941, there was only one Soviet diplomatic mission in Latin America (in Colombia), but by 1947, fourteen Latin American states had recognized the Soviet régime. The Communists, independently or in coalition, elected Senators and Deputies to the Congresses of several of the Latin American countries. In May of 1944, the Communists were involved in the *coup d'état* that overthrew the government of Ecuador, and a Communist participated in the resulting government *junta*, which eventually turned over power to President Velasco Ibarra, who then governed with Communist support. In 1946, the Communists, allied with the Liberal and Radical parties, won the Presidential elections in Chile and, thus, were assigned three of the nine positions in the cabinet of President González Videla. Expulsion of the Communists from the Chilean cabinet, in April of 1947, may be taken as a symbolic date for the decline of Communist fortunes in the hemisphere immediately following the end of the war. The newly respectable Communist parties were outlawed once again in many countries, electoral alliances were broken, votes were lost, and, by 1954, only three countries, Mexico, Argentina, and Uruguay, maintained diplomatic contacts with the Soviets. Communist influence declined in the labor movement as well. Although the Communists maintained their control of the CTAL, that confederation steadily lost strength and membership after 1948. In that year, under the leadership of the Peruvian *Apristas,* an anti-Communist labor confederation was established, and was superseded, in 1951, by the formation of the *Organización Regional Interamericana de Trabajadores* (ORIT). With the encouragement of their governments, which in most of Latin America have great power over the labor unions, many national federations broke with the CTAL and joined ORIT. Another powerful rival arose, in 1952, with the formation of the Peronist confederation ATLAS (*Agrupación de Trabajadores Latinoamericanos Sindicalizados*). In 1953, the CTAL held a Congress and offered an alliance to ATLAS. The offer was refused. When ATLAS collapsed, with the fall of Peron, in 1955, most of its former affiliated unions either remained independent or joined ORIT, rather than the CTAL. Police and military suppression of the Communists was severe, and from a high of, perhaps, 330,000 members in 1947, party enrollment had dropped, by 1952, to about 200,000.

The only country in Latin America where the Communist momentum that had built up during the 1941–47 period continued, grew stronger, and, eventually, almost succeeded in taking power was Guatemala. A rebellion had occurred in that country in 1944, which overthrew the long-term dictatorship of General Jorge Ubico, and after a period of confusion, a reformist civilian-military junta was installed. Elections were held in 1945, which resulted in the inauguration of Juan José Arévalo as President in 1946. Arévalo was a utopian socialist who had been living in exile in Argentina. Thus, a reformist rebel group took power in Guatemala, following a long period of repressive dictatorship in a country with absolutely no tradition of democratic institutions or processes, just at the time when Soviet and Communist prestige, with the blessing of the hemisphere paramount, was at its height. Another important factor in the eventual Communist near-takeover in Guatemala was that no indigenous, powerful party of the Democratic Left had developed, either within the country or in exile. There was no available leader of the stature of a Figueres, a Betancourt, an Haya de la Torre, or a Paz Estenssoro, who could command sufficient personal prestige to govern a revolutionary régime without turning to the Communists for organizational support and foreign funds.

Arévalo's political ideas were fuzzily socialistic, and during his term of office, various not-very-important reforms were promulgated. The basic semi-feudal social fabric of the country remained intact, and the military, two members of which had been on the three-man *junta* of 1945, was untouched. At this time, the principal Communist gains (the party was officially banned) were in the labor movement. There had been no labor unions in Guatemala prior to 1945, and when he took office, Arévalo invited Vicente Lombardo Toledano, Mexican head of the CTAL to come to Guatemala and found a labor movement.[1] Not surprisingly, Lombardo Toledano saw to it that the movement was Communist-controlled. One of the key elements in this campaign was the teachers' union, which was soon heavily infiltrated.

In the meantime, the United States had made the situation worse by ignoring Arévalo's cautious attempts at reform, and by providing full support to the outrageous pretentions of the United Fruit Company, which had signed a highly unfavorable agreement with Ubico that Arévalo wanted to revise. Matters were made worse by a succession of incompetent, narrow-minded political appointees as United States ambassador. At one point, Ambassador Patterson is reported to have told President Arévalo: "I will do my utmost to see that you do not get a single pair of boots, a single cent from my government, unless you stop persecuting American

---

[1] It should be remembered that the CTAL was, at that time, the only labor confederation existing in Latin America.

companies." [2] Resentment against these humiliations grew as confusion, bickering, and corruption increased in the government ranks, and in the government political parties. As the elections of 1950 approached, the two principal claimants to the revolutionary mantle were the two military members of the original revolutionary *junta,* Cols. Javier Arana and Jacobo Arbenz Guzmán. Col. Arana, known as a moderate and an anti-Communist, had been Arévalo's heir apparent, but, in 1949, he quarreled with the President, and Guatemala was rife with rumors of an impending *coup* to be led by Col. Arana, who was at the time head of the armed forces. In July, Col. Arana was ambushed and shot to death. Communist involvement in the assassination has been proven, and there is speculation that it was engineered by Arbenz, with, at least, the tacit consent of Arévalo. Be that as it may, the result was to leave the way clear for Arbenz, who, as candidate of all the revolutionary parties, won an easy victory in 1950, and took office in 1951.

Arbenz allowed the Communists to completely dominate the labor movement, the agrarian movement, and education. They were also able to infiltrate the government to such an extent that it was practically powerless to move against them. The Agrarian Reform Act, passed by Congress in 1954, though not Communistic in form, was used by the Communists to build a peasant base for the party. Agrarian reform committees took over in the countryside and openly defied the central governmental agency set up to implement the law.

> During the four years from May 1950 to May 1954 alone the Communist Party in Guatemala grew from a small clandestine nucleus of a few dozen labor leaders and intellectuals to a well-organized national party which could boast of nearly 4000 members.
> . . .
> It would appear that Arbenz favored the Communists more for their abilities and virtues than from any belief in Communism. Although Marxist doctrine did serve to give his régime some degree of ideological underpinning, he was more concerned with the immediate problems than with the shape of things to come. [3]

The incipient takeover of Guatemala by the Communists after 1951 was the classic, original example of their use of Jacobin Left leaders and movements—first to gain influence by proxy, and then, gradually, as their superior organization and administrative skill became apparent, to move into the positions of control.

In March, 1954, the Tenth Inter-American Conference met in Caracas, Venezuela. It was obvious from the outset that the United States came to the conference with the single purpose of having a resolution passed that would declare infiltration of an American government by

---

[2] *The New York Times,* June 30, 1950.
[3] Ronald M. Schneider, *Communism in Guatemala 1944–1954* (New York, 1959), pp. 44 & 197.

the international Communist movement "aggression" under the terms of the Rio Treaty (see Chapter 4). It was equally obvious that the Latin American delegates were much more interested in possible progress toward inter-governmental programs of economic aid and financing. Some, indeed, were openly opposed to the resolution as presented. The United States, however, despite obstructive Guatemalan tactics, succeeded in having an anti-Communist resolution passed by a vote of seventeen to one, with two abstentions (Guatemala voted against, Mexico and Argentina abstained, and Costa Rica was absent from the Conference in protest against Venezuela's dictatorial régime). The operative element of the Caracas resolution reads as follows:

> . . . the domination or control of the political institutions of any American state by the international communist movement, extending to this Hemisphere the political system of an extracontinental power, would constitute a threat to the sovereignty and political independence of the American States, endangering the peace of America, and would call for a Meeting of Consultation to consider the adoption of appropriate action in accordance with existing treaties.[4]

Thus for the first time the situation emerged that would arise again and again in the years following 1954, as the United States attempted to mobilize its client organization to meet a threat that had not been envisioned at the time the basic structure of that organization was erected. These attempts at mobilization would be met by resistance as the clients tried to avoid interference in their internal affairs, avoid assuming responsibilities that they felt should be discharged by the paramount, and tried to use the paramount struggle to increase their own maneuverability in the international arena, and to extract a larger amount of paramount economic assistance. After the final vote at Caracas, the Uruguayan delegate stated: "We contributed our approval without enthusiasm, without optimism, without joy, and without the feeling that we were contributing to a constructive measure." [5]

In the meantime, the Guatemalan Government had been annoying neighboring Central American governments, and, to a lesser extent, other Latin American governments. Certain Guatemalan diplomats were declared *personae non gratae* for spreading Communist propaganda. Guatemala openly encouraged and supported a strike in Honduras against the United Fruit Company. Nicaragua finally broke diplomatic relations completely. In May of 1954, the United States announced that Guatemala had received a shipment of arms from behind the Iron Curtain, in the Swedish steamer *Alfhelm*. The arms were intended for the peasant militia that Arbenz hoped to establish as a counterweight to the army, but the army confiscated them when they were landed in Puerto Barrios. In re-

---

[4] For the full text of the Caracas Declaration, see Appendix E.
[5] *The New York Times*, March 16, 1954, p. 8.

sponse, the United States requested permission of other governments to search their ships destined for Guatemala (in a clear foreshadowing of the "selective embargo" of 1962), signed hasty Mutual Assistance pacts with Honduras and Nicaragua, and air-shipped to those countries arms intended, in part, for the small Guatemalan exile invasion force being assembled in Honduras by former Guatemalan army Colonel, Carlos Castillo Armas. Inside Guatemala, the government opened a reign of terror against anti-Communist organizations and individuals.

Finally, on June 17, 1954, Guatemala was invaded by Col. Castillo Armas' "Liberation Army." Rebel planes bombed Puerto Barrios and Guatemala City, and dropped leaflets and arms in the interior. On June 19, the Guatemalan Government cabled the President of the Security Council of the United Nations and asked him to convene a meeting of the Council, thus initiating a futile attempt to use the United Nations as a counterweight to neutralize the Organization of American States, an attempt repeated (also unsuccessfully) in 1962 and 1965 (see Chapter 7). On the same day, Alfredo Chocano, *Chargé d'Affaires* of Guatemala in Washington, called for a meeting of the Inter-American Peace Committee "to avert a violation of the peace of the American continent." The Committee met and prepared to depart for Central America on June 20. On that day, however, the Guatemalan Government requested that the Committee postpone its departure, pending Security Council action. Following the failure of the U.N. to act, Honduras, on the 22nd, requested that the IAPC take up the issue once again and was seconded, on the 23rd, by Nicaragua, both countries having been accused of aggression by Guatemala. On June 25, Guatemala rejected IAPC involvement on the grounds that a new appeal was being made to the U.N. When Guatemala was again unable to obtain U.N. action, it agreed to an investigation by the IAPC, which was to leave Washington for Central America on June 27, to be in Guatemala the next day.

The Inter-American Peace Committee never reached Guatemala. On June 27, the Arbenz régime was overthrown, not by the rebels, who in ten days had not been able to advance more than twelve miles into Guatemalan territory, but by a *junta* of its own army officers, headed by Col. Carlos Enrique Díaz. On June 28, eleven days after the invasion began, the Council of the OAS finally met on the demand of ten member states (Peru, Nicaragua, Cuba, Honduras, the United States, Panama, Haiti, the Dominican Republic, Brazil, and Costa Rica), invoking the Rio Treaty, and requesting that a Meeting of Consultation be held to investigate the infiltration of international Communism into the institutions of Guatemala. Uruguay demanded that Guatemala's charges of aggression also be heard, but was defeated by a vote of five to seven, with eight abstentions. A Meeting of Consultation was called to meet on July 7 in Rio de Janeiro.

On June 28, the IAPC asked the new Guatemalan Government if it wished the investigation to proceed. Col. Díaz replied affirmatively, and the Committee left Washington on June 29. On the same day, however, the Díaz Government was forced out of office by a new *junta,* under the leadership of Col. Elfego Monzón. On June 30, the new government asked the Committee, by now in Mexico, not to proceed to Guatemala. On July 2, the Council of the OAS met and postponed indefinitely the Meeting of Consultation set for July 7. The meeting was never subsequently held.

That the United States supported and aided the attack on Guatemala cannot be doubted. The rebels were armed with American weapons sent to Honduras and Nicaragua. The army of invasion was concentrated by local affiliates of Pan American Airways. The bombings were carried out by DC-3's manned by American pilots. A Honduran ship carrying American arms was sunk in the port of Puerto Barrios by the Guatemalan Government. The American Ambassador (Peurifoy) was continuously implicated in various plots to overthrow the Arbenz Government internally, once the invasion got bogged down, and he met on several occasions with army officers plotting the overthrow of the government to which he was accredited. At one point, he declared to the press ". . . people are complaining that I was forty-five minutes off schedule. . . ." in overthrowing Arbenz.[6] Díaz was unacceptable to Peurifoy as a replacement for Arbenz, and the Ambassador personally saw to his ouster, with a pistol strapped to his waist and accompanied by armed Marines. Just in case the invasion bogged down (which it did), and it proved impossible to generate an internal *coup,* American Marines were moved from Puerto Rico to the waters near Jamaica to be ready to assist the invading forces. Their orders were to land at Puerto Barrios if Castillo Armas and Peurifoy both failed. Thus the United States faced its first Cold War challenge by the Soviet Union in the Western Hemisphere by countering the Soviet strategy of internal subversion with the same strategy, supplemented by propaganda, the potential mobilization of clients, and in reserve, the use of military force. The combination worked in the Guatemalan case, and the United States Government settled down to enjoy hemispheric normalcy. What it thought was a conclusion, however, turned out to be merely a prelude.

Communist strategies failed in the period 1918–54, principally because the Communists were dogmatic, servile, inflexible, and unimaginative. The Communist movement was afflicted with colorless leadership, and neglected the countryside and the potentially explosive landless peasantry to concentrate on organized urban labor, which subsequently proved to be peculiarly susceptible to *embourgeoisement.* In their short period of ascendancy in Guatemala, however, they learned many lessons which they were later able to put into effect elsewhere in Latin America, because of the greater autonomy and flexibility they were allowed by the Soviets following the death of Stalin. They learned that they could compensate for their lack of charisma and mass following by supporting movements of the Jacobin Left, riding to power on the coattails of popular and demagogic, but unorganized, and susceptible, leaders, gradually occupying

[6] Flora Lewis, "Ambassador Extraordinary: John Peurifoy," *The New York Times Magazine,* July 18, 1954, p. 9.

positions of power with their own well-organized cadres, making themselves indispensable, and eventually gaining absolute power. They learned that they had to destroy the regular armed forces and all other real and potential power blocs in society, and they had to do it quickly and thoroughly. They learned that terror was not a sometime thing to be turned on and off, but must be a permanent, ubiquitous element, if it is to be successful. They learned to divide their parties, with some Communists supporting the dictatorial or bourgeois democratic governments, and other Communists working along with opposition elements against the government, so that, whatever happened, their organization could survive. And finally, they learned to make alliances with the most reactionary elements, the feudalists, the landowners, and the technocratic militarists, who are also anti-democratic, anti-liberal, and anti-American (see Chapter 2). Thus, as in 1954 in Guatemala, where only the genuinely democratic elements suffered at the hands of the military dictatorship imposed upon that country by Col. Castillo Armas, the Communists can escape to plot another day. All of these lessons were put to good use five years later elsewhere in the Caribbean.

B / COMMUNISM IN LATIN AMERICA, 1954–66

Latin America is the closest client system of the United States, geographically and strategically, and, until 1954, had appeared to be the closest politically as well. An attack on this client system is an attack on the very heart of the international position of the United States. This is most particularly true of the Caribbean. Although it is doubtful that at any time before 1960–61 the Soviet Union really believed that it could break the Latin American client system, and gain clients for itself in the Western Hemisphere, the Guatemalan experience appears to have convinced the Soviets that a major offensive in the region could severely embarrass the United States, and divert its attention from other areas of the world where the Soviets planned Cold War initiatives. Be that as it may, the year 1954, as has been mentioned, marked, not the end, but the beginning, of a major effort on the part of the Soviets to gain influence in Latin America and make better use of the region's Communist parties in creating and utilizing unrest, confusion, and opportunities for covert or overt control. Because of its inherent limitations of operations, the principal strategies employed by the Soviet Union were economic, diplomatic, propagandistic, and subversive.

In 1953, only two per cent of Communist bloc broadcasting was directed toward Latin America, or a total of just over 31 hours per week. By 1961, six per cent of total broadcasting was beamed toward Latin

America, or a total of 219 hours per week, to be added to 130 hours beamed from Cuba. Latin America was flooded with cheap books and publications from the Soviet Union, Communist China, Eastern Europe, and eventually, Cuba. Exchange of persons increased many times, and scores of Latin American labor leaders, peasant leaders, intellectuals, professionals and politicians visited Russia and China. Cultural agreements were signed with several Latin American states, and Russian and Chinese, as well as East European, orchestras, musical groups, theatrical companies, and so forth, toured the sub-continent. Scholarships were passed out lavishly to Latin Americans to study in the universities of the bloc. In 1959, the highest-ranking Soviet official ever to come to the Western Hemisphere visited Mexico, when Deputy Premier Anastas Mikoyan came to inaugurate a Soviet trade fair. In 1962, a Latin American Institute was founded in Moscow as part of the Soviet Academy of Sciences.

The Soviets were less successful in their diplomatic offensive. Although Brazil temporarily established diplomatic relations with Moscow (under the governments of Quadros and Goulart), by 1966, only one Soviet diplomatic mission (Cuba) had been added to the three existing in 1955. Nevertheless, many embassies, legations, and consulates were opened by the East European satellites, particularly Poland and Czechoslovakia, with the latter country becoming the center of Latin America operations for the bloc, symbolized by the opening in Prague of a Latin American studies center.

Czechoslovakia also became a principal Soviet bloc trading partner with Latin America, as part of the Communist economic strategies employed during this time. In 1953, economic relations between the Soviet bloc and Latin America were almost nil. By 1961, the bloc had signed some thirty economic, trade, and technical assistance agreements with various Latin American countries (this total excludes Cuba, by that time already a Soviet client). The problems of the Latin American countries, with their terms of trade and their balance of payments, caused them to be particularly receptive to any opportunities to find new markets for their primary products and new sources of capital imports. With tremendous fanfare, a $75 million trade agreement was signed by the Soviet Union with Argentina in 1953. As part of the package, a $30 million export credit was also provided by the Soviets. In succeeding years, further agreements were signed, and the bloc percentage of total trade turnover reached respectable proportions with a limited number of Latin American countries. Between 1948 and 1961, this percentage was 5.6 for Argentina, 3.4 for Brazil, 10.0 for Cuba, and 7.3 for Uruguay. Those four countries accounted for the bulk of bloc–Latin American trade, and, on the Communist side, almost the sole trading partners of any importance whatever were the Soviet Union, Poland, and Czechoslovakia. Total credits proffered by the bloc in the period up to 1961 (excluding Cuba), totaled between 120 and 150 million dollars, relatively little of which, as we shall see, was actually forthcoming, and despite numerous technical assistance agreements signed, very few bloc technicians actually materialized in Latin America, except for Cuba. It is significant that the Soviet economic offensive has concentrated on Argentina and Brazil, the two principal claimants to Latin American sub-paramountcy.[7]

Following the death of Stalin in 1953, and the lessons of the Guatemalan débâcle in 1954, the Latin American Communist parties gradually gained a large measure of local autonomy and greater flexibility of strategy and tactics. Soviet assistance to the local parties increased greatly as well, and it is estimated that between fifty and one hundred million dollars were sent by the Soviet Union to its Latin American parties and agents between the fall of Arbenz and 1960. Communist parties, in countries where they were illegal, split, with one branch supporting the incumbent government, and the other establishing ties with opposition groups. Dogmatism was suppressed, and a concerted effort was made to display the Communists in the light of good nationalists who were perfectly willing to support Jacobin Leftists to the point of self-effacement. Anti-Americanism was stressed, and this posture was used to cement many temporary working agreements with the forces of the Traditional Right in order to weaken democratic leftist and neoliberal forces and try to identify them as "Yankee-lovers." [8] The United States was attacked as imperialistic and exploitative toward, and, at the same time, not sufficiently benevolent to, its clients. The lessons learned in Guatemala, and assiduously applied throughout the sub-continent, bore fruit in Cuba.

Prior to 1959, Cuba was, perhaps, the closest of America's clients in the hemisphere. Indeed, until the abrogation of the Platt Amendment (see Chapter 3), Cuba held more the position of a protectorate or satellite than that of a client. Two factors, however, served from the beginning to cause some bitterness in Cuban-American relations. The first was the fact that, prior to the American entry into the island, the Cubans themselves had been doing well enough in their war of liberation to force Spain to offer them almost complete internal autonomy. The claim is therefore made (and cannot be proved or disproved, of course), that in a very short time the Spaniards would have had to withdraw, in any case, and that Cuba would have become independent with no strings attached to the United States, other than those made imperative by Cuba's geographic and strategic position. After an initial period of occupation, the Americans intervened three more times under the Platt Amendment, but the second factor that has most galled many Cubans was the American diplomatic intervention to assure the downfall of the mildly reformist administration of Grau San Martín in 1933–34, following the ouster of Gerardo Machado, who had been dictator for six years. After 1933,

---

[7] Increased trade with Uruguay was due entirely to domestic Soviet reasons—the shortage of meat and a temporary cutoff of wool imports from Australia due to the breaking of diplomatic relations.

[8] For page after page of such "marriages of convenience," see Víctor Alba, *Alliance Without Allies* (New York, 1965), pp. 1-74. Similar alliances of the reactionaries and the ultra-revolutionaries against the democrats and liberals have been common elsewhere. See H. Rogger and E. Weber (eds.), *The European Right* (Berkeley, 1965).

Cuban politics swung between benevolent dictatorships, headed by army chief Fulgencio Batista, and periods of constitutional, but extremely corrupt, civilian government. Prior to the elections scheduled for 1952, General Batista staged a *coup* against President Prío Socarrás, who fled the country without a struggle. Universal revulsion over Batista's seizure of power was tempered by the mildness of the early period of his second dictatorship and hopes for eventual return to constitutional government when the general got tired of ruling, as had already happened once in 1944.

As early as July 26, 1953, a group of students, led by Jacobin lawyer Fidel Castro, staged a brave, but futile, attack upon the Moncada army barracks in Santiago de Cuba. Many were killed, and others sent to prison. Among the latter was Castro. In 1955, under a general amnesty, Castro was released, and, after a short time, went into exile in Mexico with his younger brother Raúl. There he met the Argentine physician-adventurer-Communist Ernesto (Ché) Guevara, and these three men (two of whom were Communists, and one, the leader, a Jacobin), set about preparing for a landing in Cuba under the guidance and training of the Spanish Communist and ex-Civil War Commander, Alberto Bayo.

Several raids by the Mexican security police convinced the Castros and Guevara that they had to leave, and they landed in Cuba with eighty-two men on December 2, 1956. By the time they reached the hills there were only a dozen or so left, including the Castros and Guevara. Slightly more than two years later, they controlled Cuba.

Cuba, by 1956, was an urbanized, prosperous country, that only by a stretch of the imagination could be called economically underdeveloped. The standard of living had been rising rapidly and, by the late fifties, was higher than Japan's and about the level of Italy's.[9] American ownership of Cuban sugar production had dropped from 75% in the 1930's to about 35% in 1958. It is true, of course, that about 30% of Cuba's population, minifundium farmers, and seasonal sugar workers, had a very low standard of living, but Cuba certainly did not have the semi-feudal rural economy found in various other Latin American countries. Furthermore, the Batista régime was never defeated militarily. His political defeat was due to multiple causes, the most important of which, perhaps, were the political humiliation of the Cuban people; the completely unnecessary interruption of the democratic process; the apparent lack of intention on the part of the dictator to relinquish power except under duress; the romanticism of the bearded rebels in the mountains and the domestic and foreign publicity they received; rural poverty; deception on the part of the rebels with reference to their goals, once having achieved power; and, finally, American intervention—when, in December of 1958, Batista was told that his term, in effect, was at an end, and that United States support, which had been ended earlier in 1958, would now be changed to open opposition.

The most startling thing about 1959, the first year of Castro's rule,

[9] Theodore Draper, *Castro's Revolution* (New York, 1962), pp. 21-22.

was the rapidity with which the original aims of the revolution, at least as they had been presented to the Cuban people and the world, were subverted. By the end of that year, the Cuban revolution had already been clearly diverted from a middle-class revolution, primarily concerned with the restoration of democratic rights in the political field, and the fulfillment of the terms of the constitution of 1940. It became a revolution *against* the middle class, as well as the organized urban proletariat, which canceled all elections forever, destroyed the press and all other independent organs of public opinion, abrogated the constitution of 1940 and replaced it with no other, and systematically began the destruction of all independent foci of association of whatever type—economic, commercial, industrial, cultural, social, professional, or political. It is now clear that Castro intended from the beginning to transform Cuba into a Jacobin, totalitarian state, and finding the Communists (who had supported his rebellion only at the last minute and who had collaborated with Batista under the "division" tactic) the only organized, disciplined group willing and anxious to collaborate with him in this effort, accepted their support and consolidated them into his extremely loose and chaotic revolutionary apparatus. This decision was announced by Ché Guevara at a secret meeting of government officials in the summer of 1959,[10] and, from that time on, it was relatively easy for the Communists to establish effective control over the apparatus, and, to a large extent, over the direction of the Cuban Revolution.[11] By the end of 1959 and the first months of 1960, Castro sent into exile, imprisoned, or had shot, his own President, Prime Minister, Minister of Public Works, Minister of Agriculture, Army Commander of Camagüey, Air Force Commander, leader of the Havana resistance to Batista, leader of the second front of Escambray, President of the National Bank of Cuba, Quartermaster General of the Army, leader of the Labor Movement, as well as countless editors, publishers, officers, officials, professionals, and others. All public liberties were destroyed, and a start was made on the eventually almost complete collectivization of agriculture, and the nationalization of foreign and domestic commerce and industry. By the end of the year, also, expressions of anti-Communism were declared "anti-revolutionary" and punishable, and the Communist Party was the only political body allowed to operate openly.

Nineteen sixty was the year of Soviet bloc entry into the Cuban situation, politically, economically, and militarily. On February 4, 1960, Mikoyan traveled to Cuba, and, on February 13, the first Cuban-Russian trade agreement was signed. Similar agreements were signed with East Germany on February 20, and Poland on March 31. On May 8, Cuba reestablished diplomatic relations with the Soviet Union. Finally, on June 9, just one-and-a-half years after Castro's triumphant entry into Havana, the Soviet Union detached Cuba from the client system of the United States, and brought that country into the Soviet client system, by

[10] As reported by Manuel Artime, present at the meeting, who later defected.
[11] Castro's personal charisma was, for some time, a force sufficient to maintain certain policy decisions the Communists might disapprove of.

offering Cuba military protection against American attack. The offer was accepted by Cuba and in the following month Soviet arms began to arrive. On June 10, a trade agreement was signed with Czechoslovakia, and, on July 23, with Communist China. On June 29, the Cuban Government seized the foreign-owned oil refineries. On July 3, the United States took its first retaliatory action, reducing the Cuban sugar quota and convening the San José Meeting of Foreign Ministers (see below). On October 19, the United States established a partial economic embargo of Cuba, and, on December 19, in a joint communiqué signed by Castro and Mikoyan, Cuba formally aligned itself with the Soviet bloc. Thus, in two years, the Communist tactics worked out after 1954 had been completely successful in drawing into the Soviet orbit a Caribbean island state on the doorstep of the United States, whose paramount status in the area only a few months before had appeared unquestionable.

The evidence indicates that the Soviet Union, while delighted at the embarrassment it was causing the United States, did not expect to retain its new client, until the failure of the newly installed Kennedy Administration to give sufficient support to the exile invasion at the Bay of Pigs, in April of 1961, to provide the invading force with some chance of success, convinced the Communists that they could proceed with the incorporation of Cuba into the Communist bloc, and with its utilization for international bloc purposes. Nineteen sixty-one was a year of final consolidation of totalitarian power within Cuba and increased dependence upon the Soviet Union for military, financial, and economic assistance. Castro's declaration, on December 2, 1961, that he was a Communist was curiously anti-climactic under the circumstances.

It is obvious that one use to which the new client could be put was as a base for propaganda and subversion in the rest of the hemisphere, and soon, broadcasts, agents, publications, money, and arms were flowing from Cuba to the other Latin American countries, met by a reverse flow of visitors and agents coming to Cuba to view the "socialist" revolution and to receive instructions and training. The Soviet leaders, however, thought they saw another, potentially much more important use to which the island could be put.

Since the end of World War II and the beginning of the Cold War, the United States had ringed the Soviet Union with military and air bases, many by 1962 equipped with intermediate range missiles. By 1962, also, the missile gap in favor of the United States amounted, according to the British Institute for Strategic Studies, to a five to one ratio, with the likelihood of this ratio widening, instead of narrowing, because of the disparate economic and financial capabilities of the two paramounts.[12] At the same time, the Soviet Union, and the bloc in general, were going through a severe economic crisis, resulting in the raising of food prices, the necessity of importing large quantities of wheat, and even in open unrest and rioting in certain industrial centers. It is clear that the Soviet political-military

[12] B. Beedham, "Cuba and the Balance of Power," *World Today,* January, 1963, p. 39.

policy-makers decided that, at least to some extent, the strategic imbalance and economic strains caused by the American system of bases and the missile gap, could be righted by placing intermediate range missiles in Cuba, *within* the American defense perimeter. It was apparently also believed that if the missile bases could be erected rapidly enough, and the United States faced with a *fait accompli,* there would be no reaction beyond ineffectual protest.

Initial implementation of this policy decision came on September 2, 1962, when Cuba and the Soviet Union signed a new arms-supply agreement. It was not, of course, announced that the arms to be supplied included nuclear missiles, but immediately rumors to that effect began to circulate. On September 25, Castro announced that plans were being made to construct a port in Cuba for the Soviet Atlantic fishing fleet. Since the Soviet fishing fleet is used as much for espionage and subversion as for fishing, this amounted to a direct violation of the Lodge Corollary to the Monroe Doctrine (see Chapter 3). In October, American intelligence sources confirmed the existence of missile bases in Cuba, and President Kennedy, on October 22, imposed a selective blockade of Cuba to prevent further entry of missiles and jet bombers. At the same time, he ordered a partial mobilization of the armed forces of the United States to be prepared to invade Cuba, should the missile buildup continue and the Soviets refuse to withdraw the missiles already present. Following unanimous ratification of these decisions, on October 23, by the Council of the OAS acting as Provisional Organ of Consultation, the orders were signed putting them into effect. When it became obvious that the United States was prepared to invade Cuba unless the missiles were removed, thus detaching the new Western Hemisphere Soviet client and rendering it useless for *any* Soviet purpose, the Soviet Government, on October 26 (in a secret note that has not been made public), agreed to withdraw the missiles.

The spectacular success of the new Communist tactics in Cuba has meant that, since 1954, there have been no changes of great consequence in these tactics. A series of Communist setbacks in late 1963 and 1964, however, resulted in a meeting of Communist leaders of the hemisphere in Havana, in November of 1964, and again in April, 1965. A combination of Democratic Leftist and Neoliberal forces had prevented a major Communist push in Venezuela from achieving success, and Raúl Leoni succeeded Rómulo Betancourt as President of that country through peaceful elections. In Brazil a Neoliberal-military alliance deposed the extremely promising Jacobin Leftist Government of João Goulart, and cut short, at least temporarily, an excellent opportunity to exert substantial influence in and, perhaps, eventually control, Latin America's largest and most politically important country. In Chile, Christian Democrat Eduardo Frei had defeated the candidate of the Communists and their allies in free elections. In addition, since 1961, the Sino-Soviet split within the bloc had affected the efficiency of Communist operations in the hemisphere, as the two Communist powers jockeyed for influence. It has been suggested that this split was one of the most important factors preventing the Andes from becoming the Sierra Maestra of South America during this period. Soviet unhappiness over this situation is reflected in the following statement, by a Colombian Soviet-line Communist official:

> No little difficulties have been caused in this field [unity] by the leaders of the Communist Party of China, who are seeking to interfere with the work of our Party and cause confusion by the same methods they are employing in the entire world communist movement. Patronizing the small groups of "ultra-revolutionaries" embodying the most negative petty-bourgeois trends, they encourage anarchic subjectivism which tragically persists in artificially and even forcibly pushing the people into battles the meaning of which they do not yet understand, and are not yet prepared to wage.[13]

As a result of these factors, the Communists, at the November and April meetings, decided to abandon the former "shotgun" approach, which involved dispersing their efforts all over the hemisphere, in favor of a "pinpointing" tactic: concentrating effort and resources on those countries which seemed for the moment most promising.[14] In addition, the leaders of the various Soviet-, Chinese-, and Cuban-dominated Communist movements agreed to engage in united action, at least during the period of preparation and takeover, and, in the meantime, to stop fighting among themselves. In practice, this has resulted in a strengthening of the Soviet position, because of the greater resources it can bring to bear. At these meetings, as well as at the so-called Tricontinental Congress, held in Havana in January of 1966, and attended by delegates from Latin America, Africa, and Asia, the previous Soviet line against violent revolutionary action except in extraordinary circumstances was modified, and armed struggle was proclaimed, once again, a prime strategy of Communist takeover.

C / UNITED STATES RESPONSE, 1954–66

Following the passage of the Caracas Declaration and the overthrow of the Arbenz regime in Guatemala, the United States showed no understanding of the fact that the Communist offensive in Latin America was beginning, not ending. Between 1954 and 1959, there was no serious attempt to counter Soviet moves either economically, politically, or propagandistically. A small amount of money was given to Guatemala for rebuilding,

[13] José Cardona Hoyos, "Colombian Communists Building Popular Unity," *Information Bulletin,* no. 30, p. 52.
[14] This tactic, of course, has the disadvantage of informing the enemy where you are going to concentrate your efforts.

and was allowed to be swallowed up in graft by the Castillo Armas Government, which also busied itself with repealing the agrarian reform, reducing the rights of urban labor, importing wormy corn from Mexico, and arresting the sister of one-time *junta* member Elfego Monzón for practicing witchcraft against President Castillo. All of this went on without protest, or even, seemingly, interest, on the part of the United States. On the other side of the coin, the Latin Americans displayed *their* blind spots when a Mexican judge refused the Guatemalan request for the extradition of Rogelio Cruz Wer and Jaime Rosenberg, former Arbenz police chiefs, responsible for the execution of the last-minute terror in June-July, 1954, and the killing and torture of hundreds of people. When Vice-President Nixon was greeted with rocks and spittle on his trip to Latin America in 1958, the administration in Washington showed some signs of coming to the realization that all was not well in Latin America, but effective action was not taken until after the triumph of Castro in Cuba in 1959.

From 1959 until 1966, United States response to the paramount threat from the Soviet Union in Latin America was largely in the political military, and economic fields. American propaganda was stepped up, and a diplomatic offensive launched, but economic strategies, military display, and subversion were the principal elements in United States counterstrategy.

The diplomatic and political offensive against Cuba took place largely through the agency of the Organization of American States, in multiple efforts by the United States to mobilize its clients to meet the new threat. The record of the OAS in this crisis will be examined in the succeeding section as part of the general discussion of the future of that organization.

Subversion of hostile, or potentially hostile, régimes and military intervention have been part of the American strategic mix in dealing with the Soviet challenge since 1954. Just as the absence of all serious threat enabled the United States in the 1930's to abandon intervention as a strategy, the emergence of a new and powerful threat in the 1950's has brought the strategy back, with the difference that, in the meantime, the United States has signed international treaties and conventions ostensibly forbidding intervention, and can, thus, be accused of illegal behavior when it occurs. We have seen how the United States combined an exile invasion with subversion of the Guatemalan military establishment and preparations for Marine intervention in 1954. The tactical mix then was successful. In 1961, exile invasion was used alone, without auxiliary elements, or readiness for direct intervention, and was unsuccessful in Cuba. The missile crisis of October, 1962, provided another opportunity for armed intervention, and the United States mobilized, but quick Soviet agreement to remove the missiles prevented deployment. Diplomatic and economic intervention has taken place in Peru, Honduras, the Dominican Republic, Brazil, and elsewhere, and all these interventions were intended either to prevent a Communist or Jacobin-Communist takeover, or conversely, to prevent a militaristic-traditional rightist *coup,* that it was feared would lead to an extreme-leftist reaction.

By 1967, direct military intervention had taken place only in the Dominican Republic. In understanding the events of 1965 in that country, it must be recognized that, as of 1960, the United States had decided that long-term despot Rafael Trujillo, who had governed the republic since 1930, would have to go, especially in the light of the moves contemplated against the Castro Government in Cuba at the same time. The United States supported the imposition of economic sanctions upon the Dominican Republic in August of 1960 (see below), and went beyond those measures actually voted by the OAS. Before it was determined whether the sanctions would be sufficient to bring down the government, Trujillo was assassinated in May of 1961. Whether or not the United States had a direct hand in the assassination, its new attitude toward Trujillo undoubtedly encouraged his assassins. Following the assassination, the OAS, with the United States in the forefront, intervened extensively in the Dominican Republic, largely through the Sanctions Committee of the OAS Council and the Human Rights Commission. In August of 1961, an OAS technical mission revised the republic's electoral machinery; and, in November, American warships ensured the definitive departure of the Trujillo family. In January of 1962, the OAS lifted the sanctions and Rafael Bonnelly headed a council of government which supervised elections in December of the same year, resulting in the election of Juan Bosch. Thus, in a little over three years, the United States and the OAS successfully engineered the transition of the Dominican Republic from a particularly harsh dictatorship to an elected, constitutional government. Seven months after taking office, however, Bosch was overthrown by a military *coup,* after having proven himself a poor administrator and politician. The resulting confusion eventually resolved itself into a civilian *junta* headed by prominent businessman and Neoliberal Donald Reid Cabral. The Reid Government attempted to deal with the economic stagnation which the country had been experiencing since 1960, and, in early 1965, Reid attempted to eliminate certain import privileges high-ranking members of the armed forces had been using for personal enrichment. On April 19, Reid learned of a military plot against his government and on April 24, he attempted to have several officers arrested. Instead, the army rose in rebellion against him. The Reid Government was quickly overthrown, but immediately afterward the military rebels split into pro- and anti-Bosch factions. The American Ambassador was out of the country at the time the rebellion broke out. On April 25, the pro-Bosch rebels distributed some 12,000 small arms to the populace of Santo Domingo, but as armored forces moved against them, many pro-Bosch leaders took asylum in Latin American embassies. In the meantime, Bosch himself made no move to return to the Dominican Republic from exile in Puerto Rico. Had he done so, it is probable that he would have dominated the situation on April 26 and 27, since the rebel forces favorable to his return began to gain the upper hand militarily. On April 27, the United States

Ambassador returned to Santo Domingo, and, on the next day, met with the pro-Bosch rebels. On the same day, American Marines landed to protect American lives and provide for the evacuation of American citizens. Ambassador Bennett reported to Washington that the fighting was out of hand, and that, with the absence of Bosch, the moderate leaders of the rebellion had abdicated (several more entered embassies on April 28), and the Communists were taking over. As a result of this information, and at the request of the Loyalist *junta,* the only government existing at the time, on April 30, American paratroops entered the Dominican Republic, and the Embassy released a list of some fifty-three Communists involved in the insurrection. On May 2, former Ambassador Martin, a close friend of Bosch, declared that the rebellion was now definitely Communist-dominated, and President Johnson, in a television speech, reiterated the Dulles Doctrine to justify the armed intervention.[14] On May 4, a pro-Bosch government was inaugurated, and, on May 7, an anti-Bosch government. The United States troops (augmented later by Latin American troops under the terms of the May sixth resolution of the Tenth Meeting of Consultation—see below) separated the armed forces of the two camps, and a long process of negotiation began, finally ending in the Agreement of August 31, 1965, establishing a caretaker civilian government which would hold elections in July, 1966. In the meantime, former President Bosch had returned to the country under the protection of American bayonets. Latin American reaction to the Dominican intervention was generally unfavorable.

Other military actions taken by the United States, since 1960, to counter the threat of Communist subversion in the hemisphere, have included the training of Latin American military officers at Fort Gulick in the Canal Zone, and Fort Bragg, North Carolina, and the establishment of the Inter-American Police Academy at Fort Davis in the Canal Zone. Both of these programs were begun in 1962.

The establishment of the Inter-American Development Bank (IADB) was the first concrete result of the United States economic counter-offensive against the Soviet challenge in the hemisphere. Ever since the first Inter-American Conference in 1889–90, the Latin American states had been agitating for the establishment of some kind of hemispheric bank. This proposal had always been opposed by the United States on the grounds that it was unnecessary. After World War II, this argument took the form of stating that the World Bank could take care of Latin America's needs. The Inter-American Bank began its operations in January of 1960 with an initial capitalization of one billion dollars ($500 million contributed by the United States) and empowered to make both hard and soft loans. In 1961, the Central American Bank for Economic Integration was founded. The United States contributed $2 million of its initial $9 million capitalization.

[14] In November, 1965, following an intensive investigation, the OAS Consultative Committee on Security concluded that the Communists were in imminent danger of taking over the constitutionalist movement in the Dominican Republic in April, 1965.

In bilateral foreign aid, the United States, at a meeting of the Economic Ministers of the American republics in Bogotá in September of 1960, offered $500 million to Latin America in soft loans for social purposes. Part of this money was to be administered by the Inter-American Development Bank. The Act of Bogotá was issued proclaiming Inter-American cooperation to improve rural living and land use, housing and community facilities, educational systems and training facilities, public health, and the mobilization of domestic resources (for the full text of the Act of Bogotá, see Appendix F). Cuba voted against the Act of Bogotá, as it had previously refused to participate in the IADB. In March of 1961, President Kennedy raised the level of paramount benevolence another notch, when he announced to the assembled Ambassadors of the Latin American countries that the United States was willing to collaborate in an Alliance for Progress. According to the terms of the Alliance, as spelled out at a meeting of the Inter-American Economic and Social Council in August of the same year, one hundred billion dollars would be invested over a ten-year period in the economic development of Latin America. Eighty percent of this would come from the Latin Americans themselves, through private and public investment. Another ten percent was to come from private sources, the European countries, and Japan. The United States Government itself pledged to put one billion dollars a year into Latin America over the ten-year period. The alliance was officially launched at Punta del Este, Uruguay, in January of 1962, where a Meeting of Consultation of Foreign Ministers adopted the Charter of Punta del Este. Besides spelling out the goals of the aid program, the Charter pledges the Latin American countries to carry out agrarian and tax reforms and formulate detailed and feasible development plans. The Punta del Este meeting also, however, voted down the establishment of a public relations organization to publicize the Alliance in Latin America and the establishment of a seven-man panel to give some direction and coordination to the operation, replacing the proposed panel with a purely consultative body. In this way, the Alliance was weakened from the very beginning, resulting in a dispersed, and relatively inefficient, utilization of the funds and a minimal propaganda advantage. The scope of the new United States aid commitments to Latin America, however, can be gauged by the fact that, between 1945 and 1960, economic aid to Latin America had amounted to $2,897,000,000 altogether (less than that to Yugoslavia alone), plus a half-billion in military aid. Until 1960, only about two percent of United States aid went to Latin America, and the 1958 allotment was a mere $35 million. At the Second Special Inter-American Conference in Rio de Janeiro, in November, 1965, the United States extended its Alliance for Progress commitment indefinitely (see Tables VI and VII).

According to the terms of the Alliance for Progress, American private investment in Latin America was to provide fifteen percent of the twenty billion dollars that was to come from sources outside Latin America. This annual $300 million goal has never been achieved. The figure was, perhaps, based on the fact that, between 1950 and 1959, there

TABLE VI—U.S. ECONOMIC GRANTS AND LOANS TO LATIN AMERICA, 1945–
64. (EXCLUSIVE OF PARTICIPATION IN INTER-AMERICAN INSTITUTIONS,
IN MILLIONS OF DOLLARS)

Argentina	$ 389	Dominican Rep	$ 92	Nicaragua	$ 61
Bolivia	322	Ecuador	106	Panama	91
Brazil	1,517	El Salvador	45	Paraguay	63
Chile	634	Guatemala	148	Peru	222
Colombia	383	Haiti	92	Uruguay	58
Costa Rica	83	Honduras	46	Venezuela	111
Cuba	41	Mexico	365	Other	64
				Total	$4,931

Source: U.S. Dept. of Commerce, *Foreign Grants and Credits by the United States Government,* 1964.

was a mean net United States private investment in Latin America annually of $330 million. However, since 1959, there has been a substantial decrease in investment in petroleum in Venezuela, a complete drying-up, of course, of investment in Cuba, and a very low rate of investment in Argentina and Brazil, due to domestic political and economic crises. As a result, between 1960 and 1962, mean annual investment declined to $45 million. If Venezuela is excluded, however, the figure is $168 million, down only slightly from a 1950–59 figure, excluding Venezuela and Cuba, of $178 million.[15] In order to increase the flow of private funds, the United States Government has launched an extensive program of investment guarantees, which protect the investor against devaluation, nationalization, and war, and which now cover most of Latin America (see Table VIII).

The United States, in the post-1959 period, also abandoned its opposition to two other Latin American economic goals: commodity price stabilization and economic integration. As a result, the United States became a party to the International Coffee Agreement in 1962, and

TABLE VII—U.S. MILITARY ASSISTANCE TO LATIN AMERICA, 1945–54
(GRANTS ONLY, IN MILLIONS OF DOLLARS)

Argentina	$ 41	Ecuador	$ 38	Paraguay	$ 3
Bolivia	11	El Salvador	3	Peru	96
Brazil	228	Guatemala	9	Uruguay	36
Chile	100	Haiti	4	Venezuela	9
Colombia	67	Honduras	3	Regional	197
Costa Rica	1	Mexico	1	Total	$882
Cuba	16	Nicaragua	6		
Dominican Rep	12	Panama	1		

Source: U.S. Dept. of Commerce, *Foreign Grants and Credits by the United States Government,* 1964.

15 Leland L. Johnson, *The Course of U.S. Private Investment in Latin America Since the Rise of Castro,* Memorandum RM-4091-ISA, May, 1964, The Rand Corporation, p. 6.

TABLE VIII—UNITED STATES DIRECT PRIVATE INVESTMENT IN LATIN AMERICA, YEAR END, 1964 (IN MILLIONS OF DOLLARS)

Mexico	$1,035	Chile	$ 788
Panama	663	Colombia	520
Central America &		Peru	460
West Indies	594	Venezuela	2,808
Argentina	883	Other	186
Brazil	994	Total	$8,932

Source: United States Department of Commerce, *Survey of Current Business,* September, 1965.

supported the formation of the Central American Common Market and the Latin American Free Trade Area (see (Chapter 8).

With all this, however, total United States trade with Latin America remained fairly stagnant, leading to suggestions at the November, 1965 Rio meeting of the OAS that preferential trading arrangements be made between the United States and Latin America, similar to those between the European trading blocs and certain African countries (see Table IX).

TABLE IX—UNITED STATES–LATIN AMERICAN TRADE, 1950–64 (IN MILLIONS OF DOLLARS)

U.S. Exports to Latin America		U.S. Imports from Latin America	
1950	$2,819	1950	$3,102
1955	3,416	1955	3,607
1960	3,769	1960	3,961
1962	3,582	1962	3,340
1963	3,195	1963	3,382
1964	3,714	1964	3,475

Source: *Statistical Abstract of the United States, 1965.*

D / THE ORGANIZATION OF AMERICAN STATES, 1954–66

The Organization of American States, between 1954 and 1966, has not, of course, been solely concerned with the Soviet challenge to American paramountcy in the Western Hemisphere. Between 1954 and 1959, the organization reflected the unconcern of Washington, and after the Guatemalan fiasco busied itself with settling the type of dispute it had been so successful in handling earlier (see Chapter 4). In 1955, for example, the OAS halted an exile invasion of Costa Rica originating in Nicaragua. It also quieted a potentially explosive dispute between Ecuador and Peru (although this dispute, over their mutual boundary, is far from

TABLE X—INVOCATIONS OF THE RIO TREATY 1954–1966 NOT INVOLVING
THE COLD WAR

1955:	Costa Rica *vs.* Nicaragua
1955:	Ecuador *vs.* Peru
1957:	Honduras *vs.* Nicaragua
1960:	Venezuela *vs.* Dominican Republic
1963:	Haiti *vs.* Dominican Republic

settled, and was partially the cause of the multiple postponements of the Eleventh Inter-American Conference, scheduled to meet in Quito). In 1957, the OAS was instrumental in stopping a pocket war between Honduras and Nicaragua in connection with their long-standing boundary dispute, and got both sides to submit the question to the International Court of Justice. The OAS also supervised the eventual transfer of territory. Even after 1959, the OAS has, of course, continued to fulfill its function of maintaining the *Pax Americana,* a job which has included imposing diplomatic and economic sanctions on the Dominican Republic at the Sixth Meeting of Consultation (San José, 1960), for involvement in an attempted assassination of President Betancourt of Venezuela, and, in 1963, mediating in a dispute between the Dominican Republic and Haiti. In December of 1964, The First Special Conference of American States was held in Washington to facilitate the entry of new states into the organization. Jamaica and Trinidad had applied for admission in 1962, but their applications had been blocked by Guatemala because of the Belice dispute. As of 1966, the two new Caribbean states had not seen fit to reapply.

Nevertheless, the principal concern of the organization since 1959, as foreshadowed at Caracas in 1954, has been the series of attempts on the part of the United States to mobilize its client organization to support it in meeting the Soviet challenge, and the resistance to this mobilization by the Latin American countries in order to maintain their new freedom of foreign-policy action, and to avoid being drawn into matters that they believe should be the concern of, and handled by, the paramount itself.

TABLE XI—INTER-AMERICAN CONFERENCES, 1954–65

First Special Conference of American States
December 16-18, 1964
Washington, D. C.
Consideration of the procedures for admitting new members.
Act of Washington, setting forth procedure for admitting
new members (two-thirds vote of the Council), but excluding
territories which are subject to claim by an American state.

Second Special Conference of American States
November 15-30, 1965
Rio de Janeiro
Consideration of Charter revision.
Adoption of various resolutions to be ratified by a subsequent conference.

In early 1959, the Council of the OAS, acting as provisional organ of consultation, had dealt with complaints by Panama and Nicaragua of invasions by Cuban-supported exiles. When a similar complaint was received from the Dominican Republic, a formal Meeting of Consultation of Foreign Ministers was called to deal with the entire question of unrest in the Caribbean. This meeting reiterated the principle of nonintervention, and empowered the Inter-American Peace Committee to investigate the whole Caribbean situation, at the request of member states, or on its own initiative. This resolution was so innocuous that it received unanimous approval and was quite ineffective. The Santiago meeting also provided for the establishment of an Inter-American Commission on Human Rights. By August, when this meeting took place, the decision to turn Cuba into a totalitarian state in close collaboration with the Communists had apparently already been made by the Castro Government (see above).

When it became apparent that its paramountcy was being directly challenged (following Cuban acceptance of the Soviet offer of Military protection in June, 1960), the United States called a Meeting of Consultation which met in August in San José. It proved impossible to pass a resolution condemning the Cuban action, and, finally, the United States had to settle for a declaration merely deploring ". . . the attempt of the Sino-Soviet powers to make use of the political, economic or social situation of any American state, ...", reiterating nonintervention and reaffirming that the Inter-American system is ". . . incompatible with any form of totalitarianism. . . ." This Declaration was approved by 19 votes to 0 (the Dominican Republic and Cuba having walked out of the meeting). Even so, Mexico and Venezuela approved the declaration with extreme reluctance, and the Venezuelan and Peruvian foreign ministers refused to sign, and had to be replaced by other delegation members.

The Eighth Meeting of Consultation met at Punta del Este, Uruguay, in January of 1962, and, by a bare fourteen-state two-thirds majority, voted to bar participation of the Castro Government in the OAS, eliminate Cuban participation in the Inter-American Defense Board, embargo arms traffic with Cuba, and recommend interruption of other commerce. Mexico, Ecuador, Brazil, Bolivia, Argentina, Chile, and Cuba voted against the anti-Cuban measures and it was only with the greatest of difficulty, and by means of economic inducements, that the favorable votes of Haiti and Uruguay were obtained. There is little doubt that one of the reasons for the American difficulties at Punta del Este, despite the recent launching of the Alliance for Progress, was the loss of face suffered at the Bay of Pigs, and the resulting Latin American fear that the paramount was weakening and was trying to get them to assume its proper responsibilities. The Punta del Este meeting did declare that the doctrine of legitimate self-defense applied to threats to peace and security arising from subversive activities, and, to police such threats, established the Special Committee of Consultation on Security, which has since reported

TABLE XIA—MEETINGS OF CONSULTATION, 1959–66

Meeting	Location	Date	Major Agenda Items	Outcome
Fifth	Santiago, Chile	August 12–18, 1959 (after April–June disturbances in Caribbean)	Consideration of problems of unrest in the Caribbean; discussion of problems of democracy and human rights in Latin America.	Declaration of Santiago, concerning principles of democracy and respect for human rights; special temporary power assigned to Inter-American Peace Committee to investigate and conciliate in cases of invasion by foreign-based rebels.
Sixth	San José, Costa Rica	August 16–21, 1960 (after attempt on life of Venezuelan President Betancourt)	Request of Venezuelan Government regarding policy of intervention of the Dominican Republic (attempt to kill President Betancourt).	Breaking of diplomatic relations and partial interruption of economic relations with the Dominican Republic.
Seventh	San José, Costa Rica	August 22–29, 1960 (Cuban question)	Continental solidarity; defense of the inter-American system and of democratic principles.	Declaration of San José de Costa Rica regarding restatement of inter-American principles; establishment of a Committee of Good Offices.
Eighth	Punta del Este, Uruguay	January 22–31, 1962 (after increased Cuban tension)	Cuban, Soviet, and Communist Chinese subversive activities; general threat to continental unity and to democratic institutions.	Exclusion of the present Cuban Government from the inter-American system; exclusion of Cuba from the Inter-American Defense Board; prohibition of any armament trade with Cuba and request to the Council of the OAS to extend this prohibition possibly also to other commercial goods; establishment of

				the Special Consultative Committee on Security (SCCS) against Communist subversion; recommendation for amendment of the Statutes to the Inter-American Commission on Human Rights.
Ninth	Washington, D.C., United States	July 21–26, 1964	Venezuelan request for sanction against Cuba in view of Cuban complicity in terrorist activities in Venezuela.	Breaking of diplomatic and consular relations with Cuba; interruption of commercial and maritime relations with Cuba; expression of sympathy for the Cuban people; regional and international economic cooperation within the framework of the Charter of Alta Gracia.
Tenth	Washington, D.C., United States	May, 1965	Infiltration of Communism into Dominican revolt.	Establishment of a mediatory commission with military force.

Source: U.S. Senate, Committee on Foreign Relations, *United States–Latin American Relations. The Organization of American States* (Washington, D.C.: Government Printing Office, 1959), p. 11.

TABLE XII—ACTIVITIES OF THE INTER-AMERICAN PEACE COMMITTEE, 1954–65

Situation	Date Request for Action Received	Date Action Terminated	Charges by Country Initiating Action or Reasons for Requesting Action	Outcome	Countries Involved in the Situation
9. Cuba-Dominican Republic situation	February 27, 1956	April 20, 1956	Cuba requested Committee meet to study certain difficulties existing between it and the Dominican Republic.	Committee expressed its hope that parties arrive at solution through regular diplomatic channels.	Cuba, Dominican Republic
10. Request by Haiti	August 17, 1959	There was no formal termination. Case was settled in October, 1959.	Haiti asked the Foreign Ministers of the OAS to study invasion of Haiti by group coming from Cuba.	Matter was studied by Committee operating under new *ad hoc* powers granted at Santiago. Since the Cuban invasion was unsuccessful and Haiti did not accuse Cuba directly, the matter had no consequences.	Haiti, Cuba
11. Anti-Venezuelan leaflets over Curaçao	November 25, 1959	There was no formal termination of the case, since further charges were leveled against the Dominican regime by Venezuela and Ecuador.	A U.S. plane with Cuban pilots threw leaflets on Curaçao calling on the Venezuelan Army to rise up against the Betancourt regime. The leaflets were supposed to come down on Venezuelan territory. The plane, however, made a forced landing in Aruba.	The Committee found that the Dominican Government was implicated in the matter (stopover of plane in Santo Domingo).	Venezuela, Dominican Republic

12. Ecuador-Dominican Republic situation	February 16, 1960	April 12, 1960	Controversy between Ecuador and the Dominican Republic regarding thirteen Dominican citizens who had been granted asylum in the Embassy of Ecuador in Santo Domingo. Dominican measures which affected this right of asylum.	The attempt of direct negotiations between Ecuador and the Dominican Republic failed, since the Dominican Government refused to accept the "bases of agreement." The Committee then expressed the hope that the matter might find a bilateral solution.	Ecuador, Dominican Republic
13. Violation of human rights in the Dominican Republic	February 17, 1960	June 6, 1960	Venezuela requested the Committee "to examine the flagrant violation of human rights in the Dominican Republic," since it increased the tension in the Caribbean area. However, the Dominican Government did not authorize a visit of the Committee.	The Committee came to the conclusion that the tensions in the Caribbean area had increased through the violation of human rights by the Dominican Republic (Report of the Committee dated June 6, 1960).	Venezuela, Dominican Republic
14. Violation of human rights and international tensions in the Caribbean area	August, 1959	August 16, 1960 (Seventh Meeting of Consultation, August 22-29, 1960, San José, Costa Rica)	The Fifth Meeting of Consultation in Santiago, Chile, August, 1959, instructed the Inter-American Peace Committee to examine the reason for the existing tensions in the Caribbean area, apart from specific individual cases, and to report about it to the next IA Conference or Meeting of Consultation.	The Committee came to the conclusion that there existed on the American continent a serious crisis which made itself felt most acutely in the Caribbean area. It had economic and social causes —the peoples were dissatisfied with their lot— and was directed against any kind of dictatorial tutelage (Special Report dated April 14, 1960, and condensed Final Report of August 5, 1960).*	Latin America in general, with special reference to the Caribbean area.

TABLE XII—CONTINUED

Situation	Date Request for Action Received	Date Action Terminated	Charges by Country Initiating Action or Reasons for Requesting Action	Outcome	Countries Involved in the Situation
15. Request by Nicaragua	February 16, 1961	December, 1962	Guarantee of the execution of the decision of the International Court of Justice of November 18, 1960, regarding the validity of the arbitration award of the King of Spain (December 23, 1906).	The case was terminated in 1962 after the requested assistance was given. (The final solution of this controversy had been made at The Hague in favor of Honduras.)	Honduras, Nicaragua
16. Request by Mexico	June 2, 1961	June 5, 1961	Charges by Guatemala regarding the alleged training of Communist agents on Mexican territory were to be examined by the Committee.	The case needed no examination, since the IAPC came to the conclusion that a visit to Mexico was not required because Mexico was keeping its international obligations.	Mexico, Guatemala
17. Request by Peru	November 27, 1961	January 22, 1962	Examination of various arbitrary acts in Cuba; Communist subversion in Latin America.	The IAPC reported to the Eighth Meeting of Consultation in Punta del Este as follows: The ideological and political links of the Cuban Government were in contradiction to the principles of the Charter of the OAS; there was syste-	Peru, Cuba

matic violation of human rights by Cuba; subversive activities of the Soviets and of Cuba were equivalent to political aggression.

| 18. Request by Panama | January 10, 1964 | January 15, 1964 | Panama requested the assistance of the IAPC after the Canal Zone riots, which were related to the flag controversy. | On January 15, 1964, after arriving in Panama City, the IAPC announced that the immediate crisis had terminated and that it was therefore possible to begin negotiations regarding a revision of U.S. control rights. | Panama, the United States |

*This more general activity of the IAPC on the basis of the mandate of the Fifth Meeting of Consultation of Ministers of Foreign Affairs is closely linked to cases 10-13.

Source: U.S. Senate, Committee on Foreign Relations, *United States–Latin American Relations. The Organization of American States* (Washington, D.C.: Government Printing Office, 1959), p. 28.

to the Council of the OAS a number of times on cases of Communist subversion.

In October of the same year, on the other hand, when the United States proved itself capable of moving swiftly and effectively to counter a direct military threat to the hemisphere, the Council of the OAS voted unanimously to support American moves in the Caribbean to assure removal of Soviet missiles from Cuba. Several Latin American states offered naval assistance and some participated in the blockade.

Cuban involvement in subversive activities was charged by the Venezuelan Government, and, as a result, the Ninth Meeting of Consultation was called in Washington, in July of 1964. Despite the presentation of overwhelming evidence in support of the Venezuelan complaint, only a fifteen-to-four vote could be obtained for the application of diplomatic and economic sanctions against Cuba. Diplomatic relations were to be broken off, and economic and commercial relations interrupted, along with transport and communications links. Despite the obligatory nature of the vote, Mexico has refused to apply the sanctions.[16]

Finally, with the greatest of difficulty, a bare two-thirds majority was obtained at the Tenth Meeting of Consultation of the OAS, in May of 1965, for the establishment of an Inter-American Police Force for the purpose of intervening in the Dominican crisis (American troops were already there, of course).[17] Chile, Ecuador, Mexico, Peru, and Uruguay voted against the resolution, and Venezuela abstained. The United States had to depend on the vote of a Dominican representative without a government to get the measure passed. Eventually, 2,000 Latin American troops from five countries joined 9,000 United States troops in the Inter-American force. It is interesting to note that aspiring sub-paramount Brazil provided, by far, the largest Latin American contingent. For the first time in Inter-American history, an OAS commission with military force at its command was authorized to intervene in a largely domestic situation.

The United States, at the Second Special Inter-American Conference (Rio de Janeiro, November, 1965), was interested in trying to make the Inter-American Force permanent, as part of the changes in the Inter-American system to be considered at the Conference. In this aim, the United States was unsuccessful. Nevertheless, the Rio Conference did, for the first time, acknowledge that the structure of the OAS was inadequate to deal with the special regional problems created by the Cold War.

As a result, the Rio Conference passed a number of resolutions recommending various modifications of the Charter of the OAS, to be formally adopted at another meeting to be held in 1966. Since most of

---

[16] Mexico was at the time, and has continued to be, actively involved in attempting to spread its influence in the Caribbean, and, perhaps, eventually achieve the position of regional sub-paramount. It was felt that maintaining contact with Cuba was essential to this effort, as well as displaying a salutary but cautious defiance of the United States.

[17] It was impossible to actually convene the Foreign Ministers on such short notice. The members of the OAS Council acted as special delegates.

the recommendations were adopted unanimously, it is most likely that they will eventually be incorporated into the Inter-American system. Accordingly, the Inter-American Conferences, which have not met since 1954, will be put on a regular basis of annual meetings, to be supplemented by emergency meetings of Foreign Ministers whenever the necessity should arise. The Inter-American Economic and Social Council and the Inter-American Council on Culture and Education will become coordinate with the Council of the OAS, which will be renamed "Permanent Council." The term of the Secretary-General and the Assistant Secretary-General will be reduced from ten to five years, but they will be authorized to take the initiative in bringing matters to the attention of the various Councils. The

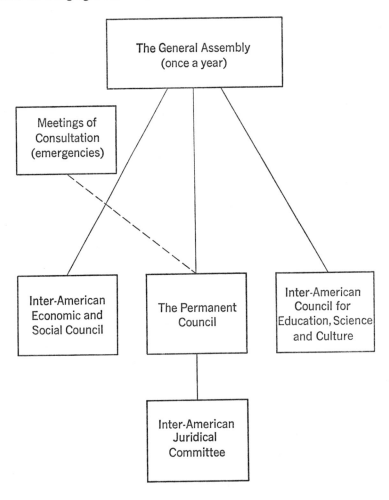

Fig. 8 — Structure of the Organization of American States as Envisioned by the Second Special Inter-American Conference

Permanent Council will have the authority to initiate procedures of peaceful settlement in hemispheric disputes, such as boundary controversies. (This resolution was adopted by a vote of twelve to six.) An Inter-American emergency aid fund will be established for emergency assistance. The United States extended the Alliance for Progress and reiterated support for stabilized commodity prices, compensatory financing for balance of payments problems, mutual economic security, a Latin American common market, and trade preferences without reciprocity.

Thus, since 1959, several new organs have been created within the Organization of American States, all, without exception, founded as a result of the Soviet challenge to American paramountcy in the hemisphere. The Inter-American Commission on Human Rights, established at Santiago in 1959, has issued reports on the violation of human rights in Haiti, the Dominican Republic, Nicaragua, Paraguay, and Cuba. The Special Consultative Committee on Security, established in 1962, in April, 1963, was authorized to investigate subversion in any member state, even if not invited. (This authorization was granted by a vote of thirteen in favor, one against [Brazil], and six abstaining.) The Inter-American Committee on the Alliance for Progress reports to the Inter-American Economic and Social Council on the progress of the Alliance. These changes, and those proposed at Rio in 1965, should modernize the OAS and render it more efficient when it is given a clear policy direction. Nevertheless, it must at all times be remembered that the OAS is an organization of clients and that its functions are to mobilize support for the paramount, funnel paramount assistance to the clients, and provide them with a formal channel for complaints and requests. Until such time as United States paramountcy is again unchallenged in Latin America, the Latin American states will continue to use the paramount clash to broaden their freedom of international action, and will continue to resist taking prior responsibilities in the Cold War. The OAS can continue to function effectively in many ways, however: in the traditional tasks of maintaining the *Pax Americana* with reference to intra-regional disputes not involving the Cold War, in the channeling of economic assistance, in the strengthening of cultural relations, and so forth. Even in the Cold War, the OAS can function in the purely formal ratification of *necessarily unilateral* acts of the United States in cases which do involve extra-continental concerns (as in the missile crisis of 1962), so long as the sensibilities of the clients are taken into account when making and timing such requests.

E / CONCLUSIONS

Given the overwhelming strategic advantages the United States enjoys in the Western Hemisphere, a successful Soviet challenge to its paramount position was, by no means, obvious, or even likely. The fact that such a challenge was, and is, being made, leading to the actual detachment of one of the Latin American clients and its incorporation into the Soviet bloc is due to several factors. First in time and in importance, was the neglect of Latin America, following World War II, by a United States, for the first time in its history, politically involved throughout the world. "The Western Hemisphere idea lost its meaning because the leading nation in the Americas became engaged in international politics in all the hemispheres." [18] Secondly, under-reaction by the United States to the Soviet takeover of Cuba led to a loss of face in Latin America, and a loss of faith in the ability of the paramount to defend its own interests and offer protection to its clients. It is instructive to compare the Latin American reaction to the Bay of Pigs with the tremendous enthusiasm and support which greeted the missile blockade. Thirdly, the United States, in Latin America as elsewhere, has often been trapped by its own propaganda, and, thus, finds itself in the position, for example, of calling intervention nonintervention, and preventive action curative action, as illustrated by some of the truly ludicrous statements made at the time of the Dominican crisis of 1965. Candor is not, by any means, always the best propaganda tactic to follow in international politics, but it often may be when dealing with Latin America, due to the mental preconceptions of the *patrón-peón* complex (see Chapter 2). Finally, the United States is still immature as a paramount and its responsibilities are immense. Latin America does not occupy the central position in American foreign policy that it did until 1941, and, perhaps, never will again.

On the Latin American side, the Cold War can be, and is, used against the paramount to gain some international flexibility and a higher level of paramount benevolence, but the Cold War cannot be used against reality. The Latin American states, separately or together, are and will be for the foreseeable future, clients. Cuba has shown, if such proof is necessary, that if they are not clients of the United States, they will be clients of another paramount.

How may we assess the position of Latin America in the Cold War as of 1966? There are, perhaps, some 300,000 to 350,000 Communists in the region, including Cuba. They are supported by, or support, an indeterminate mass of Marxist intellectuals, Jacobin Leftists, dispossessed urban and rural dwellers, and cynical and opportunistic feudalists. Following its failure to establish a military presence in 1962, the Soviet Union still must base its strategy mix on propaganda, economic tactics, and subversion. For the mix to be most effective, it must neutralize the effects of the Sino-Soviet split to the extent that it can. In Latin America, the Soviet Union has a great advantage over China, and this was reflected at the Havana meeting of November, 1964 (see above), and at the Tricontinental Havana Conference of January, 1966, which was, in effect, a Soviet *festschrift* at the expense of the Chinese. The disappear-

---

[18] G. Lagos, *op. cit.,* p. 79.

ance of pro-Chinese Ché Guevara from Cuba was another indication of the tightening hold of the Soviets.

The usefulness of economic strategy to the Soviets is inherently limited. Soviet credits have turned out to be illusory, and its technical assistance practically nonexistent. The $30 million credit offered Argentina in 1953 with such fanfare was reduced two years later to $4 million. A subsequent Czech offer of $15 million was similarly reduced to $2 million. In 1958, the Soviets offered Argentina a $100 million credit to purchase oil exploration equipment. Only $30 million was ever used and that was used only to offset the $30 million trade surplus Argentina had built up with the Soviet Union. In 1954, Uruguay signed a trade agreement with the Soviet Union providing for $19 million worth of trade both ways. In the subsequent year, Uruguay shipped the Soviets $19 million worth of goods and received in return $22,000 worth! Thus, in effect, Uruguay supplied the Soviet Union with $18.9 million worth of short-term credit. The Communist bloc supplies credits only on a bilateral basis, and in nonconvertible currencies which may be expended only in the bloc country supplying it. If a surplus in trade is developed favorable to Latin America (and this is generally the case), the surplus will have to be used to purchase goods at higher than market cost, thereby worsening the very terms of trade and balance-of-payments problems economic relations with the Soviet bloc were supposed to ameliorate. Soviet trade is erratic and unreliable. In 1959, 59% of Uruguayan wool exports went to the Soviet Union. In 1961, none. In 1961, the highest percentage of trade turnover of any Latin American country with the Soviet bloc (excluding Cuba) was the Brazilian figure of 5.4%. In any case, bloc trade with Argentina and Uruguay following the initial post-1953 surge has been stagnant, and only with Cuba has it steadily increased, until now the bloc is Cuba's principal trading partner. Essentially, the problem, aside from the limited resources of the bloc, is that Latin America produces what the bloc doesn't want or doesn't need. A startling example of this is the spectacle of the world's largest sugar producer (Cuba) sending huge quantities of sugar to the world's second-largest sugar producer (the Soviet Union).

> The objective results of the new foreign economic policy of the Soviet Union and the Soviet bloc in Latin America have been nil in terms of any kind of economic, military or technical assistance.
> . . .
> Thus, not only has the Soviet bloc failed to make credits available to Latin America for general development, the Soviet bloc has not even provided credit. Instead . . . it has been Latin America which has extended credit to the Soviet bloc, primarily via the trade accounts.[19]

[19] Ronald James Clark, *Latin American Economic Relations With the Soviet Bloc 1954–1961* (Doctoral Dissertation, Indiana University, 1963), pp. 159 and 169.

Thus, since propaganda is essentially a supplementary strategy, the principal Soviet strategy vis-à-vis Latin America in the Cold War will continue to be subversion, and, as long as it is successful, it will continue to employ the tactics of division of the party, temporary alliances with the Traditional Right, support of, and infiltration of, Jacobin Left movements and parties, extreme nationalism, and anti-Yankeeism. It will continue to try to neutralize the Neoliberals through blackmail where it controls the labor unions, and will continue to weaken the Democratic Left by proclaiming that the democrats sell out to the United States.

In its response to the Soviet challenge, the United States must beware not only of underreaction, as has already been mentioned, but also of overreaction. As far back as 1827, John Quincy Adams, in a letter to Richard Rush, suggested that the best way to deal with Latin America was through ". . . an observing and persevering system of kindness, moderation and forbearance, ...". It is perhaps better to wait until Communist involvement in a situation is obvious before taking action, and then to take that action only after notifying the OAS (but not necessarily waiting for it to act). There is little doubt, for instance, that American reaction to the Dominican crisis was precipitate, and might have eventually proven to have been unnecessary. To the Latin American states, gestures mean a great deal when coming from the paramount, and it costs little and gains much (to cite a recent example) to offer a new treaty to Panama over a canal which is, in any case, rapidly becoming obsolete. Nevertheless, none of this is meant to suggest that forceful anti-subversive action should not continue to be taken. It has been observed many times that active repression of the organized Communist movement is effective in damaging its effectiveness and its popular influence.

> The appeal of Communism does not elicit a favorable response where the party lacks legal status, *de facto* or *de jure,* to compete or cooperate as peers with the non-communist parties.[20]

The United States has still not found the proper formula for dealing with subversion, either directly or through the agency of the Organization of American States. In terms of the American economic and propaganda counter-offensives, there must be an understanding that what is socially required in Latin America is nothing less than a revolution in those countries that still have a semi-feudal structure. This revolution need not, of course, be violent, but the land must be freed and the productive capacities of the country liberated, as was partially done in Mexico and Bolivia through bloody revolution. The Alliance may build thousands of schools and clinics, and achieve, thereby, very little except to free local funds for flight capital, overbearing bureaucracy, and the purchase of arms. The Alliance funds should, rather, be used to soften the economic dislocation that will undoubtedly temporarily occur at the time of the revolution. In

[20] Rollie Poppino, *International Communism in Latin America* (New York, 1964), p. 221.

fact, that is what it was intended for—the disbursement of funds was to be accompanied by basic social change, but in most countries the Traditional Right and the state bureaucracy have been able to get the money, while preventing the change. The indigenous models of Mexico, Bolivia, Venezuela, and, perhaps after April, 1964, Brazil, hold many lessons for the hemisphere in the various ways of staging and carrying out this revolution. The alliance of the Democratic Left with the Neoliberal universe holds, perhaps, the key to making the revolution and making it work. The Jacobins and Communists are aware of this, and do all they can to prevent the alliance from taking place elsewhere, as it has already successfully taken place in Venezuela. Referring to the organized Neoliberals Ché Guevara said:

> For some years now, imperialism has been preparing an organized repression of the peoples of Latin America. In several countries an International of repression has been formed. . . . But the International of repression will be met inevitably and naturally by the International of proletarians and peasants against the common enemy.[21]

For several years following the end of World War II, the Latin American client system, as organized in the OAS, was overshadowed by new United States, European, Middle Eastern, and Asian client systems organized in NATO, CENTO, SEATO, and the Anzus Pact. As these organizations become moribund and tend to distintegrate, and with the emergence of a powerful and potentially paramount Europe, there are signs that ". . . the United States could gradually resume its traditional policy of emphasis on the Western Hemisphere and the dreams and ideals of those great statesmen who founded our nation and guided it safely through the critical decades of the first century of its existence." [22] Certainly, the gleefully or sorrowfully announced demise of the OAS has proven to be premature, and the November, 1965, meetings at Rio de Janeiro may have marked the beginnings of the painful process of reconstituting the Inter-American system on the basis of contemporary reality.

Selected Bibliography

Especially since 1959, a tremendous mass of material has appeared on the subject of Latin America in the Cold War. As a result, this Bibliography will be more selective

[21] Norman Gall, "A Red Insurgency Jolts Latin America," *The Wall Street Journal*, November 8, 1965, p. 16 (quoting a Guevara interview in the journal *Révolution Africaine*, Algiers).
[22] J. F. Rippy, *Globe and Hemisphere, op. cit.*, pp. 239-240.

than those for the other chapters in PARTS II and III. The events of the Dominican crisis of 1965 were too recent when this book was being written to allow for the development of sufficiently meaningful criteria to be applied to the selection of material. The interested investigator can consult the bibliographies in the works cited below for further material on the topics discussed.

It is impossible, of course, to attempt to survey the material on the Cold War in general. For a particularly perceptive analysis of the roots of the Cold War, however, see Sigmund Neumann, *Permanent Revolution* (2nd ed., New York, 1965). A work which appeared prior to the major Soviet offensive in Latin America, but which is still worth consulting, is Walter M. Daniels, *Latin America in the Cold War* (New York, 1952). A more recent work by a man of great intelligence and analytical ability who has been personally close to many of the events of the Cold War in Latin America is Adolf A. Berle, Jr., *Latin America—Diplomacy and Reality* (New York, 1962). On the general subject of Latin America in the Cold War, see also Salvador de Madariaga, *Latin America Between the Eagle and the Bear* (New York, 1962); Irving Peter Pflaum, *Arena of Decision: Latin America in Crisis* (Englewood Cliffs, 1964); Jules Dubois, *Operation America; The Communist Conspiracy in Latin America* (New York, 1963), and the chapters by Grace, Ravines, Bailey (on "Neoliberalism"), Ayres, and Brandenburg in the book edited by the author cited previously in the Selected Bibliography for Chapter 3.

On the history of Communism in Latin America, material is rather sparse. The best accounts are Robert J. Alexander, *Communism in Latin America* (New Brunswick, 1957); Rollie Poppino, *International Communism in Latin America* (New York, 1964); Victor Alba, *Historia del Comunismo en América Latina* (Mexico, 1954), and a personal account by a man who was for many years one of the principal Comintern agents in Latin America, *The Yenan Way,* by Eudocio Ravines (New York, 1951). A very complete, scholarly, and perceptive account of the Communist involvement in Guatemala, between 1944 and 1954, is Ronald M. Schneider, *Communism in Guatemala, 1944–1954* (New York, 1959). See also the detailed account by Theodore Geiger, *Communism vs. Progress in Guatemala* (National Planning Association, 1953). The most intelligent of the many *apologias* for the Arbenz régime written after its overthrow is Guillermo Toriello, *La Batalla de Guatemala* (Mexico, 1955). It is of great interest to trace the development of a Democratic Leftist into a Jacobin. To do this, read in sequence the following three books by Juan José Arévalo: *Discursos en la Presidencia, 1945–1948* (Guatemala, 1948); *Guatemala, la Democracia y el Imperio* (Santiago de Chile, 1954), and *The Shark and the Sardines* (New York, 1961).

Some aspects of the Soviet diplomatic and propaganda offensives after 1954 are detailed in Dorothy Dillon, *International Communism and Latin America* (Gainesville, 1962). Some background on economic strategy in general can be gained from reading Yuan-li Wu, *Economic Warfare* (New York, 1952), and on Soviet economic strategy in particular by reading Robert Loring Allen, *Soviet Economic Warfare* (Washington, 1960), and Milton Kovner, *The Challenge of Coexistence: A Study of Soviet Economic Diplomacy* (Washington, 1961). On the Soviet economic offensive in Latin America, see Robert L. Allen, *Soviet Influence in Latin America: The Role of Economic Relations* (Washington, 1959), and, particularly, the very fine analysis in Ronald James Clark, *Latin American Economic Relations with the Soviet Bloc 1954–1961* (Doctoral Dissertation, Indiana University, 1963).

Useful background on the incorporation of Cuba into the Soviet client system can be obtained from Robert F. Smith, *The United States and Cuba: Business and Diplomacy 1917–1960* (New York, 1960) and Grupo Cubano de Investigaciones Económicas, *Un Estudio Sobre Cuba: Colonia—República—Experimento Socialista* (Coral Gables, 1963). On the Castro period, see Boris Goldenberg, *The Cuban Revolution and Latin America* (New York, 1965); E. Dudley Seers, *et al., Cuba: The Economic and Social Revolution* (Chapel Hill, 1964); Theodore Draper, *Castro's Revolution, Myths and Realities* (New York, 1962); *Idem., Castroism: Theory and Practice* (New York, 1965), and Irving Peter Pflaum, *Tragic Island: How Communism Came to Cuba* (Prentice-Hall: Englewood Cliffs, 1964). A book on the Cuban revolution by the man who for decades has headed the Communist apparatus in Cuba is *The Fundamental Principles of Socialism in Cuba,* by Blas Roca [Francisco Calderío] (Washington, 1962). There are also numerous volumes, mostly journalistic, on the Bay of Pigs invasion and the missile crisis.

Two books on the Organization of American States which concentrate on the involvement of that organization in the Cold War are William Manger, *Pan America in Crisis: The Future of the OAS* (Washington, 1961), and John Dreier, *The Organization of American States and the Hemisphere Crisis* (New York, 1962). In addition, consult the official OAS publications listed in the Selected Bibliography for Chapter 4 for the period following 1954.

Arms and Politics in Latin America, by Edwin Lieuwen (New York, 1960), includes a lengthy section on United States military assistance to Latin America. Lincoln Gordon's *A New Deal for Latin America: The Alliance for Progress* (Cambridge, Mass., 1963) is a good example of the official rationale of the Alliance. Uneven discussions are provided in W. Manger, ed., *The Alliance for Progress: A Critical Appraisal* (Washington, 1963), and John Dreier, *The Alliance for Progress: Problems and Perspectives* (Baltimore, 1962). An annual issue of the journal *Inter-American Economic Affairs* is devoted to Simon G. Hanson's bitter criticisms of the Alliance, and *Alliance Without Allies,* by Víctor Alba (New York, 1965) provides an extremely perceptive and provocative analysis of what has gone wrong with the Alliance.

Finally, Juan José Arévalo's *Anti-Kommunism in Latin America* (New York, 1963) is an example in English of the Jacobin counterattack against the Democratic Left and the Neoliberals.

Part Three **/ THE RESPONSE**

6 / *STRENGTH THROUGH LAW*

> *. . . cette règle [non-intervention] et comme l'épine dorsale du droit international au nouveau monde.*
>
> *. . . This rule [non-intervention] is like the backbone of international law in the new world.*
>
> J.-M. YEPES

We have seen, in PARTS I and II, that the internal and external settings within which the Latin American states must operate in international society determine that their overriding international challenge will arise from their relations with the hemispheric paramount. As a consequence of this presently inescapable fact, and with the exception of purely Latin American matters, their international activities must largely consist of various forms of response to this challenge; that is, attempts to protect themselves, singly or jointly, from the paramount, or to revise or adjust the paramount-client relationship, so that it is on balance more favorable to what they consider to be their interests.

In an ordered, domestic society, the weaker units protect themselves largely through two means: law and organization. To the extent that they can organize into larger and more powerful groups, weak units can alter the structure of power in society, and this altered structure will sooner or later be codified in the legal system, which will then reflect more closely their interests and goals.

Within international (quasi-anarchic) society, the Latin American states have also attempted to use law and organization to protect themselves and their interests and to make their weight felt in international councils. Besides the basic, controlling fact that international society is not centrally ordered, however, they have, until very recently, placed greater emphasis on law than on organization, an order of priorities that, even in domestic society, is relatively ineffective if the goal is a change in the political structure.

The eminent Chilean jurist Alejandro Álvarez (1868–1960), long a judge of the International Court of Justice, first developed the formal concept of a special or separate Inter-American public international law. The roots of such a concept, however, go back, at least, to the Mexican call in 1834 for an Inter-American congress which would establish and codify an American international law for the new states of the hemisphere.[1] In 1866, Bolivia, Chile, Ecuador, and Peru actually signed a treaty embodying special regional rules of international law, but the treaty was not ratified. In the 1880's, the jurist Amancio Alcorta engaged in a polemic with Carlos Calvo (see below) concerning the existence of special American rules.[2] Finally, with the publication, in the early years of the twentieth century, of Álvarez' *Histoire Diplomatique des Républiques Américaines* and his *Le Droit International Américain,* what was already reality was put into theory.[3]

Inter-American public international law can be divided into three general categories. By far the most important, the most controversial, and the least effective, are those rules and doctrines intended to protect the Latin American states from their paramount and introduce a higher degree of predictability into the paramount-client relationship. Secondly, there is a body of rules intended to regulate matters of more or less purely Latin American concern. Finally, there are matters of individual interest to various Latin American countries, which other Latin American countries, as a matter of comity, have, by and large, agreed to support as general rules of Inter-American public international law.

A / DEFENSE AGAINST THE PARAMOUNT

As naïve as it may appear, the main Latin American legal offensive against paramount dominance has been through the doctrine of nonintervention—in other words, a frontal attack, outlawing, in effect, paramount dominance. The doctrine of nonintervention first appeared in rudimentary

[1] This was the first indication of dissatisfaction with eighteenth- and nineteenth-century international law as promulgated and enforced by the European paramounts. The rejection, in the twentieth century, of this international law, first by the Communist states, and, then, by the newly independent countries of Africa and Asia, has meant, for all practical purposes, the demise of the then-existing international legal system.

[2] Note, however, that Calvo did not deny the existence of these rules, but, rather, claimed that they were part of the general law of nations, a position in which he was quite mistaken.

[3] Álvarez, however, based his concept upon the "Western Hemisphere idea" and assumed that the United States shared the Latin American conception of international law. This, of course, is not the case. Since about the third quarter of the nineteenth century, the United States generally supported the European concept of international law.

form in the Treaty of League signed at the Panama Congress of 1826 (see Chapter 8), and was reiterated in the Treaty of Confederation signed at Lima in 1848. Neither of these treaties was ratified by a sufficient number of signatories to bring it into effect. The Calvo and Drago doctrines, which will be discussed later, were also expressions of opposition to intervention. All of these treaties and doctrines were directed against European intervention.

After the United States became paramount, Latin American interest in a presumed international rule of nonintervention redoubled. The United States was close, young, brash, and immensely powerful, and it proceeded to interfere vigorously, not only with the external affairs, but also with the internal affairs of the countries of the Caribbean (see Chapter 3). As a result the Fifth Inter-American Conference, in 1923, created a Commission of Jurists and instructed it to draw up a code of American international law. As part of its report, submitted in 1927, the Commission stated: "No state has a right to interfere in the internal affairs of another." This was the mildest form the doctrine of nonintervention was ever to take in the twentieth century, since it implicitly recognized that states *must* interfere in at least the external affairs of other states. Even in this form, however, the resolution was unacceptable to the United States at the Sixth Inter-American Conference at Havana in 1928, where the United States delegate, Secretary of State Charles Evans Hughes, forcefully restated the traditional rule of nineteenth-century European international law that, under certain circumstances, intervention was not only a right but a duty:

> Let us face the facts. The difficulty, if there is any, . . . is an internal difficulty. . . . From time to time there arises a situation most deplorable and regrettable in which sovereignty is not at work, in which for a time . . . there is no government at all, ...
>
> Now it is the principle of international law that in such a case a government is fully justified in taking action—I would call it interposition of a temporary character—for the purpose of protecting the lives and property of its nationals. . . . International law cannot be changed by the resolutions of this Conference. . . . We cannot codify international law and ignore the duties of States, by setting up the impossible reign of self-will without any recognition upon the part of a State of its obligations to its neighbors. . . .[4]

By 1933, however, the United States felt itself sufficiently secure in its paramountcy, as we have seen, to abjure open, armed intervention, and, thus, Secretary of State Cordell Hull, at the Seventh Inter-American Conference, held in Montevideo, signed the Convention on Rights and Duties of States, Article 8 of which states that: "No state has the right to intervene in the internal *or external* affairs of another." (Italics mine.) Thus, for the first time, the impossible injunction applied to external

[4] As quoted in Henry P. de Vries and José Rodríguez-Novás, *The Law of the Americas* (New York, 1965), pp. 17–18.

affairs was included in the doctrine of nonintervention, and the concept began to lose all meaning other than purely propagandistic. Secretary Hull, it is true, appended a reservation referring to ". . . the law of nations as generally recognized and accepted." Even this possible escape channel was closed, however, when, in 1936, the United States signed, without reservation, the Additional Protocol Relative to Nonintervention, which states in Article 1: "The High Contracting Parties declare inadmissible the intervention of any one of them, directly or indirectly, and for whatever reason, in the internal or external affairs of any other of the parties.", thereby adding indirect, as well as direct, intervention to the doctrine as previously stated, and declaring that no justification of whatever kind could excuse intervention.

Even before the doctrine was carried to its ultimate unreality in the Charter of the OAS, however, some of the Latin American states were beginning to have doubts as to either its effectiveness or its desirability. In 1945, the Foreign Minister of Uruguay circulated a note, which has since come to be known as the Larreta Doctrine: ". . . the principles of non-intervention [do] not protect unlimitedly the notorious and repeated violation by any republic of elementary rights of man." [5] Only four other Latin American states agreed with Larreta's premature declaration, but, two years later, in the Rio Treaty, collective intervention by the OAS in both the internal and external affairs of member states was clearly foreshadowed (and has since taken place on various occasions). Despite the fact that the Doctrine was already proving unworkable, however, Article 15 of the Charter of the OAS set it forth in its most extreme form: "No State *or group of States* has the right to intervene, directly or indirectly, for any reason whatever, in the internal or external affairs of any other State. The foregoing principle prohibits not only armed force but also *any other form of interference* or attempted threat *against the personality of the State* or against its *political, economic and cultural elements."* (Italics mine.)

The signing of the Charter in 1948 marked the high-water point of the doctrine of nonintervention. Since that time, and, especially since the United States has once again felt its hemispheric paramountcy threatened (see Chapter 5), nonintervention, which never, in any case, even in its mildest form, had any validity beyond the willingness of the United States to abide by it, and, in its more extreme forms, never had any validity at all, has in reality become nonexistent as a rule of Inter-American public international law. Nevertheless, Latin American statesmen still deal, verbally, in the shibboleths of the 1930's, so that "nonintervention" as a propaganda device is still a force to be dealt with. It is obvious, and needs no further elaboration, that states interfere with each other in a thousand ways every day, and that a paramount such as the United States will affect other states no matter what it does, or does not do. It has become clearly established that the OAS may intervene in the external

[5] As quoted in C. Neale Ronning, *Law and Politics in Inter-American Diplomacy* (New York, 1963), p. 68.

affairs of its member states, as foreshadowed in Article 19 of the OAS Charter: "Measures adopted for the maintenance of peace and security in accordance with existing treaties do not constitute a violation of the principles set forth in Articles 15 and 17." As a result of the Dominican crisis of 1965 the OAS has, for the first time, decided to intervene openly in the *internal* affairs of a member state, by sending a Commission charged with the establishment of a new government, and providing that Commission with military force. It has become equally clear that, if the United States cannot count upon the OAS for those interventions within the hemisphere which it feels are necessary to safeguard its security, it will not hesitate to act unilaterally, as it did in 1961 (Bay of Pigs) and 1965 (Dominican Republic). Thus self-defense, consent on the part of the intervened state, and collective security can all be, and have been, used as excuses for intervention, and will probably continue to be in the future.

In addition, even those Latin American states formally most attached to the doctrine of nonintervention, especially those with Democratic Leftist governments, themselves advocate a policy of encouraging democratic governments in other Latin American states, which cannot be considered anything other than intervention, as clearly foreshadowed by Larreta in 1945. A wave of political arrests in the Dominican Republic led to a Venezuelan demand in February, 1960, for OAS intervention. Caleo Dávila, Honduran delegate to the Council of the OAS, on this occasion declared: "We must take a forward step here. We should not use the principle of nonintervention to close the door." The Inter-American Peace Committee, in June of 1960, condemned these violations of human rights, but did so because the violations "aggravated tensions" in the Caribbean. When the Dominican Republic was condemned at the Sixth Meeting of Consultation of Foreign Ministers in August of the same year, and sanctions applied, the formal reason was the attempt on the life of Venezuelan President Rómulo Betancourt. Attempts to sanction intervention on behalf of democracy and human rights have continued, however, and these initiatives from Latin America, coupled with the chilling winds of Cold War reality from the north, have, between them, rendered the doctrine of nonintervention meaningless and void.

The antecedents of the doctrine of nonintervention developed as a result of the tentative plans of the Holy Alliance to help Spain regain her lost colonies (see Chapter 3). As the nineteenth century wore on, however, and as fears of direct reconquest faded, this danger was replaced by recurrent European interventions to secure payment on defaulted debt, or redress for damage to aliens and/or their property. As a result, a unique Inter-American public international law developed concerning public debt, and the protection of aliens and their property. This sub-category of the general nonintervention doctrine has actually had a longer and more successful life than the doctrine itself, due, no doubt, to the fact that its goals are more modest and attainable.

European international law concerning the protection of aliens was codified in the eighteenth century. The Swiss jurist Emmerich Vattel, in

Le Droit des Gens (1758), expressed the dictum that an injury to the citizen of a state is an injury to the state itself, thereby giving the theoretical legal basis to a whole series of European interventions in Africa, the Middle East, Asia, and Latin America in the succeeding century and a half. The Latin American experience with interventions undertaken under cover of this dictum, finally led, in 1902 (on the occasion of the joint British-Italian-German blockade of Venezuela), to the issuance of a circular note by the Argentine Foreign Minister, Luis Drago. This note, which has since become known as the Drago Doctrine, stated that: ". . . the public debt of an American State cannot occasion armed intervention . . . by a European power." Besides being a statement of what Drago hoped would become part of American international law, the note was an obvious appeal to the new hemispheric paramount to protect its Latin American clients from recurrent European intervention. The new paramount responded to the appeal, both formally and informally. Informally, the Venezuelan blockade was, in fact, the last armed European intervention in Latin America until the 1960's. Formally, at the Hague Peace Conference of 1907 (the first international conference to have any Latin American representation), the United States sponsored, and the Conference adopted, the so-called Porter Convention. The Porter Convention embodied as much of the Drago Doctrine as the European powers which dominated the Conference would swallow, providing that default on public debt could not occasion armed intervention, unless the defaulting state either refused to arbitrate the dispute or refused to accept the judgment of an arbitral tribunal. Because of the assertion of U.S. paramountcy, however, the provisos were inoperative in fact, and no armed intervention, or even threat of armed intervention, from Europe occurred during the wholesale Latin American defaults of the 1930's. Drago may be accused of opening Pandora's box, however, since many of the U.S. interventions in the first three decades of the twentieth century were undertaken under the guise of preventing European intervention.

Drago's doctrine dealt only with public debt, but the Latin American states had been equally plagued, during the nineteenth century, with interventions undertaken to obtain redress for injury to aliens and their property. In response, the Argentine jurist Carlos Calvo, in his monumental work *Le Droit International Théorique et Pratique* (five editions between 1868 and 1896), stated the following "rule" of international law:

> According to strict international law, the recovery of debts and the pursuit of private claims does not justify *de plano* the armed intervention of governments, and, since European states invariably follow this rule in their reciprocal relations, there is no reason why they should not also impose it upon themselves in their relations with the nations of the new world.[6]

[6] 1896 edition, vol. I, pp. 350–351.

This rule was, of course, not a rule at all; at least, not a rule of European international law, and the reason why the European states did not use armed intervention among themselves to obtain redress for injury to their nationals is because the rule of injury to a citizen being injury to the state was *their* rule—meant to be applied to others.[7] Nevertheless, Calvo's dictum, known as the Calvo Doctrine, was immediately taken up by the Latin American states, and has been supported by them ever since. With reference to Europe, of course, the Calvo Doctrine has been quite successful, for the same reason the Drago Doctrine has been—the European states have been prevented from forcibly intervening by the new hemispheric paramount. The United States itself, of course, intervened extensively until the 1930's. During that decade, two test cases, the Bolivian and Mexican expropriations of American oil companies, marked the turning point in armed intervention to protect the property of citizens. Despite clamorous domestic agitation for intervention, the United States Government confined itself to diplomatic protest. Since that time, although interventions have occurred on grounds of national security, none has occurred on grounds of protecting U.S. citizens, or corporations or their property, the United States having apparently adopted the general nineteenth-century British approach, that people travel and investors invest largely at their own risk.

The Latin American countries have made various efforts to legislate the Calvo Doctrine into effect, through treaties, constitutions, and domestic legal codes. All these efforts have failed, however. Only treaties among the Latin American states themselves have incorporated the doctrine,[8] and national constitutions and laws cannot amend international law. One device of considerable effectiveness has been hit upon, however—the so-called Calvo Clause. This is a clause inserted in a government contract with a foreign individual or company, in which the foreign contractor promises, in case of dispute over the contract, not to apply for redress to his own government. Although almost universally discounted by international jurists, the Calvo Clause is, in reality, fairly effective. The argument against the clause is that a citizen cannot limit his own state. The argument for it is that a citizen can limit his own action in bringing an issue to his state, and, if he does so through having signed a contract including the Calvo Clause, he is guilty of breach of contract, if he then requests diplomatic intervention. The latter is the position now generally followed in international claims cases, following the precedent set in the North American Dredging Co. case (1926).

The possible and actual use of recognition or nonrecognition of governments, as a means of intervention, has given rise to contradictory

[7] It may also be argued that such incidents were less likely to occur in Europe, or that redress in the local courts in case of such injury was more likely to be expeditious and thorough. Such argument is questionable, however, when applied to the then-new states of Eastern Europe.

[8] Article VII of the Pact of Bogotá is a statement of the Calvo Doctrine, but the Pact is a purely American instrument, and has been ratified only by Latin American states.

Latin American doctrines, due to the conflicting interests of Latin American governments in attempting to protect themselves from violent domestic overthrow, and, at the same time, trying to prevent the paramount from using its power of recognition as a threat. There are two basic approaches that can be taken to the problem of recognition: that of recognizing any government that is in effective control, and willing and able to fulfill its international obligations, and that of recognizing only those governments that fulfill some concept of legitimacy held by the recognizing government. The United States, itself the product of revolution, held to the concept of automatic recognition throughout the nineteenth century and until the administration of Woodrow Wilson. Wilson applied a rather vague test of constitutionality to governments before he would recognize them. This policy was quashed in the 1920's, and returned in the 1930's in the form of the Stimson Doctrine. It was held to, during the war years, and was applied to the Nazi-oriented governments of Villarroel in Bolivia (1943) and Farrell in Argentina (1944). Some test of legitimacy (a fluctuating one depending on the administration in office in Washington) continued through the administration of President Kennedy, but the Johnson Administration returned to automatic recognition except in the case of a Communist or pro-Communist government.

At first, domestic concerns won out over international doctrine in Latin America on the issue of recognition, and, in 1907, the Foreign Minister of Ecuador circularized the governments of the hemisphere, suggesting that no governments coming to power by violence be recognized by the other states of the hemisphere. This Tobar Doctrine was applied in the Central American treaties of 1907 and 1923, which provided for nonrecognition of *coup* governments. The Irigoyen Government in Argentina (1916–20) applied the doctrine, and, since World War II, most democratic leftist regimes in Latin America have refused, at least for a time, to recognize governments coming to power through the overthrow of constitutional authorities.

It is significant that it was one of the most stable of the Latin American states, Mexico, that first stated the opposite thesis, through a note circularized in 1930 by its Foreign Minister. The Estrada Doctrine declares that the recognition of a new government should be automatic, and that not even a declaration of recognition is necessary (Mexico was Wilson's favorite nonrecognition target). There is, thus, no consensus in Latin America as to the relative weight to be accorded to domestic *vs.* international factors involved in the question of the recognition of governments. Even individual states are inconsistent in their attitude, as witness Mexico's continued recognition of the Spanish Republican Government, nonexistent for almost three decades.

The inconsistencies, as well as the consistencies, of Inter-American public international law as it deals with the questions of nonintervention, protection of alien persons and property, and recognition of governments, are due to the fact that these "rules" are really intended to be applied only to the paramount, or secondarily, on occasion, by a weaker Latin American state against a stronger. The Latin American states violate all these "rules" constantly in their relations with each other, and are generally indifferent as to their application outside the Western Hemisphere.

B / REGIONAL ORDERING

For obvious reasons, those rules of Inter-American public international law meant to regulate intra-Latin American concerns have been generally more successfully applied than those meant to "regulate" the paramount. Among these, the most important are the practice of diplomatic asylum and the applicability of unratified treaties.

The granting of diplomatic asylum to political refugees has long been a common practice in Spain, and, due in part to this heritage, the states of Latin America have recognized and supported the right of asylum ever since they gained their independence. Their history, full of revolution and chaos, has strengthened, rather than weakened, their support of the practice. There have been countless occasions where the granting of asylum to political enemies was not only tolerated, but often encouraged by the men of the government in power, since in the next week, month, or year they might be the ones seeking a place of refuge.

There have been many attempts made by the Latin American countries to regularize and give official sanction to the practice of diplomatic asylum. The first protocol on the subject was signed in Lima in 1865, and other declarations and agreements were signed in 1889, 1907, and 1911. Since 1928, three formal treaties have been signed at Inter-American conferences regulating and formalizing diplomatic asylum. The first was the Convention on Asylum signed at the 1928 Havana Conference. This Convention bans asylum for ordinary criminals, and political asylum is limited in various ways. For political asylum to be granted, the case must be urgent; the territorial government must be informed of the asylum; the refugee must be sent out of the country if the government requests; the refugee shall not be landed in the territory of his own state; care must be taken to see that the refugee does not conspire against his government; and finally, the legation or embassy must pay all expenses. By 1964, this convention had been ratified by fifteen of the twenty Latin American states. A second Convention, signed in Montevideo in 1933, made the following changes in the Havana Convention: the state offering asylum has the right to decide whether the case is political or criminal; the granting of asylum is not subject to reciprocity; and the asylum conventions may be denounced on a year's notice, although they remain in effect among the other parties. This convention had also been ratified by fifteen states as of 1964. In 1954, in Caracas, a new Convention codifying the previous two was signed and has been ratified by nine states.[9]

The United States does not officially recognize the practice of diplomatic asylum, but, in fact, practices it whenever it finds it in its national interest to do so, as with the asylum granted in 1945 to the Bulgarian peasant leader Dimitroff in the American Legation in Sofia, and to Cardinal Mindszenty in the American Legation in Budapest in 1956. The same can be said of most of the European states. Officially, they do not recognize asylum, but, in practice, they grant it when they find it in their interest, as during the Spanish Civil War and World War II. The United States signed the Havana Treaty but did not ratify it, and did not sign either the Montevideo or the Caracas treaties.

The most interesting recent case involving diplomatic asylum, which clearly demonstrates the existence of a special American international law, was that of Víctor Raúl Haya de la Torre, contested by Peru and Colombia between 1948 and 1954. On January 3, 1949, Haya de la Torre, leader of the then-outlawed A.P.R.A. party in Peru, was granted asylum in the Colombian Embassy. Peru refused to grant him safe conduct out of the country and, instead, demanded his delivery to the authorities. After several notes were exchanged, the two states agreed, on August 31, 1949, to take the case to the International Court of Justice.[10] In defending its grant of asylum, Colombia claimed that it was clearly its prerogative to determine whether Haya was, or was not, a political refugee, and cited the 1928 and 1933 conventions to this effect. The court ruled, however, that the Havana Convention did not grant the right of unilateral qualification of the crime, and, although the Montevideo Convention did, Peru had not ratified the Convention and, therefore, its provisions were not binding on Peru (on this issue, see below). On the second point, it was decided that since Peru had not asked for the departure of Haya, it did not have to grant him safe conduct.

The Peruvian Government submitted a further brief claiming that Haya was a common criminal and, therefore, not entitled to asylum, and that the case could no longer be considered one of urgency under the Havana Convention. The court decided that Haya was indeed a political refugee, but, by a vote of ten to six, it ruled that since the government of Col. Odría had been securely in power for two years, Peru was right in claiming that the case was no longer urgent. These decisions were handed down on November 20, 1950.

In order to clarify these ambiguous rulings, in December, 1950, Peru and Colombia submitted further briefs. This time, the single issue was whether or not, under the previous decisions of the court, Colombia should surrender Haya to Peru. After studying the provisions of the

---

[9] For the texts of the asylum conventions, see de Vries, *op. cit.*, pp. 269-277.
[10] On the Peruvian-Colombian cases, consult Manley O. Hudson, "The Thirtieth Year of the World Court," *American Journal of International Law,* Jan., 1952, and "International Court of Justice: Colombian-Peruvian Asylum Case," *International Organization,* Feb., May, Aug., 1951.

Havana convention, the court decided that, since the asylum was in violation of Article II, Part 2 of the Convention (the urgency clause), the asylum should cease, but that, since the Convention did not stipulate how asylums should be terminated, Colombia was not bound to surrender the refugee. These completely unhelpful decisions were subsequently ignored by Colombia and Peru, which continued to negotiate bilaterally. Haya was finally given safe conduct by the Peruvian Government, in May of 1954, in a purely political decision, and the right of asylum was upheld.

The right of diplomatic asylum has a definite place in Latin American practice and in American international law. Asylum can be justified on purely humanitarian grounds, at least in Latin America, and probably elsewhere as well. Asylum is often granted by the legate state with no thought as to the fugitive's political beliefs. Haya de la Torre, a radical political figure, asked for and was given asylum by a country whose conservative government abhorred the principles for which he stood. And yet, this same government fought steadily for five years to establish its right to grant him asylum, and, in the end, achieved its purpose. Diplomatic asylum in Latin America has served that area well in preventing acts of injustice and barbarity on the part of a group of politicians or army officers pursuing their personal vendettas against the "outs." Any successful attempt to terminate the practice could only have the unfortunate effect of further adding to the political instability with which these countries are already too much afflicted.

The contention of the International Court of Justice that the provisions of the Asylum Convention of 1933 were not binding on Peru, because that country had not ratified it, points up another aspect of Inter-American public international law meant to regulate regional affairs—the often-binding effect of unratified treaties. For various reasons, the Latin American countries have a very bad record in the ratification of any but the most important and far-reaching treaties and conventions. As a consequence, the doctrine developed that organizational instruments would be applied, whether ratified or not, and substantive instruments would be considered binding on all, when ratified by a substantial number of Latin American states. Examples of this are the application of the provisions of the 1928 Convention regulating the Inter-American system, despite the lack of sufficient ratifications, application of the provisions of the Charter of the OAS before sufficient ratifications had been received to put it formally into effect, participation of non-ratifying states for years in the organs of the OAS, and the application of treaties such as the Asylum Conventions of 1928 and 1933, ratified by three-fourths of the Latin American states, even to countries which had not formally ratified them. In his dissenting opinion to the decisions of the International Court in the first Colombian-Peruvian case, Judge Philadelpho Azevedo of Brazil stated these principles as follows:

> . . . It will be sufficient to emphasize that treaties often embody principles already established by custom, and thus have a declara-

tory effect with regard to customary rules. This role is greater in a system where the field of written law is progressively extended by the reception of new practices which have manifested themselves in the interval.

It is then very dangerous for a State to proclaim that it is bound only by the treaties which it has signed and ratified. . . .

Thus, in a course at the Academy of International Law, Professor Balladore Pallieri referred to the current observation to the effect that "a large number of Pan American conventions are observed, even by States which did not ratify them, and that they often become common and general law for America." [11]

From the time of the first Inter-American conference in 1890, the idea of the establishment of an Inter-American Court to apply American international law, and, thus, avoid fiascoes such as the Peruvian-Colombian asylum cases has been broached. Between 1907 and 1917, such a court did exist in Central America. More recently, the project has been formulated in such a way that the projected court would not only deal with cases brought by states under public international law, but also with cases brought by individuals alleging violations of human rights. The opposition to the first concept by the United States, which fears that the court will be used as a forum for the airing of client grievances, and by dictatorial Latin American régimes to the second idea have, thus far, been sufficient to ensure their failure.

C / INDIVIDUAL INTEREST

Certain individual Latin American countries have attempted to incorporate into Inter-American public international law certain "rules" that favor their special interests. In this, they are generally, although not particularly enthusiastically, supported by other Latin American countries on grounds of comity. When the individual interests of other Latin American countries conflict, however, such regional comity quickly disappears.

The states that made and enforced European international law generally found it to their interest to proclaim a short limit of territorial waters, usually three miles, to further their own maritime, naval, and commercial freedom. The so-called three-mile limit has, in the twentieth century, been so extensively challenged that no such rule can be said to exist, except as a minimum limit of territorial waters recognized by all states. Various Latin American countries claim jurisdiction over the open sea from six to two hundred miles offshore, for the purpose of controlling fishing and offshore resources. What minimal consensus exists was

[11] As quoted in de Vries, *op. cit.,* pp. 54-55.

expressed in a report of the Inter-American Council of Jurists in 1956. Fifteen Latin American states voted in favor of the report, and five abstained. The report generally declares the caducity of the three-mile limit, and each state was declared free to establish its own territorial waters "within reasonable limits." The report declared that coastal states could establish extensive regulation and control of offshore resources, even outside the limits of territorial waters, so long as navigation is not interfered with. The United States has also declared its control of certain offshore resources, such as oil, and has averred its willingness to consider an extension of the international limit to twelve miles. Nevertheless, it does not recognize the more extreme claims of some Latin American countries such as El Salvador, Ecuador, and Chile. The Latin American countries themselves ignore each other's claims when they find it suitable to do so, and, at one point, Guatemalan Air Force planes bombed and sank Mexican fishing boats operating within the self-proclaimed Guatemalan twelve-mile limit, precipitating an international incident. Mexico recognized only a nine-mile limit.

Chile and Argentina claim large contiguous and overlapping areas of the Antarctic Continent, and, because solidarity costs them nothing in this case, the claims are generally supported by the other Latin American countries. The United States recognizes no claims to Antarctic territory, and the Chilean and Argentine claims are disputed by Great Britain, which has claimed more or less the same territory since 1908.

The international rule of *uti posseditis* has been invoked by Argentina and Guatemala to support their claims to the Falkland Islands and Belice, respectively. The Spanish Crown was undeniably sovereign over both territories at the time of independence, and Argentina and Guatemala claim sovereignty as successor states to Spain. The Guatemalan case is complicated by the fact that northern Belice was administratively part of the Captaincy-General of Yucatán at the time of independence, for which Mexico was the successor-state, and by the existence of a treaty of cession with Great Britain. Guatemala claims unfulfillment of the terms of the treaty by Britain and, thus, the invalidity of the cession.

As we have already noted (Chapter 1), law is the codification, somewhat delayed, of the power structure in a given society. Since 1914, international society has had no power structure that could agree on an extensive body of rules of behavior, and, thus, international law, in the twentieth century, has been largely inoperative. The power structure of the society of Latin American states, has, on the other hand, agreed on a very limited number of rules, such as diplomatic asylum and the applicability of certain unratified instruments. These, coupled with support of some special interest rules proclaimed by individual states, and such limited concessions as they can induce the paramount to make, as in the case of the Calvo Clause, represent the body of what is called Inter-American public international law. On the other hand, their attempt to apply, internationally, the principle that Chief Justice Coke proclaimed to his sovereign, Henry VIII (that the King is subject to the law), has been almost completely unsuccessful as regards the hemisphere paramount, except as a propaganda device for domestic consumption.

Selected Bibliography

There is relatively little material on Inter-American public international law published in English. In contrast, there are literally thousands of treatises in Spanish, Portuguese, and French written by a legion of jurists and international lawyers in Latin America. Unfortunately, much of this material is polemical, and most of it, repetitive and declaratory of "rules" of law that simply do not exist except in the wishes of the writer.

Some notion of the general Latin American concept of the role and function of law can be found in Helen L. Clagett, *The Administration of Justice in Latin America* (New York, 1952) and Phanor J. Eder, *A Comparative Survey of Anglo-American and Latin American Law* (New York, 1950), as well as in Chapter III of the volume by de Vries and Rodríguez-Novás noted below.

The following books can be enthusiastically recommended on the general subject of Inter-American public international law, in English: Henry P. de Vries and José Rodríguez-Novás, *The Law of the Americas* (New York, 1965); C. Neale Ronning, *Law and Politics in Inter-American Diplomacy* (New York, 1963); and H. B. Jacobini, *A Study of the Philosophy of International Law as Seen in Works of Latin American Writers* (The Hague, 1954). Some of the classic Latin American statements of the concept of a unique American international law are found in Alejandro Álvarez, *L'Histoire Diplomatique des Républiques Américaines* (Paris, 1902) and *Le Droit International Américain* (Paris, 1910), and in Jesús-María Yepes (a disciple of Álvarez), *El Panamericanismo y el Derecho Internacional* (Bogotá, 1930) and *La Codificación del Derecho Internacional Americano* (Bogotá, 1927). See also the excellent summary and account in Italian, *Panamericanesimo e Diritto Internazionale* (Milan, 1939) by Carlo Cereti.

From the North American standpoint, the subject of nonintervention has been thoroughly and competently surveyed in Ann van Wynen Thomas and A. J. Thomas, Jr., *Non-Intervention: The Law and Its Import in the Americas* (Dallas, 1956). Among dozens of other books on the subject the Latin American viewpoint can be absorbed from *Intervención* (Mexicc, 1959) by Isidro Fabela.

The general subject of the protection of alien persons and property is surveyed in F. S. Dunn, *The Protection of Nationals* (Baltimore, 1932), and in the excellent study of the Calvo Doctrine and Clause, *The Calvo Clause: A Problem of Inter-American and International Law and Diplomacy* (Minneapolis, 1955), by Donald R. Shea.

The development of the concept of diplomatic asylum as practiced in the Latin American sub-continent is treated in Carlos Urrutia Aparicio, *Diplomatic Asylum in Latin America* (Guatemala, 1960), and in C. Neale Ronning, *The Legal Status of the Institution of Diplomatic Asylum in Latin America as Determined by Treaties and Practice* (Doctoral Dissertation, 1958).

The British-Guatemalan dispute over Belice is competently analyzed in L. M. Bloomfield, *The British Honduras-Guatemala Dispute* (Toronto, 1958). In addition to the works cited in this limited Bibliography, there are many others in Spanish and Portuguese on all the subjects covered in Chapter 6.

7 / STRENGTH THROUGH ASSOCIATION

> *As an American, I am alarmed especially by one thing: the fear that San Francisco may have weakened the continental solidarity strengthened at Chapultepec.*
>
> MIGUEL ÁNGEL CAMPA (1945)
>
> *. . . we are now confronted with a draft resolution asking that Guatemala's complaint should be referred to the very Organization of American States which the State Department is planning to use to settle its accounts with Guatemala.*
>
> SEMYON TSARAPKIN (1954)

We have seen, in Chapter 6, that recourse to "law" by the Latin American states has been fairly effective in regulating their internal affairs and quite unsuccessful in restraining the paramount, or bringing a higher degree of regularity and predictability into the paramount-client relationship. We have seen that this result was inevitable, given the imperatives of a quasi-anarchic society.

The Latin American states have also attempted to use association to gain the same ends. Because of the lack of political international organizations in the nineteenth century, however, the use of law antedated the use of association, and the proliferation of international organizations, in the twentieth century, has proceeded simultaneously with the debilitation of European international law, which accounts for much of the confusion of goals and rules within which these organizations have operated.

The Latin American states have made use of international organizations (the response of association), as they have of international law, to attempt to accomplish two purposes: the restriction and regulation of the paramount, and the furtherance of regional and individual state interests. As a rule, the first goal has been pursued in general political organizations (principally the League of Nations and the United Nations), and the second, in both general organizations, insofar as they are concerned with economic, social, and cultural matters, and in the many functional international organizations.

A / LATIN AMERICA IN THE LEAGUE OF NATIONS AND IN FUNCTIONAL ORGANIZATIONS

As has already been mentioned, no Latin American state participated in an international conference until the Hague Peace Conference of 1907, and then, only the largest Latin American countries were invited, and their participation in the deliberations of the Conference was relatively unimportant, except with reference to the adoption of the Porter Convention. All of the Latin American states, however, were either signatories to the Versailles Treaty, including the Covenant of the League of Nations, or were invited to adhere to the Covenant immediately after. Nevertheless, Latin American participation in the League was sketchy and intermittent, due to various factors, including the failure of the United States to join the League and the costs involved in membership for the smaller states. At the time of the first League Assembly, that organization had fifteen Latin American members, and at its last meeting in 1945, there were ten Latin American members. In between those dates (1920–45), all the Latin American states were, at one time or another, members of the League, but at no one time were they all members simultaneously. Argentina, although remaining a member, ceased participating in League activities in 1920, over the issue of universal membership. Later, Argentina began participating once again, only to repeat its walkout, when its delegate was not elected Assembly President. Brazil withdrew its membership in 1926 (effective 1928), when it was not made a permanent member of the League Council. Costa Rica withdrew at the same time. Mexico did not join until 1931, withdrew in 1933, and then returned. Ecuador did not join until 1934. Paraguay withdrew during the Chaco War over the issue of the selective League arms embargo (see below). Many Latin American states, though remaining League members, did not, in fact, participate in League meetings or organs. This was true of most of the Central American republics. Peru did not participate between 1921 and 1929, and Bolivia also withdrew for a time. The high point of Latin American participation in the League was in 1934, with eighteen Latin American members (all but Brazil and Costa Rica) actively participating, because of League involvement in the Leticia Incident and the Chaco War.

A Latin American bloc formed in the League, principally to present a united front in Assembly and Council elections, and to pressure for the allocation of more Secretariat positions to Latin Americans. In these activities the Latin Americans were quite successful—the President of the Assembly, for example, was often a Latin American. Latin American participation in the nonpermanent seats of the League Council was steadily increased, from one seat in 1920–22 to two seats in 1922–26, and three seats after 1926.

Latin American efforts to use the League of Nations to further their regional and individual economic and social interests were unimportant, both because such activities were secondary to the League and because Latin American participation in these League activities was weak and intermittent. Efforts to use the League as a counterweight to the United States and its Inter-American client system were also generally unsuccessful. To protect its hemispheric interests, the United States had insisted upon inclusion in the League Covenant of reference to the Monroe Doctrine in the famous Article 21: "Nothing in this Covenant shall be deemed to affect the validity of international engagements, such as treaties of arbitration or regional understandings like the Monroe Doctrine, for securing the maintenance of peace." In this way, the *Pax Americana* was officially recognized by the organized international community. Many of the Latin American states were understandably unhappy over this, but various requests by them for interpretation, or repudiation, of Article 21 by the Assembly or Council of the League were uniformly denied. In 1920, Peru and Bolivia requested that the League investigate the validity of the Treaty of Ancón with Chile. The United States asked Brazil to request the League to refuse to consider this petition, and the League complied. In 1921, a boundary conflict between Panama and Costa Rica, which had led to military action, was brought to the attention of the League, but the United States intervened, and, itself, settled the matter by mediation.

The League *did* intervene in two internal Inter-American conflicts, with success in the Leticia Incident between Peru and Colombia (1932–35), and unsuccessfully in the Chaco War between Paraguay and Bolivia (1928–38). Colombia and Peru signed a treaty, in 1922, fixing the boundary between them. This treaty assigned the Amazon River port of Leticia to Colombia. Ratification procedures were completed in 1928, and, in 1930, Colombia occupied Leticia. In September, 1932, Peruvian irregulars seized the town. The Peruvian Government, at first, disavowed the act, but, after the Peruvian army commander in the region declared his support of the movement and ordered regular troops into Leticia, the government at Lima reversed its position, and declared the boundary treaty invalid. Peru suggested submitting the dispute to conciliation under the terms of the Gondra Treaty (see Chapter 4), but Colombia refused. In January, 1933, Brazil offered mediation but the offer was refused. In February, the two countries severed diplomatic relations and Colombia sent a military expedition up the Amazon to Leticia, but failed to retake the town.

On February 17, Colombia appealed to the League Council. The Council asked the Chaco Commission (see below), to proceed to Leticia to see if it could settle that dispute. The Commission went to the disputed area, and, on February 25, recommended that the League itself administer the area until a direct settlement could be reached. United States' permission was asked for and granted, and a Special Commission for Leticia was established, consisting of a Spaniard, a Brazilian, and an American, to administer Leticia (note that neither Brazil nor the United States was a member of the League, and, since Brazil at the time was acting as United States sub-paramount in Latin America, the United States actually controlled the League Commission). On June 23, the Commission took over the area and administered it for slightly less than one year, at which time it was returned to Colombia, according to a Peruvian-Colombian agreement reached as a result of Brazilian mediation.

The boundary between Paraguay and Bolivia had been in dispute throughout the entire nineteenth century and the first quarter of the twentieth century. Various attempts to settle the dispute failed, as one side or the other refused to ratify negotiated boundary settlements. Finally, the controversy became serious, due to the discovery of oil in the Chaco, and the desire of the German military mission in Bolivia to test Panzer tactics (the Chief of the Bolivian General Staff at the beginning of the Chaco War was General Hans Kundt. He discovered that Panzer tactics do *not* work in a swamp.) The first serious armed incident between forces of the two countries occurred in February, 1927. Argentine good offices failed to settle the matter, and, in December, 1928, another incident occurred. Paraguay invoked the Gondra Treaty, but Bolivia refused conciliation, and diplomatic relations were broken. The International Conference of American States on Conciliation and Arbitration was meeting in Washington at the time, and formed a Chaco Committee which offered good offices. Paraguay and Bolivia accepted, and, in September, 1929, agreed to return to the *status quo ante*. In 1930, fresh hostilities broke out, but were stopped, and, in May, diplomatic relations were resumed. In June of 1931, border clashes began again and Ambassadors were withdrawn. In July, 1932, Bolivia attacked in earnest, and Paraguay replied. Both the League of Nations and the Inter-American Chaco Committee urged arbitration. Paraguay accepted, but Bolivia refused. In September, 1932, the League Council established a Commission to deal with the Chaco War (comprised of delegates from Ireland, Spain, and Guatemala). In December, 1932, the Inter-American Committee presented a plan of settlement, accepted by Bolivia, but rejected by Paraguay (which was momentarily doing well in the war). In February, 1933, Argentina, Brazil, Chile, and Peru offered another settlement, this time rejected by Bolivia, which had taken the offensive. At this point, the Inter-American Committee retired from the scene and deferred to the League Commission. Bolivia and Paraguay, however, requested that the neighboring countries again try to settle the dispute, but, by October, 1933, it was obvious they could not do so, and, in November, the League Commission left for the scene of hostilities. Great Paraguayan victories were registered during December, 1933, and on the promptings of the Seventh Inter-American Conference meeting in Montevideo, Paraguay offered peace, leading to an armistice during December, 1933, and January, 1934. During this time, the League Commission suggested terms of settlement. The terms were rejected and the war resumed. In May, 1934, the United States embargoed arms exports to the belligerents. In November, the League Council ordered an arms embargo and suggested a settlement, which Paraguay rejected. By December, Paraguay was clearly winning the war and the League Council lifted the embargo as to Bolivia, precipitating

Paraguayan withdrawal from the League. At the same time, the League Assembly suggested terms of settlement rejected by Paraguay. This was the last important League action in the Chaco War. By 1936, both belligerents were exhausted, with Paraguay holding most of the disputed area. In May, a Mediatory American Commission was established which produced an acceptable armistice plan in June. A Peace Conference met in Buenos Aires, in October, but the belligerents could not agree on a settlement. A prisoner exchange was arranged, however, and the armistice continued. In May of 1938, new proposals were accepted by Bolivia, but rejected by Paraguay. In July, the United States finally intervened directly, and, in the same month, the belligerents signed a treaty of peace according to the so-called Roosevelt Formula, which provided for arbitration of the boundary dispute *ex aequo et bono*. In October of 1938, the arbitral award was made, awarding most of the Chaco to Paraguay.[1]

Throughout the record of Latin American participation in the League of Nations, the single most obvious thread is extreme League deference to the United States with reference to all Inter-American questions. Even in the two matters where the League was most heavily involved, the "League" Commission, which administered the settlement in the Leticia dispute was dominated by the United States, and, in the Chaco War, a settlement was finally reached by U.S. mediation, following complete League failure. Thus the Latin American states failed in their efforts to use the League as a counterweight to the hemispheric paramount. "The ambiguous situation of the Latin American states in the League of Nations is due, in great part, to the absence of the United States." [2]

Since the nineteenth century, the Latin American states have participated actively and constructively in the work of various functional international organizations, such as the Universal Postal Union, the International Labour Organization, the World Health Organization, the United Nations Educational, Scientific, and Cultural Organization, the Food and Agriculture Organization, and others. All of these agencies assist the Latin American states in solving their regional and individual economic, social, and cultural problems, and they do not interfere in the structure of the international hierarchy, or in the governing element of international politics, interstate conflict. As such, they are the most successful form of international organization (see Chapter 1). The problem of overlapping and duplication between international and Inter-American functional agencies has been quite satisfactorily solved, with the possible exception of duplication of effort and conflict between the Economic Commission for Latin America of the United Nations and the Inter-American Economic and Social Council (see below).

[1] Subsequently, however, the only substantial quantities of oil were found in the region retained by Bolivia. By the time of the settlement, Bolivia had expropriated American oil companies, and there had been several *coups* in both Paraguay and Bolivia.
[2] Manuel Pérez-Guerrero, *Les Relations des États de L'Amérique Latine avec la Société des Nations* (Paris, 1936), p. 208.

B / LATIN AMERICA AND THE UNITED NATIONS

Initial Latin American reaction to the United Nations was quite cautious and negative, due to the failure of the League of Nations as an instrument for furthering their foreign policy interests, coupled with the aftereffects of the Good Neighbor Policy, the seeming omnipotence of the United States, and the potential threat of the Soviet Union. Chances of using the incipient organization as a counterweight to the United States were considered minimal, and cooperation with the paramount in the hope of increasing the flow of assistance was thought to be the only possible choice. As time went on, the relative permanence and stability of the U.N. and its much greater universality (compared with the League), caused this feeling to be substantially altered, and, by the 1950's, the U.N. was being used by the Latin American states for the same purposes and with the same pattern of success and failure as the League was earlier.

As early as 1942, the Juridical Committee of the Pan American Union issued recommendations concerning the establishment of a universal organization to replace the League. Among the recommendations was one that any projected organization must be reconciled with the reality of local regional groupings. The attitude of the United States toward this point of view, under the influence of the universalists among President Roosevelt's advisors, was essentially negative, and the Pan American Union was not kept informed of developments. From the beginning, Secretary of State Cordell Hull had led this tendency, being tenaciously opposed, at first by Under-Secretary of State Sumner Welles, and later, by Assistant Secretary of State Nelson Rockefeller and Senator Arthur Vandenberg. President Roosevelt generally supported the universalist position, on the assumption that cooperation with the Soviet Union would continue into the post-war period. At the Dumbarton Oaks Conference in 1944, the universalist tendency clearly won the day over the opposition of British Prime Minister Winston Churchill, who, with his customary realism, argued for strong regional groupings. According to the conclusions of the Conference, the Security Council of the projected organization was to encourage settlement of local disputes through regional agencies and use them where appropriate for enforcement action. However, such regional agencies were not to take any enforcement action without Council authorization, and were to keep the Council fully informed of their activities.

Upon the conclusion of the Conference, Secretary Hull met with Latin American Ambassadors in Washington to inform them of the results of the Conference. It was quickly clear that the Latin American states were dissatisfied with the veto power of the paramounts in the Security Council, and with what they saw as a threat to the Inter-American system. They placed great emphasis on the need for prior recourse to Inter-American procedures before going to the Security Council. The Juridical Committee of the Pan American Union published a formal report on

Dumbarton Oaks late in 1944. Realistically, it supported the concept of the veto, but demanded recognition of Pan-Americanism, and attacked the Security Council's monopoly over enforcement measures.

The Chapultepec Conference, in 1945, was held partially as a result of Latin American dissatisfaction with the results of Dumbarton Oaks. The Latin American states were determined to strengthen the Inter-American system before the United Nations was inaugurated. Aside from those measures (see Chapter 4) foreshadowing the passage of a collective security treaty and a charter for the Inter-American system, the Chapultepec Conference passed, over the opposition of the United States, Resolution XXX concerning the United Nations, which recommended, among other things, that the role of the General Assembly be amplified, and that intra-regional disputes be settled ". . . preferably in accordance with inter-American methods and procedures. . . ." The resolution also demanded "adequate" Latin American representation on the Security Council.

At the San Francisco Conference, the Latin American states were united in opposition to the veto, an issue on which they and the other small states lost. They also threatened to walk out of the Conference if Argentina were not admitted as a founding member of the United Nations (Argentina had declared war on the Axis at the last minute), and, on this issue, they eventually won, over the strong opposition of the Soviet Union. They concentrated their attention, however, on amending the Dumbarton Oaks proposals on regional agencies. The first concern was to achieve as broad a definition of regionalism as possible. Secondly, they attempted to limit the competence of the Security Council, so that it could act only if a regional organization failed to settle an intra-regional dispute successfully, or if action were requested by the regional agency involved. Finally, an attempt was made to see that the regional agencies were not limited in their use of coercive measures. Chile, Colombia, Costa Rica, Ecuador, Peru, Brazil, Cuba, Guatemala, Mexico, Paraguay, and Venezuela all introduced individual or joint amendments to the Dumbarton Oaks draft to incorporate these ideas. Only Bolivia broke the united Latin American bloc, by suggesting that regional organizations be limited even more than envisioned at Dumbarton Oaks. The Soviet Union was bitterly opposed to these suggestions, as were several other delegations, who feared that the new world agency would be crippled, from the start, by regionalism. A real impasse developed, which threatened the success of the entire Conference. The United States delegation was divided once again. Finally, the case was taken to President Truman. The proponents of a strong regional organization argued that, under the existing draft, the Security Council's interests would be safeguarded through the provision for reporting of regional action. Opponents pointed out that any exemption for regional organizations would weaken the entire structure of the fledgling international agency, and that the Monroe Doctrine was sufficiently safeguarded by the provisions on self-defense. A compromise was proposed by President Truman, and accepted, finally, by all parties, resulting in the wording of Chapter VII of the U.N. Charter.[3]

The states of Latin America, thus, did the United States an inestimable service at San Francisco, not only by making possible hemispheric enforcement action, with a minimum of interference by the United Nations, but also providing a legal cover in Article 51 for the later formation of NATO, SEATO, CENTO, and the Anzus Pact.

The pattern of Latin American participation in the United Nations has been quite different from that in the League. All the Latin American states have been members of the U.N. from the beginning, and have actively participated in U.N. meetings and organs. Latin America has been allocated two seats in the Security Council from the beginning, the General Assembly often has a Latin American President, and always a Latin American Vice-President, and the proportion of Latin Americans in the U.N. Secretariat is higher than it was in the League Secretariat. There has been a Latin American bloc in the U.N. since its inception, and, since the ninth Session of the General Assembly, the Latin American states have had a formal caucusing group, with meetings every other week during the sessions of the General Assembly, and chaired by the Latin American Vice-President of the Assembly. These meetings are formalized in procedure, and serve to form a large measure of agreement upon goals, strategies, and tactics, although decisions are not binding upon members. The Latin American bloc has been powerful in the U.N., not only because of the number of votes involved, but also because the Latin American delegates to the U.N. are often given very broad instructions by their Foreign Offices, granting them unusual flexibility in making individual decisions on issues before the Assembly.[4] The Latin American bloc votes unanimously on about half the issues before the Assembly, with the highest degree of unanimity on economic and social matters, and the least on matters of international law and the financing of the organization.[5] Within the bloc, ephemeral groupings form and dissolve, largely with reference to the type of government in power in the various countries at any given time. There is no significant pattern in these shifts, however. So far, the Latin American states seem to have avoided, much more than the new countries of Africa and Asia, the illusion that their voting strength in the General Assembly of the United Nations reflects international reality.

On security matters involving the Cold War, solidarity of the Latin American bloc with the United States has been quite strong, as one would expect from a client system:

> On matters that involved "security" considerations in the cold war, nearly all, if not all, of the Latin-American Members voted together and with the United States. This cohesion was tightest when

[3] For excerpts from the Charter of the United Nations, see Appendix H.
[4] This is a reflection of the relative independence enjoyed by the generally apolitical Latin American Foreign Services.
[5] Thomas Hovet, Jr., *Bloc Politics in the United Nations* (Cambridge, Mass., 1960), p. 67.

the issue between the United States and the Soviet Union was sharpest and clearest; it was looser when such an issue was less clearly defined; and it became increasingly unsure as the apparent or alleged danger to the national security of the Latin American states became more remote. . . .

The first [hypothesis] was that security considerations moved the Latin-American Members to stick closely to the United States on "political" questions, especially on those issues that produced sharp conflict between the two poles of power, the United States and the Soviet Union. This hypothesis, based upon the nature of power politics in the world, was overwhelmingly substantiated by the record of voting.[6]

On security votes, Brazil has generally supported the United States very closely, in accordance with its pursuit of sub-paramountcy. Following a period of intransigence, lasting until about 1954, Argentina, due to its economic and political weakness, has, since that time, also followed the United States lead closely. Mexico, on the other hand, has shown considerable independence, as did Guatemala before 1954. Cuba, of course, since 1960, has been a member of the Soviet, rather than the Latin American, bloc in the United Nations.

On matters of regional concern, Latin American solidarity has been most marked with reference to elections to U.N. organs and conferences, on the issue of dependent peoples (with the notable exception of general Brazilian support for the Portuguese position, with reference to Portuguese Africa and Asia), theoretical discussions and resolutions concerning discrimination and human rights, and matters concerning economic development and international trade. With reference to the latter, Latin America, and the underdeveloped regions in general, have been much more successful in using the United Nations for their own purposes than they were in the League. Impelled by ECLA (see below), the Latin Americans have taken the lead in this effort. From their own standpoint, the U.N. is principally useful in extracting a yet higher level of paramount benevolence, and in getting a share of the economic assistance supplied by other industrialized countries.

Efforts by the Latin American states to use the United Nations as a counterweight to the hemispheric paramount have naturally centered around Inter-American issues involving the Cold War—in other words, issues in which unilateral paramount action is most likely to occur, and where OAS action is least likely to be successful. As a result, three principal efforts have been made, in the Guatemalan crisis of 1954, the Cuban crises of 1961 and 1962, and the Dominican crisis of 1965.

The Guatemalan crisis set the pattern for the others, and, for the first time, the implications of the efforts of the Latin American countries at San Francisco became clear, both to their perpetrators and to their beneficiary, the United States. "A profound irony lay in the fact that

[6] William G. Cornelius, "The 'Latin-American Bloc' in the United Nations," *Journal of Inter-American Studies,* vol. III, no. 3, July, 1961, pp. 421 and 433.

whereas at San Francisco, the great Latin American concern had been that an appeal to the regional enforcement machinery might be paralyzed by a Security Council veto, in the Guatemalan case the plaintiff sought most urgently to avert any regional action whatsoever and to restrict consideration of the case to the United Nations." [7] Following the invasion of June 17-18, 1954 (see Chapter 5), the Guatemalan Government cabled the President of the Security Council (Henry Cabot Lodge of the United States), and asked him to convene a meeting of the Council, alleging aggression on the part of Honduras and Nicaragua, and asking the Council to send an investigating commission. Lodge attempted to postpone the meeting until June 21, but finally gave in to the insistence of the Guatemalan delegate to the U.N., and convened the Council on June 20. At the June 20 meeting, the cable and accusations of Guatemala, as well as the denial of Honduras, were noted and the agenda was adopted. After statement of the Guatemalan case, the Honduran delegate said: "Too many years have passed for us to doubt the great benefits which mankind can derive from the proper functioning of the United Nations. I therefore believe that the most suitable action in the present case will be to refer the matter completely to the appropriate jurisdiction, that is, the Organization of American States." [8] Aside from the non sequitur inherent in this statement, it was the first inkling of the line that was eventually to be followed in the Guatemalan case, and in similar cases in the future. Colombia and Brazil, the two Latin American members of the Security Council at the time, submitted a joint draft resolution providing for the referral of the whole matter to the OAS. Those delegations supporting referral based their support principally on Articles 33, 52, and 53 of the U.N. Charter. The Guatemalan delegate, in speaking against the draft resolution, claimed that Articles 33, 52, and 53 were inoperative because the case was not one of a dispute, but of aggression. He appealed instead to Articles 34, 35, 39, which provide that the Council may investigate any dispute, that any member of the U.N. may bring any dispute to the attention of the Council, and that the Security Council will determine the existence of any breach of the peace. He finished by citing Article 103, which states that obligations under the U.N. Charter prevail over all others. Although the vote was ten to one in favor of the Brazil-Colombia resolution, the Soviet Union's negative vote constituted a veto. A French resolution calling for a cease-fire was then passed unanimously.

On June 23, Guatemala requested another Council meeting, stating that the June 20 cease-fire resolution had not been honored. The Council met on June 25, but the substantive issue was never discussed, since the Council ended by refusing to place the question on its agenda. In the course of debate, Soviet delegate Tsarapkin stated: "Either we have a Charter which is binding on all Members of the United Nations, or in actual fact

---

[7] John A. Houston, *Latin America in the United Nations* (New York, 1956), p. 105.
[8] United Nations, Security Council, *Official Records,* 675th Meeting, June 20, 1954, p. 14.

. . . the United Nations will survive as a mockery." [9] The final vote on adoption of the agenda was four in favor, five opposed, and two abstentions (Brazil, Colombia, Turkey, China, and the United States voted against adoption).

The Guatemalan precedent was followed in 1961, when Cuba appealed to the Security Council for action against "aggression" by the United States and other states, in connection with the Bay of Pigs Invasion (see Chapter 5). The Security Council was unwilling to act before, or during, the invasion, and finished by taking no action. In the missile crisis of 1962, the United States took the initiative in calling a meeting of the Security Council, since, this time, *it* was alleging aggression. U.N. Secretary-General U Thant flew to Havana, but the Cuban Government rejected international inspection of the removal of Soviet missiles from Cuba (thereby incidentally releasing the United States from its promise not to attempt the overthrow of the Castro Government in return for removal). Thus, U.N. intervention was minimal and ineffective, although for the first time the Secretary-General personally intervened in Latin America, a precedent to be followed in 1965.

Until the Dominican crisis of April, 1965, support for the United States on security matters by the Latin American members of the Security Council was unfaltering. In the Dominican crisis, however, Uruguay supported the concept of U.N. intervention, thereby seriously weakening the perennial U.S. case that hemispheric matters should be left to the OAS. As a result, Secretary-General Thant was able to send personal civilian and military representatives to the Dominican Republic. In fact, however, they were unable to accomplish anything at all, and the matter was handled by the United States through the instrumentality of the OAS.

By these cases, and by other cases handled by the OAS (see Chapter 4), the precedent has been well established that the United Nations will not interfere in any effective fashion in hemispheric disputes and crises. Although the proposition that the U.N. cannot act if the OAS is already acting in a dispute is a highly questionable one, it has been followed consistently. The case for this interpretation rests largely upon Article 33 of the Charter, which states that the parties to a dispute shall seek a solution by negotiation, inquiry, mediation, conciliation, arbitration, judicial settlement, or "resort to regional agencies or arrangements," before taking the matter to the United Nations, as well as to the "collective self-defense" provisions of Article 51. It is also claimed that Article 2 of the Rio Treaty, and Article 20 of the OAS Charter, oblige members of the OAS to settle their disputes within the regional organization. It is admitted that Articles 52–54 are subject to the powers of the Security Council, in Articles 34 and 35, and that forceful measures can be used by the OAS only with U.N. authorization, except for collective self-defense. The legal division of the Pan American Union, however, has defined collective

---

[9] United Nations, Security Council, *Official Records,* 676th Meeting, June 25, 1954, p. 32.

self-defense as practically synonymous with collective security as provided for in the Rio Treaty, and this position has been followed in
practice.[10]

There is no doubt that the U.N. agency which has been most useful
to the Latin American states, both from the standpoint of their regional
interests and from the standpoint of providing a counterweight to the
United States, has been the Economic Commission for Latin America
(ECLA). In 1947, Chile proposed the creation of such a Commission as
a sub-organ of the U.N. Economic and Social Council. The United States
opposed the proposal, claiming that the Inter-American Economic and
Social Council was adequate to handle the job. A study committee was
formed, which reported early in 1948, recommending the formation of
ECLA. This report was approved by the full Council by a vote of thirteen
to nothing, with four abstentions. ECLA was founded with headquarters
in Santiago, Chile, and held its first meeting in June of 1948. At this
meeting, a coordination agreement was signed with IA-ECOSOC (ECLA
was for many years filling a vacuum, since IA-ECOSOC did not become
truly active until the 1960's), and the highly nationalistic Argentine economist Raúl Prebisch was appointed Director. Under his direction, ECLA has
acted as a sounding board for what some Latin Americans consider to be
their economic interests in contra-distinction to the United States. ECLA
has relied heavily on statistical manipulation and econometrics; has pushed
for commodity agreements on the grounds that the Latin American terms
of trade have been deteriorating for a century; and for rapid industrialization at the expense of agriculture, on the grounds that imports must be
substituted for by domestic production, even if at a high cost, to conserve
scarce foreign exchange. All of these are questionable economic proposi-
tions, but it is beyond the scope of this book to examine them.[11] ECLA has
also been the prime moving force behind the formation of common markets
and free trade areas in Latin America, but this story, relating appropriately
to strength through union, will be examined in Chapter 8.

With increasing frequency, the Latin American states have tried to
identify themselves with a "third-world" position, in association with the
extremely amorphous Afro-Asian bloc. Besides the problems given rise
to by the shifting character and instability of the "third world," however,
the economic interests of Latin America more often conflict with those
of other "underdeveloped" countries than otherwise, and, although an
anti-colonial attitude can generally be adopted without difficulty, it is no
longer the burning issue in Latin America that it is in Africa, Asia, and
the Middle East. In the final analysis, none of the Latin American states
in the foreseeable future would seem likely to be able to develop a

[10] See, for example, Manuel Canyes, *The Organization of American States and the
United Nations* (Washington, 1963).
[11] Latin American statistics are not sufficiently good to allow for much meaningful
manipulation. That the terms of trade have, in fact, deteriorated is disputed, and
commodity agreements can lead to overproduction and retard diversification. Import
substitution may lead to a high-cost, artificial economic structure and impedes the
operation of the principle of comparative advantage.

sufficient degree of foreign policy autonomy to adopt any genuine "third" position.

As with their attempts to create an Inter-American public international law to protect themselves against hemispheric paramountcy, the Latin American attempt to use association with extra-regional agencies to fulfill the same purpose has been largely unsuccessful, due to the imperatives and realities of international politics. On the other hand, the Latin American states have been quite successful, especially since World War II, in using such means to increase the quantity, and diversify the sources, of economic assistance. And what small success they have had in modifying the paramount-client relationship, in their favor, has come, in association (ECLA), as in law (the Calvo Clause), in the economic field.

Selected Bibliography

Except, of course, for the official records of the various international organizations involved, very little has been written in any language about the role of Latin America in international organizations. The participation of the Latin American states in the League of Nations is surveyed in *Latin American Relations with the League of Nations* (Boston, 1930) by Warren H. Kelchner, and in *Les Relations des États de L'Amérique Latine avec la Société des Nations* (Paris, 1936) by Manuel Pérez-Guerrero. The role of the League in the Leticia dispute is examined in Manley O. Hudson, *The Verdict of the League—Colombia and Peru at Leticia* (Boston, 1933), and its role in the Chaco War in Margaret La Foy, *The Chaco Dispute and the League of Nations* (Ann Arbor, 1946).

The only scholarly account of at least monograph length (known to the author) dealing with the role of Latin America in a functional organization is Frederick E. Kidder, *Latin America and UNESCO: The First Five Years* (Gainesville, 1960).

The story of the genesis of the United Nations is very readably told in Ruth B. Russell, *A History of the United Nations Charter* (Washington, 1958), and with greater detail and documentation in Leland M. Goodrich and Edvard Hambro, *Charter of the United Nations* (Boston, 1949). The story of Dumbarton Oaks is told in Robert E. Summers, *Dumbarton Oaks* (New York, 1945), and a very interesting, although controversial, interpretation of the relations between the United Nations, the OAS, and regional agencies in general, is found in Romain Yakemtchouk, *L'O.N.U., La Sécurité Régionale et la Problème du Régionalisme* (Paris, 1955). The author is indebted to M. Yakemtchouk for some of the points made in this Chapter and in Chapter 4.

The role of Latin America in the United Nations in general is surveyed in John A. Houston, *Latin America in the United Nations* (New York, 1956), and in Chapter III of *Bloc Politics in the United Nations* (Cambridge, Mass., 1960), by Thomas Hovet, Jr. The role of various individual Latin American states is examined by Jorge Castañeda, *Mexico and the United Nations* (New York, 1958); Lawrence O. Ealy, *The Republic of Panama in World Affairs 1903–1950* (Philadelphia, 1959); and *Uruguay and the United Nations* (New York, 1958). The official OAS view, as to its relations with the U.N., is spelled out in Manuel Canyes, *The Organization of American States and the United Nations* (Washington, 1963).

There is no full-length study of the role and influence of ECLA and Raúl Prebisch in the U.N., in Latin America, and in the world, but such a study would be of the utmost interest, especially since Dr. Prebisch has recently moved to a position of world influence, by being made director of the United Nations Conference on Trade and Development (UNCTAD), dominated by the underdeveloped countries. He left a disciple (José Antonio Mayobre of Venezuela) in charge of ECLA. An interesting attack on the Prebisch theses by a countryman of his is *La Cepal y la Realidad Económica en América Latina* (Buenos Aires, 1963), by Federico Pinedo.

Many of the serious questions concerning the role of ECLA have been hinted at in this Chapter's Footnote 11. Another is that ECLA has emphasized the role of government planning and government regulation and ownership, at the expense of private enterprise, in countries which are extremely weak in public administration. The eminent Brazilian economist, Eugenio Gudin, in replying to a paper on programming by an ECLA economist (José Antonio Mayobre, who later became Executive Secretary of ECLA), said the following:

> Macro-economic programming is naturally a governmental task, as it does not make sense without government sponsorship. This explains its invariable bias towards government intervention and direct action in the economic field. The author of the paper under discussion is therefore quite wise in expressing the fear that programming may be seriously tainted with socialization. . . .
>
> The next result is worth registering, for the example as well as for posterity. The government autarchies which replaced (in Brazil) the previously existing private companies produce today an operational deficit (twelve billions of cruzeiros) equivalent to nearly 20 per cent. of the total budget receipts of the Federal Government. Furthermore, the inefficiency of railways and shipping, together with the shortage of electric power, has been for the last ten years the worst bottleneck in the Brazilian economy. . . .
>
> This [the "Herculean task" of global programming] might perhaps not be so in the case of countries and economies of small dimensions, great stability, ample administrative capacity and first-class statistical organization, like the Netherlands or Switzerland. But in countries in the process of full development, where economic disorder is frequent either through exogenous factors or through the incapacity of governments, countries unusually vulnerable to impact from outside, countries largely dependent on export prices and on the size of harvests, countries subject to chronic inflationary pressure, it seems to me that the forecasting of demand during the next few years by far exceeds the possibilities of the courageous economists who attempt it.
>
> If, instead of concentrating its efforts and energies on the drawing up of estimates, forecasts and programmes for every element of the economic system and the rate at which the country is going to develop, the Economic Commission for Latin America were to devote its efforts: first, to the analysis of the economic situation and of the policies followed by each country; second, to the improvement of economic statistics; and third, to contributing to the solution of Latin America's two greatest economic problems— productivity and education, I contend that it would be of much greater assistance to Latin America. . . .
>
> Finally, little attention has been given to the progress and productivity of agriculture, generally considered as a sort of inferior type of economic activity. This lack of assistance to agriculture is the more regrettable because

agricultural techniques in tropical or semi-tropical countries must be developed *in loco* and cannot be copied from temperate or cold climates of the Northern Hemisphere, as can industrial techniques of transformation industries.

[Howard S. Ellis, ed., *Economic Development for Latin America* (London, 1962), pp. 45-48.]

8 / STRENGTH THROUGH UNION

> *There must be but one Fatherland and for all Americans, since in all things we have had a perfect unity.*
>
> SIMÓN BOLÍVAR

> *Arbitrary power, military and ecclesiastical, was stamped upon their education, upon their habits, and upon all their institutions. Civil dissension was infused into all of their seminal principles. War and mutual destruction was in every member of their organization: moral, political, and physical.*
>
> JOHN QUINCY ADAMS

The states of Latin America have attempted to gain in relative power and influence vis-à-vis the hemispheric paramount through law, through association with outside organizations, and through attempts to pool their strength by union. This chapter will trace through the history of these attempts at unity, their failures and their successes.

Latin America has gone through two waves of enthusiasm for union. The first began in 1826 with high hope, and sputtered to a close by 1865. During this wave, the union that was hoped for was to be political union, and was directed against what were perceived to be direct threats from various European states and, to a lesser extent, the United States. Thus it was characterized by the drawing-together often occasioned by conflict and fear.

From 1865 to 1951, the Latin American states abandoned initiatives directed toward union. They placed their reliance upon law between 1865 and 1920, and on a combination of law and association after 1920. The manifest failure of this reliance, coupled with the drive for economic development, led, in the years following 1951, to a new wave of initiatives directed toward union—this time, economic union, or the unity of cooperation, modeled upon the seemingly successful European experience. That this type of union can, and does, have political manifestations, however, we shall see below.

There is a myth abroad, among the many concerning Latin America, relating to a supposed Latin American solidarity and feeling of oneness. There is some validity to this myth, as there is with most myths. Especially

161

with relation to the paramount, and to the outside world, the Latin Americans feel a sameness. With relation to each other, however, they are just as likely, or, perhaps, more likely, to feel fear, suspicion, indifference, or dislike. Past wars and disputes rankle. Present boundary and other controversies divide them. Economic and power rivalries limit cooperative efforts. Internal political and economic chaos spills over boundaries. With these and other disruptive forces, the drive toward union must contend. The drive failed ignominiously between 1826 and 1865. Whether it will succeed in the twentieth century remains to be seen.

A / THE UNITY OF FEAR, 1826-65

Moves toward union in the nineteenth century in Latin America were beset, not only with nationalistic forces and rivalries, but with extremely powerful separatist movements within the states involved. Thus, not only was regional or sub-regional union not achieved, but the initial states, in many cases, fragmented even further. Central America broke away from Mexico in 1823, and then split up into five tiny republics in 1838. Gran Colombia, the country of the Liberator, cracked apart in 1831, becoming Venezuela, Colombia, and Ecuador. Attempts at union between Peru and Bolivia were frustrated by Chile and Argentina (see Chapter 3). The Dominican Republic split away from Haiti in 1844. In addition, strong separatist movements kept Brazil, Argentina, and Mexico in turmoil in the same period, resulting, in the case of Mexico, in loss of half the national territory, and abdication, for many years, of all pretensions to regional leadership.

Had it not been for the enormous personal prestige of Simón Bolívar, it is doubtful that there would have been any move toward union in the early years following independence. When the Latin American states broke away from Spain, men of all countries served in the revolutionary armies, and it was this first flush of kindred feeling that brought on the spate of unitary schemes leading to the Congress of Panama in 1826. The Venezuelan "Precursor," Francisco de Miranda, the Argentine Bernardino Rivadavia, the Chilean Juan Martínez de Rosas, the Central American patriot José Cecilio del Valle, and others, all advocated confederation of the new states. It was only when Bolívar became personally involved in such plans, however, that anything concrete happened.

From 1822 to 1824, Colombia, with Bolívar at its head, signed treaties of friendship and alliance with several of the other new states of the hemisphere. This network of alliances encouraged Bolívar to send out his famous circular letter of December 7, 1824, to all the Spanish-American states, Great Britain, and Brazil, inviting them to a Congress to be held in the city of Panama. In the spring of 1825, Colombia sent an invitation to the United States. The Congress convened on June 22, 1826, and adjourned on July 15. Only Colombia, Central America, Mexico, Peru, and Great Britain attended. The delegates of the United States failed to arrive in time, and the other countries either refused to attend altogether, or sent delegates too late for theim to arrive at the Congress. It is significant that Britain, having abandoned its plans for conquest, was recognized as paramount and thus invited, to be consulted on defense against the plans of the Holy Alliance and France (already a thing of the past), that the United States was invited as an afterthought, and that Argentina and Brazil, already with visions of regional leadership, refused the invitation outright, declining to recognize Colombia's initiative.

A series of treaties and conventions was signed at Panama, providing for a permanent union and league. All disputes were to be settled by peaceful means, and the territorial integrity of every member state was guaranteed. The Congress, which was to have its own troops, would meet every two years in peacetime, and every year in wartime. The next meeting was set for the following year in Tacubaya, Mexico. A secret protocol was also signed, dealing with the provision and deployment of the armed forces of the Congress. Colombia was the only state which ratified the agreements, and, thus, none of them came into effect.

The first flush of revolutionary fervor which, along with fear of the Holy Alliance, had produced the Congress of Panama, and the other schemes for a Pan American organization, soon disintegrated into petty nationalism and particularism. From 1826 to 1865, three more Latin American Congresses met to discuss union, usually as a result of foreign intervention by Spain, France, England, or the United States. Fear, alone, sustained these conferences. Certain of the Latin American countries would come together in the face of an external threat, but, when the threat had passed, such ephemeral moves toward union would collapse. At least they kept alive the feeling of unity and the ideal of confederation or cooperation; they established, though weakly, a tradition of the use of assemblies for consultation among the states, and they nurtured the ideal of the peaceful settlement of disputes.

The first congress of American states to convene after the Panama Congress of 1826, was the conference held in the city of Lima from December 11, 1847 to March 1, 1848, although Mexico had previously, on various occasions, unsuccessfully tried to reconvene the Panama Congress in Tacubaya. The Congress of 1847 was motivated by fear of Spain, which was attempting to gain back the west coast of South America and of the United States, which was at the time at war with Mexico. In all, five states were represented at Lima: Bolivia, Chile, Ecuador, New Granada (Colombia), and Peru, in other words, all the states of South America which at that time had a Pacific coastline. Venezuela, Argentina, and Brazil, also invited, declined to attend. Without authorization, New Granada issued an invitation to the United States. This invitation was refused, and, in any case, was repudiated by the Congress when it met.

The so-called American Congress of 1847–48 resulted in a treaty of confederation, a treaty of commerce and navigation, a consular convention, and a postal convention. The treaty of confederation was very loose, but it did provide for regular meetings, and set forth procedures of peaceful settlement of disputes. The purpose of the treaty, as stated in the text, was to: ". . . sustain the sovereignty and independence of all and each one, to maintain the integrity of their respective territories, to assure in them their dominance and sovereignty, to refuse to consent that they should be permitted to suffer outrage or offense." [1] Only the consular convention was eventually ratified by all the states represented at the congress and thus entered into force.

On September 15, 1856, the representatives of Peru, Ecuador, and Chile met in the city of Santiago de Chile, and signed the "Continental Treaty of 1856." This one-day meeting has been termed the Continental Congress of 1856. Again, the threat was from Spain, which had sent a renegade Ecuadorean general, Juan José Flores, to regain the Pacific coast of South America. The treaty set up a permanent league of Latin American states with a permanent congress, and the other states of Latin America were invited to adhere to the treaty. Surprisingly enough, seven countries did so: Mexico, Nicaragua, Guatemala, Honduras, Costa Rica, Bolivia, and Colombia (note that Mexico and the Central American states were, at the time, under threat of American filibustering expeditions). None of the original signers ratified it, however, and it never came into force. Again, the principal claimants to regional dominance, Brazil and Argentina, refused to have anything to do with the plan of confederation.

The Second Lima Congress was held in that city from November 14, 1864, to March 13, 1865. It was also motivated by fear of foreign intervention, and was a reaction to intervention that was actively taking place. Spain had reoccupied Santo Domingo, and was waging war against Peru and Chile. France had invaded Mexico, and set up Maximilian as puppet Emperor. The Second Lima Congress was called to discuss an "American Union." Bolivia, Chile, Ecuador, Guatemala, Peru, El Salvador, Venezuela, and Colombia were represented. Argentina and Brazil refused to attend. Peru suggested inviting the United States, but, after some discussion, the suggestion was defeated. Three conventions were signed, one providing for a defensive alliance, another for compulsory arbitration of disputes, and a third on commercial navigation and postal exchange. The defensive alliance gave up any idea of confederation, in favor of a vague sort of "family of states." Not one of the countries which signed the treaties ratified them.

At various other times during the nineteenth century, Costa Rica, Mexico, and Colombia called for conferences of the Latin American states to discuss union, but these calls never even reached the stage of actually holding a conference. As we have seen, the total result of the four conferences that did meet between 1826 and 1865 was the coming into effect of

[1] John Holladay Latané, *The United States and Latin America* (New York, 1922), p. 90.

one consular convention having nothing to do with regional union. Transportation and communications were such in nineteenth-century Latin America, that by the time a Congress could meet, deliberate, and report back to the sponsoring governments, the threat which had caused the Congress to be called had been largely dissipated. The Congresses, even if dominated by the motive of fear, were not specifically directed against the paramount, and, thus, involved only certain states at any given moment. The possibility of using the United States as a counterweight to Great Britain was not explored, and Brazil and Argentina held uniformly aloof from these early initiatives. Thus, they became mere proposals for the amalgamation of the weak into confederations that would have been, even if formed, almost equally weak.

B / THE UNITY OF COOPERATION, 1951–PRESENT

The idea of economic union had not been entirely absent from Latin America prior to 1951. For a short time in the nineteenth century, there was a customs union between Argentina and Chile. In 1939, a free trade agreement was signed between Argentina and Brazil. In 1940, at the Second Meeting of Consultation of Foreign Ministers, the idea of an Inter-American Bank, including a payments union, was formally approved. In the 1940's and 1950's bilateral payments agreements were signed among various states of the hemisphere. In 1948, at its first meeting, the Economic Commission for Latin America (ECLA), of the Economic and Social Council of the United Nations (see Chapter 7), proposed that, among other items of importance, the possibility of a customs and/or payments union in Latin America should be considered. As a result, various member states proposed a sub-regional approach to the problem, citing obvious groupings such as Mexico, Central America, and the Caribbean; Gran Colombia; Peru–Bolivia–Chile, and Argentina–Uruguay–Paraguay–Brazil. As we shall see, with the exception of Central America, the sub-regional approach was abandoned upon the urgings of ECLA. This decision has been severely criticized on economic grounds. It is contended that sub-regional markets should have been established first, later to join together in larger groupings. This, it is said, would have enabled the Latin American countries to begin the process of integration modestly, but surely, and would have obviated the difficulties that later arose, and almost destroyed the Latin American Free Trade Association. As we shall also see, however, these criticisms, to some extent, miss their mark, because the decision to try to integrate substantially all of Latin America in the same organization was, at least in part, a political one.

The idea of a Central American Common Market developed during

Map of the Central American Common Market (CACM) and the Latin
American Free Trade Association (LAFTA) as of December, 1966

the June, 1951, meetings of ECLA. In the same year, the beginnings of
an institutional framework were provided by the foundation of the Orga-
nization of Central American States (ODECA—see Chapter 4). In 1952,
ECLA established the Central American Economic Cooperation Committee, and entrusted it with the task of studying the matter. In 1958, the
Committee reported back with two draft treaties of economic integration.
In June of that year, the Central American states signed the Multilateral
Treaty of Free Trade and Economic Integration, and the Convention on
Integrated Industries. In September, these treaties were supplemented by
an Agreement on Equalization of Import Duties and Charges. All these
treaties were quickly ratified by Guatemala, Honduras, and El Salvador,
but not by Nicaragua and Costa Rica. As a result, in early 1960, the
first three countries signed a new treaty among themselves providing for
more rapid integration.

The threat of being left out induced Nicaragua and Costa Rica to join in the signing, in December, 1960, of the General Central American Treaty of Economic Integration, which consolidated and replaced the earlier treaties. The General Treaty was ratified by Guatemala, Nicaragua, and El Salvador in 1961, and, in the same year, the Central American Bank of Economic Integration and a rudimentary payments union were established. Honduras ratified the General Treaty in 1962, and, with Costa Rican ratification in 1963, the Central American Common Market was finally given regional coverage.

Top policy decisions within CACM are made by the Central American Economic Council, consisting of the Ministers of Economy of the five republics. Day-to-day decisions are made by an Executive Commission, aided by a permanent secretariat. There is a regional Advanced School of Public Administration, and an Institute for Industrial Research and Technology. The Central American Clearing House now handles the bulk of the visible trade payments within Central America, and the capital of the Central American Bank of Economic Integration has been raised to over $50 million as of 1966. As part of its campaign of penetration into Central America and the Caribbean, Mexico has joined the Clearing House, has provided funds to the bank and has lent technical advisors to various bodies within CACM.

Economically, CACM has been an undoubted success, given the fact that the region started with a very low economic base. Between 1960 and 1965, intra-regional trade in Central America expanded some 300% to a dollar volume of over one hundred million, comprising about thirteen percent of the total trade of Central America. Internal tariffs had been largely eliminated, and a common external tariff erected, by 1966, and plans were laid for uniform customs administration by 1970. Labor movement and capital movements had been freed, and a common Central American currency was planned. Mexico, as has already been mentioned, took an active interest in the new markets opening to the south, and both Panama and the Dominican Republic expressed an interest in joining. Only one aspect of CACM can be considered a failure. By 1966, only one Central American integrated industry (a tire factory in Guatemala) was in operation, and it seemed as if the program would become a dead letter. This was far from uniformly mourned, however, for many economists believe that granting industrial monopolies within a regional trading area is counterproductive, and likely to lead to a high-cost structure, due to the elimination of salutary competition, both from within and from without the trading area. This, in turn, would tend to make an expansion of industrial exports to the outside world difficult, and freeze the region in a pattern of agricultural and mineral exports.

The Central American Common Market is the one almost universally acclaimed initiative of ECLA, and the results have amply justified the acclaim. In its origins and development, CACM appeared to have only economic motivations and goals, except, perhaps, for a possible eventual political union of the Central American republics, which, after all, had, at one time, formed a single country. Should such an eventuality come to pass, it would, of course, result in a diminution of the weight of the Latin American bloc in the United Nations and other universal international organizations, and would make it more difficult for the United States to achieve a two-thirds majority of votes within the Council of the Organization of American States and the Meetings of Consultation of Foreign Ministers.

Latin American fears of the growing economic ties between Europe and Africa (threatening to exclude them from lucrative markets), plus a desire to circumvent the requirement of the General Agreement on Tariffs and Trade (GATT) that Argentina, Brazil, and other Latin American states give up the preferential agreements they had signed (see above), unless they were part of a recognized trading area, were two strong motivations toward the formation of the much larger, and more ambitious, Latin American Free Trade Association (LAFTA). In addition to these motives of state policy, were the economic and political considerations, discussed below, which impelled ECLA to discard proposals for sub-regional groupings, and push for the formation of a free trade area covering practically the entire hemispheric island. ECLA cautiously began discussions of the possibility of forming a free trade area in 1955–56. In May of 1957, the first full-scale exchange of ideas took place, and, in 1958, sub-regional groupings were definitely rejected, except in the case of Central America. An ECLA meeting in Panama City, in May of 1959, tied together the loose strings of the various proposals, and, in February of 1960, Brazil, Uruguay, Paraguay, Argentina, Chile, Peru, and Mexico signed the Treaty Establishing a Free-Trade Area and Instituting the Latin American Free-Trade Association (Montevideo Treaty). Bolivia attended the meetings in Montevideo, but did not sign the Treaty, and has not subsequently joined LAFTA. (For the text of the Montevideo Treaty, see Appendix I.) Enough ratifications were received to bring the Treaty into effect in June of 1961, and LAFTA was subsequently joined by Colombia, Ecuador, and Venezuela, so that it covered the vast bulk of the area, population, and natural resources of Latin America, and, between LAFTA and CACM, all of Latin America was economically joined together, with the exception of Bolivia, Haiti, the Dominican Republic, Cuba, and Panama.

Originally modeled on the European Free Trade Area (EFTA), but even looser, and more permissive, in its structure and operations, the LAFTA machinery was overhauled in late 1965, following the near-collapse of the organization. Steps toward the establishment of a common market were taken, including an agreement, in principle, on the eventual establishment of a common external tariff, and the formation of a Committee of Technical Advisors to make day-to-day decisions on implementation of policy. Nevertheless, a Chilean proposal that the Committee be given supra-national attributes, was rejected, being, predictably, opposed by Argentina and Brazil. Despite these changes, labor and capital movements are still restricted, and LAFTA still operates on the principle of "reciprocity," that is, the balancing of trade so as to eliminate internal regional balance-of-payments discrepancies through special concessions. This, of course, limits incentives to greater efficiency in individual countries, and limits the extent to which intra-regional trade can be expanded. Rather than being automatic, as provided for by the Rome Treaty establishing the European Economic Community (EEC), tariff negotiations still take place on a product-by-product basis. In addition, LAFTA countries can make complementarity agreements on individual industries, a program similar to the already discredited integrated-industries scheme of CACM.

The economic results of LAFTA have been, to some extent, disappointing, although it must be stated that a comparison with CACM can be misleading. LAFTA members are geographically dispersed, and many have no history of extensive trading with each other. The general industrial-commercial-agricultural base that LAFTA started with was much higher than that of CACM, so that the easy, initial developments in trade and industry were not possible. Despite these drawbacks, LAFTA regional trade increased some 85% between 1961 and 1964, about half consisting of foodstuffs, a quarter raw materials, and only about 14% semi-manufactures and manufactures.[2] It should also be pointed out that inter-regional trade had been higher in volume in certain years of the 1950's, before the inception of LAFTA, that it was even in 1964. The fact that enthusiasm for actual freeing of trade was considerably less in LAFTA than in CACM, is pointed up by the fact that the trade gains of Mexico, which increased its LAFTA exports 35%, in 1964 alone, over 1963 (for a total of $50.4 million, about two percent of total Mexican exports), almost resulted in the demise of the organization. In order to prevent this, a four-man panel was established in 1964, consisting of Raúl Prebisch, José Antonio Mayobre, Felipe Herrera of the Inter-American Development Bank, and Carlos Sanz de Santamaría of the Alliance for Progress Panel. It was this committee that made the recommendations which, in watered-down form, were adopted by the LAFTA countries in late 1965.

LAFTA cannot be assessed purely on an economic basis, however, for there is strong evidence that its political motivations are, at least, as strong. "In practice, LAFTA is treated by most member countries as a means for negotiating non-competitive preferences which discriminate against non-LAFTA countries rather than as a means for attaining a truly free and competitive trade area."[3] ECLA theorists envisioned LAFTA as a counterweight to paramount hegemony, providing the Latin American countries with an economic weapon against the United States, as,

[2] "Latin American Development and Western Hemisphere Trade," *Hearings Before the Subcommittee on Inter-American Economic Relationships of the Joint Economic Committee, Congress of the United States,* 89th Congress, First Session, September 8, 9, and 10, 1965, p. 62.
[3] John M. Porges, "Exports and Imports Between the United States and the Caribbean," paper presented at the Sixteenth Annual Conference on the Caribbean, Center for Latin American Studies, University of Florida, December 2, 1965 (mimeo), p. 12.

with the further development of trade discrimination by the Eurafrican trading bloc, the United States would be forced to turn more and more to Latin America for its supply of vital raw materials, and could, thus, be induced to join commodity agreements, raise the level of paramount benevolence, and permit greater foreign policy flexibility. Writing on the eve of the adoption of the Montevideo Treaty, an Argentine writer expressed the thought in the following way, under the subtitle "Towards a Better Understanding with the United States":

> Projected towards these great ends, economic integration, realized by means of regional markets, is the best way to overcome the inferiority complex, with its train of sensitivities and prejudices, that like a memory of colonialism, still weighs down these isolated countries. . . .
>
> All this will tend to tighten the friendly relations of the peoples of Latin America, within a regime of security and confidence, that is an attribute only of those peoples who have attained spiritual and material fulfillment.
>
> It is primarily by this route that an easy solution will be found to the problems of the useful incorporation of foreign capital and of the political relations of this group of countries with the United States. With the dangers of economic and political subjugation eliminated, nothing will prevent a sincere understanding, mutually beneficial, realized on worthy and equal bases.[4]

Later, with the development of the Alliance for Progress, those in Latin America who saw in this program another instrument of United States economic penetration and ideological pressure, turned to LAFTA to counteract those elements of the Alliance that were considered bad: "The Alliance is a political instrument. It is an effort to give Latin America U.S.-style tools for growth by helping develop some aspects of free enterprise economies on broadly represented democratic bases. ECLA's 'integration mystique' seems to represent a political stance in opposition; . . . ." [5] Rómulo Almeida, first Executive Secretary of LAFTA, posited the confrontation of the two politico-economic concepts in a speech: "The mystique of joint development in Latin America is much more important as a road toward an internal political integration in certain countries than that of combatting communism through a 'popular capitalism' promoted by the Alliance for Progress." [6]

Economically, LAFTA encompasses an area larger than the United States, with a population of roughly the same magnitude, and with a collective gross national product about one-tenth that of the United States. No one doubts the benefits to Latin America of the formation of a genuine,

---

[4] Ovidio S. Ventura, *Hacia la Integración Económica de Latino-América* (Buenos Aires, 1959), p. 17. (translation by author)
[5] Porges, *op. cit.*, p. 17.
[6] *Visión* Report, *Economic Integration in Latin America: LAFTA* (New York, 1963), p. 15. In a speech in New York, in December of 1965, Alberto Gainza Paz, editor-publisher of *La Prensa* of Buenos Aires, warned of the dangers inherent in the Alliance-LAFTA confrontation.

nondiscriminatory free trade area or common market. Whether LAFTA will become this, is questionable. The principles of reciprocity and complementarity violate the trend toward liberalization. In 1963, Chile, Colombia, Peru, and Uruguay managed to get themselves classified as "countries with insufficient markets," and, thus, qualified to receive the same preferential treatment already accorded to Ecuador and Paraguay. This agreement was not only a violation of the principles underlying liberalization, but of the letter of the Montevideo Treaty. But this is, perhaps, essentially irrelevant, as economic unity *per se* is irrelevant to international politics, unless it develops political manifestations, intended or spontaneous. And, here again, we run into the inherent disability of the collectively weak. A united Western Europe would be a power entity of the first rank, and would quickly become a paramount. A Latin America, even politically united with a unitary constitution, would not constitute a great power, although it would have the long-range potentiality to become one. An indication of this fact is that LAFTA, following the lead of ECLA, is now beginning to agitate for regional hemispheric trade preferences, as between the United States and Latin America, and, in the United States, influential voices are being raised in favor of a hemispheric free trade area or common market.[7] It is thought that such a development would be the final triumph of the new power and influence that Latin America developed by means of economic integration. Yet, paradoxically and ironically, if a system of preferences, a free trade area, or a common market, including the United States and Latin America *were* initiated, this, more than any other possible move, aside from military conquest, would assure the continued and strengthened dominance of the United States. In fact, it would make the Latin American states completely dependent upon, and, thus, subservient to, the United States, in the way that Cuba is now totally dependent upon Soviet largesse. It would make the continued development of foreign policy flexibility, through use of the Cold War and the Soviet challenge, impossible, except for the one-time terminal move of transferring from the U. S. to the Soviet client system. In short, the development that ECLA and some of the LAFTA participants see as the culmination of their political efforts would result, in reality, in exactly the opposite of the effect foreseen: "Latin America's request for preferred trade access to the U.S. market is a more difficult problem. It is inconsistent: existing preference systems involving the former British, French and Dutch possessions are colonial vestiges; most Latin American governments, of course, claim they wish to eliminate such colonial vestiges and that they wish to reduce their economic dependence on the industrial countries." [8]

It may be argued that, even if disastrous to the political hopes of Latin America, a preferential system should be supported by the United

---

[7] By Nelson Rockefeller and Jacob Javits, among others. Some provision would have to be made in any such arrangement to protect Latin American industry, which otherwise would be largely destroyed in a flood of mass-produced American manufactured goods.

[8] Porges, *op. cit.*, p. 25.

States, since it would strengthen its dominant position, in the way Europe is attempting to re-establish its dominance over Africa. But, to this, it can be replied that any such system is economically damaging, in that it creates a higher cost structure than would otherwise prevail, and that, perhaps, unlike Europe, the United States is militarily powerful enough, and its strategic position vis-à-vis Latin America is such, that further strengthening of dominance through economically counterproductive trade preference systems is unnecessary.

What, then, can we say concerning the future prospects of the twentieth-century Latin American trend toward union? Economically, one of the most difficult stumbling-blocks in the path of integration is the relatively poor transportation and communications network linking the Latin American countries to one another, compared with the excellent links to the United States and Europe. This is one of the reasons why CACM has been able to progress at a more rapid pace than LAFTA, even though the export commodities produced by the Central American countries are less complementary, one to another, than those produced by LAFTA member countries.[9] Other problems that the Latin American countries have, or will have, in attempting to create a viable economic bloc, include the formation of a common outside tariff; automatic reductions, and eventual elimination, of internal tariffs; adoption of a common customs terminology; the making of meaningful regional economic studies; the provision of export financing for the small and medium company; monetary inflation; avoidance of the phenomenon whereby the relatively rich countries get richer and the poor get poorer; excessive governmental interference in market forces; and political disruption. It will be noted that all of these problems, with the exception of the last, are actually, or potentially, of greater significance for LAFTA than for CACM. Some of them, such as automatic internal tariff elimination, and erection of a uniform external tariff, have been entirely solved by CACM, while remaining matters of bitter controversy within LAFTA. It must, thus, be concluded that the immediate economic prospects of CACM are better than those of LAFTA.

Both CACM and LAFTA, quite unintentionally, have served to stimulate the development of private initiative in Latin America. The integrated-industries scheme in Central America had the totally unexpected effect of stimulating competition, rather than deadening it, as private companies, domestic and foreign, scrambled to enter the market before monopolistic integrated industries could be established. In order to protect themselves from the statist tendency manifest in the foundation and development of LAFTA, Latin American entrepreneurs have been forced to hold various meetings, leading to the founding of various sectoral manufacturers' associations, and to the overall Latin American Industrialists' Association. Private industry has even financed the beginnings of the completion of the last remaining link of the Pan American Highway, through the Darién jungle, connecting Colombia and Panama.

[9] On the transportation and communications problem, see the *Visión* Report, *op. cit.*, pp. 23-27.

A year after the signing of the Montevideo Treaty, a report, issued by the Committee for Economic Development, suggested that the eventual success of regional economic integration in Latin America depended upon a real freeing of internal competition, freedom of payments (involving monetary stability), and care that an eventual common external tariff wall did not serve to create a closed, autarchic, high-cost, low-productivity economic bloc.[10] The fact that, between 1955 and 1964, industrial exports from Latin America increased only 17% while those from the rest of the underdeveloped world increased 46%, would indicate that the CED warning is still much to the point.

"North Americans have done little study of the LAFTA movement and this year's [1965] proposal for a Latin American Common Market. Almost without our noticing it an integration mystique is taking form in Latin America. . . . An important element of the mystique seems to be that the task of 'integration' should be exclusively Latin American, that is, U.S. influence should be minimal." [11] As we have seen, such an effort, to the extent that it is directed toward independence from the paramount, must fail, as long as the development of the movement politically looks toward an eventual special trade arrangement with that same paramount. One of the reasons for the development of the "integration mystique" has been a certain post-World War II demonstration effect upon Latin America from the new Afro-Asian countries. The Afro-Asian countries themselves are now learning that preferential economic agreements with developed countries are a two-edged sword, and it may be expected that, with a certain time lag, the same lesson may be learned in Latin America. In short, the prescription for political success of the movement toward economic integration in Latin America would appear to be the same as that for economic success. To the extent that integration is carried out in such a way as to make Latin America genuinely more prosperous and more economically independent, to that extent will it be able to follow a more flexible foreign policy line. To the extent that integration is restrictive and protectionist, Latin America will be weakened economically, and, thus, will become economically and politically more dependent upon the United States, or any other potential paramount.[12]

With the movement toward the economic union of Latin America in full flow, with the evidence yet incomplete, and with a hundred possible factors which might affect it in any direction in future months and years, it can only be said that, at this point, it would appear that both the economic and the political potentialities of CACM outstrip those of LAFTA.[13]

[10] *Cooperation for Progress in Latin America* (Washington, 1961), pp. 34–35.
[11] Porges, *op. cit.*, p. 16.
[12] As a result of these and other considerations, the United States, while enthusiastically supporting the formation of CACM, has been lukewarm toward LAFTA.
[13] Brief mention should be made of the formation, in early 1965, of a Preparatory Committee for Latin American Denuclearization, charged with the preparation of a treaty for the permanent denuclearization of Latin America. As of mid-1966, however, no acceptable treaty was in sight. Among other problems, Brazil was insisting that any treaty include Cuba and all European colonies; Argentina insisted upon extensive inter-regional inspection to ensure compliance; Chile was afraid that such inspection would infringe upon her sovereignty; and Venezuela wanted a guarantee of any eventual agreement by all the nuclear powers.

Selected Bibliography

On the subject of the nineteenth-century Latin American attempts to achieve union through fear, consult the following three works in English: Joseph Byrne Lockey, *Pan-Americanism—Its Beginning* (New York, 1926); Lockey, *Essays in Pan-Americanism* (Berkeley, 1939), and John Holladay Latané, *The United States and Latin America* (New York, 1922). See also the detailed accounts in the two books by Francisco Cuevas Cancino, and Jesús-María Yepes, both entitled *Del Congreso de Panamá a la Conferencia de Caracas 1826–1954* (Caracas, 1955) already cited in the Selected Bibliography for Chapter 4 (*q.v.*).

On the subject of the twentieth-century movement toward Latin American economic integration, see Sidney Dell, *A Latin American Common Market?* (Oxford, 1966). Otherwise, there is very little on the subject. *Inter-American Economic Affairs,* and *The Journal of Inter-American Studies* should be consulted for a few articles, and various United States banks have issued pamphlets concerning CACM and/or LAFTA. These tend to be rather narrow and technical. Prior to the Montevideo Conference, the respected Mexican economist, Víctor Urquidi, wrote a book in Spanish, later translated into English under the title, *Free Trade and Economic Integration in Latin America: Toward a Common Market* (Berkeley, 1962). The Urquidi book studies the idea of forming LAFTA and the reasons supporting its formation. It is, thus, useful for the historical background which finally led to the signing of the Montevideo Treaty. It should be noted that, at the time he wrote the book, Urquidi was head of the Mexican office of ECLA, and the work reflects pristine ECLA doctrine concerning the desirability of a common market covering substantially all of Latin America. The book also is useful for its explanation of the articles of the Montevideo Treaty. There is a chronology of events leading to Montevideo, and the text of the Treaty is provided.

For another, this time nonofficial, Latin American view of the desirability of economic integration, see Ovidio S. Ventura, *Hacia la Integración Económica de Latinoamérica* (Buenos Aires, 1959). An early ECLA study, presenting the case for Central American integration, is *La Integración Económica de Centroamérica* (United Nations, 1956). The numerous publications of the Central American Economic Cooperation Committee should also be consulted with reference to CACM, its origins and its development.

Another ECLA publication, this time giving the bases for the idea of a subcontinental common market, is *The Latin American Common Market* (United Nations, 1959), perhaps the most influential single publication in the development of the "integration mystique." A 1962 ECLA publication gives the texts of the various CACM and LAFTA treaties, protocols, etc., as well as official reports on integration: *Multilateral Economic Cooperation in Latin America,* vol. I (United Nations, 1962). A second announced volume, to provide interpretation of the documents, has not yet appeared.

Unofficial assessments of Latin American economic integration, mostly from the economic standpoint, can be found in the following publications: "Economic Integration in Latin America: The Central American Program of Economic Integration and the Latin American Free-Trade Association," *The Record of the Association of the Bar of the City of New York,* vol. 17, no. 6 (Supplement), June, 1962; "Economic Integration in Latin America: LAFTA," A *Visión* Report (New York, 1963), and "Latin American Development and Western Hemisphere Trade," *Hearings Before the Subcommittee on Inter-American Economic Relationships of the Joint Economic Committee, Congress of the United States,* 89th Congress, First Session, September 8, 9, and 10, 1965. Of all of these, by far the most useful is the report included in the last-named, "Economic Integration in Latin America: A Progress Report," by George S. Moore, pp. 57–72. All of these are listed, however, for lack of anything better. This is a prime virgin field for scholarly research.

Concluding Note / THE WORLD, THE HEMISPHERE, AND LATIN AMERICA

El estudio más digno de un americano es la América.

The study most worthy of an American is America.

JOSÉ CECILIO DEL VALLE

A / SUMMARY

All manifestations of human behavior consist of variations on the pattern of stimulus and response, taking place within some sort of framework. This book has attempted to describe the setting within which Latin America must operate in international politics, as well as the nature of the region itself. These two factors condition and, to a certain extent, determine rather rigidly the parameters of behavior within which Latin America must operate. The challenges to the Latin American states have then been described, especially those of paramount dominance, and the paramount-client relationship. Finally, the various forms of response that the challenges have evoked have been catalogued and evaluated.

International society is a quasi-anarchic society, which means that the behavior of states is fairly narrowly circumscribed, making prediction on a scientific basis somewhat more feasible than in the case of domestic politics. As in any quasi-anarchic society, the structure of international society is hierarchical. Certain states exercise paramount hegemony over others, which we have termed clients. This hegemony can range from a rather loose influence over foreign policy to tight control of both external and internal political behavior. Conflict among states is the cement of international relations (as it must be in a quasi-anarchic society)—the intensity of the conflict depending on its likelihood of escalating into a confrontation of paramounts.

As law is the codification of the power structure of a given society at a given time, there is a meaningful international law only when certain rules are agreed upon by the paramounts, and enforced with reference to the weaker states. In the nineteenth century, there was such a law, enforced by the European states. With the development, in the twentieth century, of Communist paramounts, such agreement disappeared, so that international law became, at best, a minor element in international politics. Voluntary associations in international society will last as long as the units maintain similarity of goals and complementarity of resources. Many international associations are not voluntary, but represent client associations, and these may remain in existence indefinitely, due to the power factor.

States may have a foreign policy that is predominantly one of revision, or of stasis. In implementing their foreign policies, states utilize a mix of strategies, including diplomacy, propaganda, economic strategy, military display, subversion, and war. All of these strategies, when employed, will, in turn, be implemented by a series of tactics.

The various states of Latin America differ, in many important respects, with reference to their domestic racial and ethnic structures, their natural resources and populations, their geographic position, etc. In terms of international politics, however, their similarities outweigh their differences, so that their international behavior is relatively uniform, and, thus, one can meaningfully speak of the role of Latin America, as a region, in international politics. The salient features of Latin America, from the standpoint of international politics, are its strategic position as a hemispheric island in immediate proximity to an international paramount; the fact that all the states in the region are clients with no immediate prospect of attaining paramount status; the region's indigenous heritage and Mediterranean culture-origin; the fact that all the states of the region are, or consider themselves to be, economically underdeveloped, and the fact that their mentality, or world-view, is Western.

Due to its strategic position and weakness, the principal challenge to Latin America has always been its relations with its paramount. In effect, this has meant its relations with Great Britain, between about 1823 and 1896, and its relations with the United States thereafter. Generally, Latin America was happier with Great Britain as a paramount than with the United States, primarily for two reasons. Britain, once it had given up its original dreams of conquest in the New World, did not generally interfere in the domestic concerns of the Latin American states, as long as British state interests were not directly affected. Perhaps equally important, British policy had a high level of predictability, while American policy has fluctuated widely, making client adjustment more difficult.

The United States developed the Inter-American system and the Organization of American States, for the purposes of organizing and mobilizing its Latin American clients. During the "era of interventions," relations within the Inter-American system were predictably strained, but, when the United States finally felt secure in its paramount position, and its position correspondingly looked unchallengeable to the Latin American countries, relations improved, and a high degree of cooperation was obtained.

Following World War II, the Latin American states were dissatisfied with the level of paramount benevolence directed toward them by the United States, which had suddenly fallen heir to client systems all over the world. As a result of this dissatisfaction, coupled with the ability of the Soviet Union to penetrate ideologically into the Western Hemisphere (and its surprisingly rapid development of a nuclear capability), the seemingly unshakable position of the United States was challenged, within less than a decade following the end of the war. The Soviet challenge failed in Guatemala in 1954, but succeeded in Cuba following the Castro revolution of 1959. As a result of this paramount challenge in the Western Hemisphere, relations between the United States and Latin America, and within the OAS, have once again become strained, as the Latin American states, taking advantage of the Cold War, have developed greater foreign policy flexibility. In consequence, the level of paramount benevolence has been greatly increased, and the machinery of the OAS is in the process of being overhauled (as of 1967).

In attempting to deal with the challenge of paramount dominance, the Latin American states have followed three distinguishable patterns of response, modeled upon protection-patterns utilized by weaker units in a domestic society. In the early nineteenth century, there were several efforts to gain strength through political unification, but these uniformly failed, as a result of nationalism and particularism. Later in the nineteenth century, and in the twentieth century, the Latin American states have tried to use law to protect themselves, but this effort has also failed. In the nineteenth century, they were advocating a law at variance with the international law actually enforced by the European paramounts, and, in the twentieth century, public international law is largely inoperative. With the development of the League of Nations and the United Nations, Latin America has tried to use association with organizations outside the immediate regional society as a counterweight to the paramount. Again, the realities of power and strategic position have rendered these efforts generally ineffective, although, at times, embarrassing to the paramount. In the 1950's, union was tried again, this time through economic integration, attaining concrete form in the Central American Common Market and the Latin American Free Trade Association. The inherent disability of the collectively weak makes unlikely the attainment of the political aims of such efforts, however, at least as they relate to the paramount. There is evidence, also, that the economically counterproductive elements of LAFTA, injected into that organization for political reasons, are beginning to be questioned, especially as it becomes clear that the political goals are, in any case, unlikely of attainment.[1]

[1] At the March, 1966, annual meeting of IA-ECOSOC, the economic theories of ECLA were severely criticized, especially as they relate to import substitution and neglect of agriculture. See Pan American Union, *The Future of Latin America's Development and the Alliance for Progress* (Washington, 1966). As a result, the formerly autonomous, and ECLA-dominated, Panel of Experts was reduced from nine to five members, and incorporated into the Inter-American Committee for the Alliance for Progress. In protest, the members of the Panel resigned.

B / CONCLUSIONS

In any set of conclusions concerning the role of Latin America in world politics certain assumptions must be made. The assumption here is that, despite numerous well-intentioned efforts to transform the international system into something different, it will remain essentially the same, and will continue to exhibit the characteristics of a quasi-anarchic, hierarchical society. This assumption, may not, of course, be justified. There are two other reasonable possibilities—a world state achieved through world conquest, and the creation of fully anarchic conditions through an inconclusive general nuclear war. In the first instance, we would not be dealing with international politics any longer, but with some form of domestic politics, and, thus, many of our analyses and conclusions would not apply. In the second instance, analysis of any kind would have to wait until some sort of pattern emerged from chaos.

On the assumption, then, of a continuation of the present structure of international society, the Latin American countries will remain, for the forseeable future, client states. At present, they have none of the attributes, or even preconditions, for paramountcy, and some, in recent years, have, indeed, been moving in the opposite direction, toward greater dependence on the hemisphere paramount (Argentina is the prime example of this). The struggle for sub-paramountcy will, of course, continue, expanded into a three-way contest among Brazil, Argentina, and Mexico. The re-entry of Mexico into the lists is, of course, a product of her size and population, but, perhaps to an even greater extent, of her relatively long-term political and economic stability and economic growth, contrasted with chaotic political and economic conditions in Brazil and Argentina. For Mexico to extend a substantial influence into South America will be difficult, however, and a conceivable and, perhaps even likely, eventual hemispheric configuration will find the United States using Mexico as Caribbean sub-paramount, and either Argentina or Brazil as South American sub-paramount, depending upon the final outcome of their continuing struggle for regional power and influence.

As the Latin American states will remain clients,[2] the only question is, whose clients? Again, for the forseeable future, there are only two candidates, the United States and the Soviet Union. These are the only two international paramounts presently existing. A united Europe could quickly achieve paramount status, with client systems in Africa and the Middle East, and mainland China is attempting to gain paramount status, with a client-system in Asia. Even should both these efforts eventually prove successful, however, the strategic position of Latin America makes penetration of either of these powers into the Western Hemisphere to a degree sufficient for client detachment most unlikely for many years. The only reason the Soviet Union has been able to do it in the case of Cuba, and to threaten to do the same with other Latin American countries, is the fact that

---

[2] The geographic position of Latin America makes the possibility of any of the countries of the region attaining and maintaining floater status, even for a time, most unlikely.

its missile fleet enables it, in a sense, to bypass the American Navy, and, once having obtained a client, to threaten Armageddon, should there be an attempt to reverse the move. In other words, the Soviet missiles make it possible for that country to play something of the role the British Navy made it possible for Great Britain to play in the nineteenth century.

If, then, a Latin American country is not going to be a client of the United States, it will have to be a client of the Soviet Union, as Cuba has amply demonstrated. For any government, or people, that has as its principal values the development of consensual government and economic growth (and there are those, of course, who do not), the choice between the alternatives would appear to be quite clear. Few people and few states enjoy being in a subordinate position, but states must operate within the boundary limits of reality, and the United States is a much more permissive paramount than the Soviet Union. Even should the present liberalization trend continue in the Soviet bloc, it should be noted that the Soviet Union can afford to become somewhat more permissive, with reference to its Eastern European clients, because of their proximity to Soviet power. Similar degrees of permissiveness applied to any Western Hemisphere Soviet clients would invite loss of the client, because of the proximity of American power. Secondly, the Soviet Union cannot conceivably match, or even approach, the American capacity for paramount benevolence. Cuba, alone, strains the resources of the Soviet bloc. This point is made here entirely aside from the question of the general suitability of the Communist dogma as a strategy of economic development. Even in a depression, American capability for economic assistance would far outstrip that of the Soviets.

All this does not mean, of course, that the Latin American countries cannot continue to use the existence of the Cold War and the Soviet challenge for their own purposes. The loss of another Latin American client to the Soviet Union would be a blow at American power and prestige that the United States would go to almost any lengths to avoid. Some of the manifestations of that willingness, as in the case of the Dominican Republic, in 1965, may be distasteful to the Latin Americans, but they would do well to ponder the significance of that intervention as a reflection of American policy. Effectively manipulated, this policy can increase their foreign policy flexibility, and aid in the solution of their domestic social and economic problems.

Although not the central subject of this book, there are obviously lessons here for the United States as well. I leave the task of extracting them in all their complexity to others. I will only say here, that two of the most obvious and important lessons—two that are closely interrelated—are: that attainment of our foreign policy goals vis-à-vis Latin America could be more effective and efficient if we strove to confine our interpositions to matters directly concerning our national interests, foreign policy objectives, and continental security, and ceased trying to be either the conscience of the Latin Americans themselves, or the guarantor of private interests. At the same time, however, pursuit of legitimate foreign-policy objectives and continental security must be consistent, bold, and determined.

APPENDICES

THE MONROE DOCTRINE AND ITS COROLLARIES

The No-Transfer Resolution (1811)

Taking into view the peculiar situation of Spain and of her American provinces; and considering the influence which the destiny of the territory adjoining the southern border of the United States may have upon their security, tranquillity and commerce: Therefore,

RESOLVED by the Senate and House of Representatives of the United States of America, in Congress assembled, THAT the United States under the peculiar circumstances of the existing crisis, cannot, without serious inquietude, see any part of the said territory pass into the hands of any foreign power; and that a due regard to their own safety compels them to provide, under certain contingencies, for the temporary occupation of the said territory; they, at the same time, declare that the said territory shall, in their hands, remain subject to future negotiations.

The Monroe Doctrine (1823)

. . . the American continents, by the free and independent condition which they have assumed and maintain, are henceforth not to be considered as subjects for future colonization by any European powers.

. . . we would consider any attempt on their part to extend their system to any portions of this Hemisphere, as dangerous to our peace and safety . . . with the governments who have declared their independence, and have maintained it, and whose independence we have, on great consideration, and on just principles, acknowledged, we could not view any interposition for the purpose of oppressing them, or controlling in any other manner, their destiny, by any European power, in any other light, than as the manifestation of an unfriendly disposition toward the United States.

The Polk Corollary (1845)

The United States, sincerely desirous of preserving relations of good understanding with all nations, cannot in silence permit any European interference on the North American continent, and should any such interference be attempted will be ready to resist it at any and all hazards.

The Hayes Corollary (1889)

The policy of this country is a canal under American control. The United States can not consent to the surrender of this control to any European power, or to any combination of European powers.

The Olney Declaration (1895)

Today the United States is practically sovereign on this continent, and its fiat is law upon the subjects to which it confines its interposition . . . its infinite resources combined with its isolated position render it master of the situation and practically invulnerable as against any or all other powers. . . .

The Roosevelt Corollary (1904)

All that this country desires is to see the neighboring countries stable, orderly, and prosperous. Any country whose people conduct themselves well can count upon our hearty friendship. If a nation shows that it knows how to act with reasonable efficiency and decency in social and political matters, if it keeps order and pays its obligations, it need fear no interference from the United States. Chronic wrongdoing, or an impotence which results in a general loosening of the ties of civilized society, may in America, as elsewhere, ultimately require intervention by some civilized nation, and in the Western Hemisphere the adherence of the United States to the Monroe Doctrine may force the United States, however reluctantly, in flagrant cases of such wrongdoing or impotence, to the exercise of an international police power.

The Lodge Corollary (1912)

RESOLVED, THAT when any harbor or other place in the American continents is so situated that the occupation thereof for naval or military purposes might threaten the communications or the safety of the United States, the Government of the United States could not see without grave concern the possession of such harbor or other place by any corporation or association which has such a relation to another Government, not American, as to give that Government practical power of control for naval or military purposes.

The Clark Memorandum (1928)

The Doctrine states a case of United States vs. Europe, not of United States vs. Latin America.

Such arrangements as the United States has made, for example, with Cuba, Santo Domingo, Haiti, and Nicaragua, are not within the scope of the Doctrine as it was announced by Monroe. They may be accounted for as the expression of a national policy which, like the Doctrine itself, originates in the necessities of security or self-preservation—a policy which . . . was outlined in what is known as the "Roosevelt Corollary" to the Monroe Doctrine . . . ; but such arrangements are not covered by the terms of the Doctrine itself.

The Dulles Doctrine (1954)

. . . the domination or control of the political institutions of any American state by the international communist movement, extending to this Hemisphere the political system of an extracontinental power, would constitute a threat to the sovereignty and political independence of the American States, endangering the peace of America, and would call for a Meeting of Consultation to consider the adoption of appropriate action in accordance with existing treaties.

The Johnson Corollary (1965)

The American nations cannot, must not, and will not permit the establishment of another Communist government in the Western Hemisphere.

CHARTER OF THE ORGANIZATION OF AMERICAN STATES
(1948)

IN THE NAME OF THEIR PEOPLES, THE STATES REPRESENTED AT THE NINTH INTER-NATIONAL CONFERENCE OF AMERICAN STATES,

Convinced that the historic mission of America is to offer to man a land of liberty, and a favorable environment for the development of his personality and the realization of his just aspirations;

Conscious that that mission has already inspired numerous agreements, whose essential value lies in the desire of the American peoples to live together in peace, and, through their mutual understanding and respect for the sovereignty of each one, to provide for the betterment of all, in independence, in equality and under law;

Confident that the true significance of American solidarity and good neighbor-liness can only mean the consolidation on this continent, within the framework of democratic institutions, of a system of individual liberty and social justice based on respect for the essential rights of man;

Persuaded that their welfare and their contribution to the progress and the civilization of the world will increasingly require intensive continental cooperation;

RESOLVED to persevere in the noble undertaking that humanity has conferred upon the United Nations, whose principles and purposes they solemnly reaffirm;

Convinced that juridical organization is a necessary condition for security and peace founded on moral order and on justice; and

In accordance with Resolution IX of the Inter-American Conference on Problems of War and Peace, held at Mexico City,

HAVE AGREED
upon the following
CHARTER
OF THE ORGANIZATION OF
AMERICAN STATES
PART ONE
CHAPTER I
NATURE AND PURPOSES
ARTICLE 1

The American States establish by this Charter the international organization that they have developed to achieve an order of peace and justice, to promote their solidarity, to strengthen their collaboration, and to defend their sovereignty, their territorial integrity and their independence. Within the United Nations, the Organization of American States is a regional agency.

ARTICLE 2

All American States that ratify the present Charter are Members of the Organization.

ARTICLE 3

Any new political entity that arises from the union of several Member States and that, as such, ratifies the present Charter, shall become a Member of the Organization. The entry of the new political entity into the Organization shall result in a loss of membership of each one of the States which constitute it.

ARTICLE 4

The Organization of American States, in order to put into practice the principles on which it is founded and to fulfill its regional obligations under the Charter of the United Nations, proclaims the following essential purposes:

a.) To strengthen the peace and security of the continent;

b.) To prevent possible causes of difficulties and to ensure the pacific settlement of disputes that may arise among the Member States;

c.) To provide for common action on the part of those States in the event of aggression:

d.) To seek the solution of political, juridical and economic problems that may arise among them; and

e.) To promote, by cooperative action, their economic, social and cultural development.

CHAPTER II
PRINCIPLES
ARTICLE 5

The American States reaffirm the following principles:

a.) International law is the standard of conduct of States in their reciprocal relations;

b.) International order consists essentially of respect for the personality, sovereignty and independence of States, and the faithful fulfillment of obligations derived from treaties and other sources of international law;

c.) Good faith shall govern the relations between States;

d.) The solidarity of the American States and the high aims which are sought through it require the political organization of those States on the basis of the effective exercise of representative democracy;

e.) The American States condemn wars of aggression: victory does not give rights;

f.) An act of aggression against one American State is an act of aggression against all the other American States;

g.) Controversies of an international character arising between two or more American States shall be settled by peaceful procedures;

h.) Social justice and social security are bases of lasting peace;

i.) Economic cooperation is essential to the common welfare and prosperity of the peoples of the continent;

j.) The American States proclaim the fundamental rights of the individual without distinction as to race, nationality, creed or sex;

k.) The spiritual unity of the continent is based on respect for the cultural values of the American countries and requires their close cooperation for the high purposes of civilization;

l.) The education of peoples should be directed toward justice, freedom and peace.

CHAPTER III
FUNDAMENTAL RIGHTS AND DUTIES OF STATES
ARTICLE 6

States are juridically equal, enjoy equal rights and equal capacity to exercise these rights, and have equal duties. The rights of each State depend not upon its power to ensure the exercise thereof, but upon the mere fact of its existence as a person under international law.

ARTICLE 7

Every American State has the duty to respect the rights enjoyed by every other State in accordance with international law.

ARTICLE 8

The fundamental rights of States may not be impaired in any manner whatsoever.

ARTICLE 9

The political existence of the State is independent of recognition by other States. Even before being recognized, the State has the right to defend its integrity and independence, to provide for its preservation and prosperity, and consequently to organize itself as it sees fit, to legislate concerning its interests, to administer its services, and to determine the jurisdiction and competence of its courts. The exercise of these rights is limited only by the exercise of the rights of other States in accordance with international law.

ARTICLE 10

Recognition implies that the State granting it accepts the personality of the new State, with all the rights and duties that international law prescribes for the two States.

ARTICLE 11

The right of each State to protect itself and to live its own life does not authorize it to commit unjust acts against another State.

ARTICLE 12

The jurisdiction of States within the limits of their national territory is exercised equally over all the inhabitants, whether nationals or aliens.

ARTICLE 13

Each State has the right to develop its cultural, political and economic life freely and naturally. In this free development, the State shall respect the rights of the individual and the principles of universal morality.

ARTICLE 14

Respect for and the faithful observance of treaties constitute standards for the development of peaceful relations among States. International treaties and agreements should be public.

ARTICLE 15

No State or group of States has the right to intervene, directly or indirectly, for any reason whatsoever, in the internal or external affairs of any other State. The foregoing principle prohibits not only armed force but also any other form of interference or attempted threat against the personality of the State or against its political, economic and cultural elements.

ARTICLE 16

No State may use or encourage the use of coercive measures of an economic or political character in order to force the sovereign will of another State and obtain from it advantages of any kind.

ARTICLE 17

The territory of a State is inviolable; it may not be the object, even temporarily, of military occupation or of other measures of force taken by another State, directly or indirectly, on any grounds whatever. No territorial acquisitions or special advantages obtained either by force or by other means of coercion shall be recognized.

ARTICLE 18

The American States bind themselves in their international relations not to have recourse to the use of force, except in the case of self-defense in accordance with existing treaties or in fulfillment thereof.

ARTICLE 19

Measures adopted for the maintenance of peace and security in accordance with existing treaties do not constitute a violation of the principles set forth in ARTICLES 15 and 17.

CHAPTER IV
PACIFIC SETTLEMENT OF DISPUTES
ARTICLE 20

All international disputes that may arise between American States shall be submitted to the peaceful procedures set forth in this Charter, before being referred to the Security Council of the United Nations.

ARTICLE 21

The following are peaceful procedures: direct negotiation, good offices, mediation, investigation and conciliation, judicial settlement, arbitration, and those which the parties to the dispute may especially agree upon at any time.

ARTICLE 22

In the event that a dispute arises between two or more American States which, in the opinion of one of them, cannot be settled through the usual diplomatic channels, the Parties shall agree on some other peaceful procedure that will enable them to reach a solution.

ARTICLE 23

A special treaty will establish adequate procedures for the pacific settlement of disputes and will determine the appropriate means for their application, so that no dispute between American States shall fail of definitive settlement within a reasonable period.

CHAPTER V
COLLECTIVE SECURITY
ARTICLE 24

Every act of aggression by a State against the territorial integrity or the inviolability of the territory or against the sovereignty or political independence of an American State shall be considered an act of aggression against the other American States.

ARTICLE 25

If the inviolability or the integrity of the territory or the sovereignty or political independence of any American State should be affected by an armed attack or by an act of aggression that is not an armed attack, or by an extra-continental conflict, or by a conflict between two or more American States, or by any other fact or situation that might endanger the peace of America, the American States, in furtherance of the principles of continental solidarity or collective self-defense, shall apply the measures and procedures established in the special treaties on the subject.

CHAPTER VI
ECONOMIC STANDARDS
ARTICLE 26

The Member States agree to cooperate with one another, as far as their resources may permit and their laws may provide, in the broadest spirit of good neighborliness, in order to strengthen their economic structure, develop their agriculture and mining, promote their industry and increase their trade.

ARTICLE 27
If the economy of an American State is affected by serious conditions that cannot be satisfactorily remedied by its own unaided effort, such State may place its economic problems before the Inter-American Economic and Social Council to seek through consultation the most appropriate solution for such problems.

CHAPTER VII
SOCIAL STANDARDS
ARTICLE 28
The Member States agree to cooperate with one another to achieve just and decent living conditions for their entire populations.

ARTICLE 29
The Member States agree upon the desirability of developing their social legislation on the following bases:

a.) All human beings, without distinction as to race, nationality, sex, creed or social condition, have the right to attain material wellbeing and spiritual growth under circumstances of liberty, dignity, equality of opportunity, and economic security;

b.) Work is a right and social duty; it shall not be considered as an article of commerce; it demands respect for freedom of association and for the dignity of the worker; and it is to be performed under conditions that ensure life, health and a decent standard of living, both during the working years and during old age, or when any circumstance deprives the individual of the possibility of working.

CHAPTER VIII
CULTURAL STANDARDS
ARTICLE 30
The Member States agree to promote, in accordance with their constitutional provisions and their material resources, the exercise of the right to education, on the following bases:

a.) Elementary education shall be compulsory and, when provided by the State, shall be without cost;

b.) Higher education shall be available to all, without distinction as to race, nationality, sex, language, creed or social condition.

ARTICLE 31
With due consideration for the national character of each State, the Member States undertake to facilitate free cultural interchange by every medium of expression.

PART TWO
CHAPTER IX
THE ORGANS
ARTICLE 32
The Organization of American States accomplishes its purposes by means of:

a.) The Inter-American Conference;

b.) The Meeting of Consultation of Ministers of Foreign Affairs;

c.) The Council;

d.) The Pan American Union;

e.) The Specialized Conferences; and

f.) The Specialized Organizations.

CHAPTER X

THE INTER-AMERICAN CONFERENCE

ARTICLE 33

The Inter-American Conference is the supreme organ of the Organization of American States. It decides the general action and policy of the Organization and determines the structure and functions of its Organs, and has the authority to consider any matter relating to friendly relations among the American States. These functions shall be carried out in accordance with the provisions of this Charter and of other inter-American treaties.

ARTICLE 34

All Member States have the right to be represented at the Inter-American Conference. Each State has the right to one vote.

ARTICLE 35

The Conference shall convene every five years at the time fixed by the Council of the Organization, after consultation with the government of the country where the Conference is to be held.

ARTICLE 36

In special circumstances and with the approval of two-thirds of the American Governments, a special Inter-American Conference may be held, or the date of the next regular Conference may be changed.

ARTICLE 37

Each Inter-American Conference shall designate the place of meeting of the next Conference. If for any unforeseen reason the Conference cannot be held at the place designated, the Council of the Organization shall designate a new place.

ARTICLE 38

The program and regulations of the Inter-American Conference shall be prepared by the Council of the Organization and submitted to the Member States for consideration.

CHAPTER XI

THE MEETING OF CONSULTATION OF MINISTERS OF FOREIGN AFFAIRS

ARTICLE 39

The Meeting of Consultation of Ministers of Foreign Affairs shall be held in order to consider problems of an urgent nature and of common interest to the American States, and to serve as the Organ of Consultation.

ARTICLE 40

Any Member State may request that a Meeting of Consultation be called. The request shall be addressed to the Council of the Organization, which shall decide by an absolute majority whether a meeting should be held.

ARTICLE 41

The program and regulations of the Meeting of Consultation shall be prepared by the Council of the Organization and submitted to the Member States for consideration.

ARTICLE 42

If, for exceptional reasons, a Minister of Foreign Affairs is unable to attend the meeting, he shall be represented by a special delegate.

ARTICLE 43

In case of an armed attack within the territory of an American State or within the region of security delimited by treaties in force, a Meeting of Consultation shall be held without delay. Such Meeting shall be called immediately by the Chairman of the Council of the Organization, who at the same time shall call a meeting of the Council itself.

ARTICLE 44

An Advisory Defense Committee shall be established to advise the Organ of Consultation on problems of military cooperation that may arise in connection with the application of existing special treaties on collective security.

ARTICLE 45

The Advisory Defense Committee shall be composed of the highest military authorities of the American States participating in the Meeting of Consultation. Under exceptional circumstances the Governments may appoint substitutes. Each State shall be entitled to one vote.

ARTICLE 46

The Advisory Defense Committee shall be convoked under the same conditions as the Organ of Consultation, when the latter deals with matters relating to defense against aggression.

ARTICLE 47

The Committee shall also meet when the Conference or the Meeting of Consultation or the Governments, by a two-thirds majority of the Member States, assign to it technical studies or reports on specific subjects.

CHAPTER XII
THE COUNCIL
ARTICLE 48

The Council of the Organization of American States is composed of one Representative of each Member State of the Organization, especially appointed by the respective Government, with the rank of Ambassador. The appointment may be given to the diplomatic representative accredited to the Government of the country in which the Council has its seat. During the absence of the titular Representative, the Government may appoint an interim Representative.

ARTICLE 49

The Council shall elect a Chairman and a Vice Chairman, who shall serve for one year and shall not be eligible for election to either of those positions for the term immediately following.

ARTICLE 50

The Council takes cognizance, within the limits of the present Charter and of Inter-American treaties and agreements, of any matter referred to it by the Inter-American Conference or the Meeting of Consultation of Ministers of Foreign Affairs.

ARTICLE 51

The Council shall be responsible for the proper discharge by the Pan American Union of the duties assigned to it.

ARTICLE 52

The Council shall serve provisionally as the Organ of Consultation when the circumstances contemplated in ARTICLE 43 of this Charter arise.

ARTICLE 53

It is also the duty of the Council:

a.) To draft and submit to the Governments and to the Inter-American Conference proposals for the creation of new Specialized Organizations or for the combination, adaptation or elimination of existing ones, including matters relating to the financing and support thereof:

b.) To draft recommendations to the Governments, the Inter-American Conference, the Specialized Conferences or the Specialized Organizations, for the coordination of the activities and programs of such organizations, after consultation with them;

c.) To conclude agreements with the Inter-American Specialized Organizations to determine the relations that shall exist between the respective agency and the Organization;

d.) To conclude agreements or special arrangements for cooperation with other American organizations of recognized international standing;

e.) To promote and facilitate collaboration between the Organization of American States and the United Nations, as well as between Inter-American Specialized Organizations and similar international agencies;

f.) To adopt resolutions that will enable the Secretary General to perform the duties envisaged in ARTICLE 84;

g.) To perform the other duties assigned to it by the present Charter.

ARTICLE 54

The Council shall establish the bases for fixing the quota that each Government is to contribute to the maintenance of the Pan American Union, taking into account the ability to pay of the respective countries and their determination to contribute in an equitable manner. The budget, after approval by the Council, shall be transmitted to the Governments at least six months before the first day of the fiscal year, with a statement of the annual quota of each country. Decisions on budgetary matters require the approval of two-thirds of the Members of the Council.

ARTICLE 55

The Council shall formulate its own regulations.

ARTICLE 56

The Council shall function at the seat of the Pan American Union.

ARTICLE 57

The following are organs of the Council of the Organization of American States:

a.) The Inter-American Economic and Social Council;

b.) The Inter-American Council of Jurists; and

c.) The Inter-American Cultural Council.

ARTICLE 58

The Organs referred to in the preceding ARTICLE shall have technical autonomy within the limits of this Charter; but their decisions shall not encroach upon the sphere of action of the Council of the Organization.

ARTICLE 59

The Organs of the Council of the Organization are composed of representatives of all the Member States of the Organization.

ARTICLE 60

The Organs of the Council of the Organization shall, as far as possible, render to the Governments such technical services as the latter may request; and they shall advise the Council of the Organization on matters within their jurisdiction.

ARTICLE 61

The Organs of the Council of the Organization shall, in agreement with the Council, establish cooperative relations with the corresponding organs of the United Nations and with the national or international agencies that function within their respective spheres of action.

ARTICLE 62

The Council of the Organization, with the advice of the appropriate bodies and after consultation with the Governments, shall formulate the statutes of its Organs in accordance with and in the execution of the provisions of this Charter. The Organs shall formulate their own regulations.

A.) The Inter-American Economic and Social Council

ARTICLE 63

The Inter-American Economic and Social Council has for its principal purpose the promotion of the economic and social welfare of the American nations through effective cooperation for the better utilization of their natural resources, the development of their agriculture and industry and the raising of the standards of living of their peoples.

ARTICLE 64

To accomplish this purpose the Council shall;

a.) Propose the means by which the American nations may give each other technical assistance in making studies and formulating and executing plans to carry out the purpose referred to in ARTICLE 26 and to develop and improve their social services;

b.) Act as coordinating agency for all official inter-American activities of an economic and social nature;

c.) Undertake studies on its own initiative or at the request of any Member State;

d.) Asemble and prepare reports on economic and social matters for the use of the Member States;

e.) Suggest to the Council of the Organization the advisability of holding specialized conferences on economic and social matters;

f.) Carry on such other activities as may be assigned to it by the Inter-American Conference, the Meeting of Consultation of Ministers of Foreign Affairs, or the Council of the Organization.

ARTICLE 65

The Inter-American Economic and Social Council, composed of technical delegates appointed by each Member State, shall meet on its own initiative or on that of the Council of the Organization.

ARTICLE 66

The Inter-American Economic and Social Council shall function at the seat of the Pan American Union, but it may hold meetings in any American city by a majority decision of the Member States.

B.) *The Inter-American Council of Jurists*

ARTICLE 67

The purpose of the Inter-American Council of Jurists is to serve as an advisory body on juridical matters; to promote the development and codification of public and private international law; and to study the possibility of attaining uniformity in the legislation of the various American countries, insofar as it may appear desirable.

ARTICLE 68

The Inter-American Juridical Committee of Rio de Janeiro shall be the permanent committee of the Inter-American Council of Jurists.

ARTICLE 69

The Juridical Committee shall be composed of jurists of the nine countries selected by the Inter-American Conference. The selection of the jurists shall be made by the Inter-American Council of Jurists from a panel submitted by each country chosen by the Conference. The Members of the Juridical Committee represent all Member States of the Organization. The Council of the Organization is empowered to fill any vacancies that occur during the intervals between Inter-American Conferences and between Meetings of the Inter-American Council of Jurists.

ARTICLE 70

The Juridical Committee shall undertake such studies and preparatory work as are assigned to it by the Inter-American Council of Jurists, the Inter-American Conference, the Meeting of Consultation of Ministers of Foreign Affairs, or the Council of the Organization. It may also undertake those studies and projects which, on its own initiative, it considers advisable.

ARTICLE 71

The Inter-American Council of Jurists and the Juridical Committee should seek the cooperation of national committees for the codification of international law, of institutes of international and comparative law, and of other specialized agencies.

ARTICLE 72

The Inter-American Council of Jurists shall meet when convened by the Council of the Organization, at the place determined by the Council of Jurists at its previous meeting.

C.) *The Inter-American Cultural Council*

ARTICLE 73

The purpose of the Inter-American Cultural Council is to promote friendly relations and mutual understanding among the American peoples, in order to strengthen the peaceful sentiments that have characterized the evolution of America, through the promotion of educational, scientific and cultural exchange.

ARTICLE 74

To this end the principal functions of the Council shall be:

a.) To sponsor inter-American cultural activities;

b.) To collect and supply information on cultural activities carried on in and among the American States by private and official agencies both national and international in character;

c.) To promote the adoption of basic educational programs adapted to the needs of all population groups in the American countries;

d.) To promote, in addition, the adoption of special programs of training, education and culture for the indigenous groups of the American countries;

e.) To cooperate in the protection, preservation and increase of the cultural heritage of the continent;

f.) To promote cooperation among the American nations in the fields of education, science and culture, by means of the exchange of materials for research and study, as well as the exchange of teachers, students, specialists and, in general, such other persons and materials as are useful for the realization for these ends;

g.) To encourage the education of the peoples for harmonious international relations;

h.) To carry on such other activities as may be assigned to it by the Inter-American Conference, the Meeting of Consultation of Ministers of Foreign Affairs, or the Council of the Organization.

ARTICLE 75

The Inter-American Cultural Council shall determine the place of its next meeting and shall be convened by the Council of the Organization on the date chosen by the latter in agreement with the Government of the country selected as the seat of the meeting.

ARTICLE 76

There shall be a Committee for Cultural Action of which five States, chosen at each Inter-American Conference, shall be members. The individuals composing the Committee for Cultural Action shall be selected by the Inter-American Cultural Council from a panel submitted by each country chosen by the Conference, and they shall be specialists in education or cultural matters. When the Inter-American Cultural Council and the Inter-American Conference are not in session, the Council of the Organization may fill vacancies that arise and replace those countries that find it necessary to discontinue their cooperation.

ARTICLE 77

The Committee for Cultural Action shall function as the permanent committee of the Inter-American Cultural Council, for the purpose of preparing any studies that the latter may assign to it. With respect to these studies the Council shall have the final decision.

CHAPTER XIII
THE PAN AMERICAN UNION
ARTICLE 78

The Pan American Union is the central and permanent organ of the Organization of American States and the General Secretariat of the Organization. It shall perform the duties assigned to it in other inter-American treaties and agreements.

ARTICLE 79

There shall be a Secretary General of the Organization, who shall be elected by the Council for a ten-year term and who may not be re-elected or be succeeded by a person of the same nationality. In the event of a vacancy in the office of Secretary General, the Council shall, within the next ninety days, elect a successor to fill the office for the remainder of the term, who may be re-elected if the vacancy occurs during the second half of the term.

ARTICLE 80

The Secretary General shall direct the Pan American Union and be the legal representative thereof.

ARTICLE 81

The Secretary General shall participate with voice, but without vote, in the deliberations of the Inter-American Conference, the Meeting of Consultation of Ministers of Foreign Affairs, the Specialized Conferences, and the Council and its Organs.

ARTICLE 82

The Pan American Union, through its technical and information offices, shall under the direction of the Council, promote economic, social, juridical and cultural relations among all the Member States of the Organization.

ARTICLE 83

The Pan American Union shall also perform the following functions:

a.) Transmit *ex officio* to Member States the convocation to the Inter-American Conference, the Meeting of Consultation of Ministers of Foreign Affairs, and the Specialized Conferences;

b.) Advise the Council and its Organs in the preparation of programs and regulations of the Inter-American Conference, the Meeting of Consultation of Ministers of Foreign Affairs, and the Specialized Conferences;

c.) Place, to the extent of its ability, at the disposal of the Government of the country where a conference is to be held, the technical aid and personnel which such Government may request;

d.) Serve as custodian of the documents and archives of the Inter-American Conference, of the Meeting of Consultation of Ministers of Foreign Affairs, and, insofar as possible, of the Specialized Conferences;

e.) Serve as depository of the instruments of ratification of inter-American agreements;

f.) Perform the functions entrusted to it by the Inter-American Conference and the Meeting of Consultation of Ministers of Foreign Affairs;

g.) Submit to the Council an annual report on the activities of the Organization;

h.) Submit to the Inter-American Conference a report on the work accomplished by the Organs of the Organization since the previous Conference.

ARTICLE 84

It is the duty of the Secretary General:

a.) To establish, with the approval of the Council, such technical and administrative offices of the Pan American Union as are necessary to accomplish its purposes;

b.) To determine the number of department heads, officers and employees of the Pan American Union; to appoint them, regulate their powers and duties, and fix their compensation, in accordance with general standards established by the Council.

ARTICLE 85

There shall be an Assistant Secretary General, elected by the Council for a term of ten years and eligible for re-election. In the event of a vacancy in the office of Assistant Secretary General, the Council shall, within the next ninety days, elect a successor to fill such office for the remainder of the term.

ARTICLE 86

The Assistant Secretary General shall be the Secretary of the Council. He shall perform the duties of the Secretary General during the temporary absence or disability of the latter, or during the ninety-day vacancy referred to in ARTICLE 79. He shall also serve as advisory officer to the Secretary General, with the power to act as his delegate in all matters that the Secretary General may entrust to him.

ARTICLE 87

The Council, by a two-thirds vote of its members, may remove the Secretary General or the Assistant Secretary General whenever the proper functioning of the Organization so demands.

ARTICLE 88

The heads of the respective departments of the Pan American Union, appointed by the Secretary General, shall be the Executive Secretaries of the Inter-American Economic and Social Council, the Council of Jurists and the Cultural Council.

ARTICLE 89

In the performance of their duties the personnel shall not seek or receive instructions from any Government or from any other authority outside the Pan American Union. They shall refrain from any action that might reflect upon their position as international officials responsible only to the Union.

ARTICLE 90

Every Member of the Organization of American States pledges itself to respect the exclusively international character of the responsibilities of the Secretary General and the personnel, and not to seek to influence them in the discharge of their duties.

ARTICLE 91

In selecting its personnel the Pan American Union shall give first consideration to efficiency, competence and integrity; but at the same time importance shall be given to the necessity of recruiting personnel on as broad a geographical basis as possible.

ARTICLE 92

The seat of the Pan American Union is the city of Washington.

CHAPTER XIV
THE SPECIALIZED CONFERENCES
ARTICLE 93

The Specialized Conferences shall meet to deal with special technical matters or to develop specific aspects of inter-American cooperation, when it is so decided by the Inter-American Conference or the Meeting of Consultation of Ministers of Foreign Affairs; when inter-American agreements so provide; or when the Council of the Organization considers it necessary, either on its own initiative or at the request of one of its Organs or of one of the Specialized Organizations.

ARTICLE 94

The program and regulations of the Specialized Conferences shall be prepared by the Organs of the Council of the Organization or by the Specialized Organizations concerned; they shall be submitted to the Member Governments for consideration and transmitted to the Council for its information.

CHAPTER XV
THE SPECIALIZED ORGANIZATIONS
ARTICLE 95

For the purposes of the present Charter, Inter-American Specialized Organizations are the inter-governmental organizations established by multilateral agreements and having specific functions with respect to technical matters of common interest to the American States.

ARTICLE 96
The Council shall, for the purposes stated in ARTICLE 53, maintain a register of the Organizations that fulfill the conditions set forth in the foregoing ARTICLE.

ARTICLE 97
The Specialized Organizations shall enjoy the fullest technical autonomy and shall take into account the recommendations of the Council, in conformity with the provisions of the present Charter.

ARTICLE 98
The Specialized Organizations shall submit to the Council periodic reports on the progress of their work and on their annual budgets and expenses.

ARTICLE 99
Agreements between the Council and the Specialized Organizations contemplated in Paragraph c.) of ARTICLE 53 may provide that such Organizations transmit their budgets to the Council for approval. Arrangements may also be made for the Pan American Union to receive the quotas of the contributing countries and distribute them in accordance with the said agreements.

ARTICLE 100
The Specialized Organizations shall establish cooperative relations with world agencies of the same character in order to coordinate their activities. In concluding agreements with international agencies of a world-wide character, the Inter-American Specialized Organizations shall preserve their identity and their status as integral parts of the Organization of American States, even when they perform regional functions of international agencies.

ARTICLE 101
In determining the geographic location of the Specialized Organizations the interests of all the American States shall be taken into account.

PART THREE
CHAPTER XVI
THE UNITED NATIONS
ARTICLE 102
None of the provisions of this Charter shall be construed as impairing the rights and obligations of the Member States under the Charter of the United Nations.

CHAPTER XVII
MISCELLANEOUS PROVISIONS
ARTICLE 103
The Organization of American States shall enjoy in the territory of each Member such legal capacity, privileges and immunities as are necessary for the exercise of its functions and the accomplishment of its purposes.

ARTICLE 104
The Representatives of the Governments on the Council of the Organization, the Representatives on the Organs of the Council, the personnel of their delegations, as

well as the Secretary General and the Assistant Secretary General of the Organization, shall enjoy the privileges and immunities necessary for the independent performance of their duties.

ARTICLE 105

The juridical status of the Inter-American Specialized Organizations and the privileges and immunities that should be granted to them and their personnel, as well as to the officials of the Pan American Union, shall be determined in each case through agreements between the respective Organizations and the Governments concerned.

ARTICLE 106

Correspondence of the Organization of American States, including printed matter and parcels, bearing the frank thereof, shall be carried free of charge in the mails of the Member States.

ARTICLE 107

The Organization of American States does not recognize any restriction on the eligibility of men and women to participate in the activities of the various Organs and to hold positions therein.

CHAPTER XVIII
RATIFICATION AND ENTRY INTO FORCE
ARTICLE 108

The present Charter shall remain open for signature by the American States and shall be ratified in accordance with their respective constitutional procedures. The original instrument, the Spanish, English, Portuguese and French texts of which are equally authentic, shall be deposited with the Pan American Union, which shall transmit certified copies thereof to the Governments for purposes of ratification. The instruments of ratification shall be deposited with the Pan American Union, which shall notify the signatory States of such deposit.

ARTICLE 109

The present Charter shall enter into force among the ratifying States when two-thirds of the signatory States have deposited their ratifications. It shall enter into force with respect to the remaining States in the order in which they deposit their ratifications.

ARTICLE 110

The present Charter shall be registered with the Secretariat of the United Nations through the Pan American Union.

ARTICLE 111

Amendments to the present Charter may be adopted only at an Inter-American Conference convened for that purpose. Amendments shall enter into force in accordance with the terms and the procedure set forth in ARTICLE 109.

ARTICLE 112

The present Charter shall remain in force indefinitely, but may be denounced by any Member State upon written notification to the Pan American Union, which shall communicate to all the others each notice of denunciation received. After two years from the date on which the Pan American Union receives a notice of denunciation, the present Charter shall cease to be in force with respect to the denouncing State, which shall cease to belong to the Organization after it has fulfilled the obligations arising from the present Charter.

INTER-AMERICAN TREATY
OF RECIPROCAL ASSISTANCE
(RIO TREATY, 1947)

In the name of their Peoples, the Governments represented at the Inter-American Conference for the Maintenance of Continental Peace and Security, desirous of consolidating and strengthening their relations of friendship and good neighborliness, and

CONSIDERING:

THAT Resolution VIII of the Inter-American Conference on problems of War and Peace, which met in Mexico City, recommended the conclusion of a treaty to prevent and repel threats and acts of aggression against any of the countries of America;

THAT the High Contracting Parties reiterate their will to remain united in an inter-American system consistent with the purposes and principles of the United Nations, and reaffirm the existence of the agreement which they have concluded concerning those matters relating to the maintenance of international peace and security which are appropriate for regional action;

THAT the High Contracting Parties reaffirm their adherence to the principles of inter-American solidarity and cooperation, and especially to those set forth in the preamble and declarations of the Act of Chapultepec, all of which should be understood to be accepted as standards of their mutual relations and as the juridical basis of the Inter-American System;

THAT the American States propose, in order to improve the procedures for the pacific settlement of their controversies, to conclude the treaty concerning the "Inter-American Peace System" envisaged in Resolutions IX and XXXIX of the Inter-American Conference on Problems of War and Peace,

THAT the obligation of mutual assistance and common defense of the American Republics is essentially related to their democratic ideals and to their will to cooperate permanently in the fulfillment of the principles and purposes of a policy of peace;

THAT the American regional community affirms as a manifest truth that juridical organization is a necessary prerequisite of security and peace, and that peace is founded on justice and moral order and, consequently, on the international recognition and protection of human rights and freedoms, on the indispensable well being of the people, and on the effectiveness of democracy for the international realization of justice and security,

HAVE RESOLVED, in conformity with the objectives stated above, to conclude the following Treaty, in order to assure peace, through adequate means, to provide for effective reciprocal assistance to meet armed attacks against any American State, and in order to deal with threats of aggression against any of them:

ARTICLE 1
The High Contracting Parties formally condemn war and undertake in their international relations not to resort to the threat or the use of force in any manner inconsistent with the provisions of the Charter of the United Nations or of this Treaty.

ARTICLE 2
As a consequence of the principle set forth in the preceding ARTICLE, the High Contracting Parties undertake to submit every controversy which may arise between them to methods of peaceful settlement and to endeavor to settle any such controversy among themselves by means of the procedures in force in the Inter-American System before referring it to the General Assembly or the Security Council of the United Nations.

ARTICLE 3

1.) The High Contracting Parties agree that an armed attack by any State against an American State shall be considered as an attack against all the American States and, consequently, each one of the said Contracting Parties undertakes to assist in meeting the attack in the exercise of the inherent right of individual or collective self-defense recognized by ARTICLE 51 of the Charter of the United Nations.

2.) On the request of the State or States directly attacked and until the decision of the Organ of Consultation of the Inter-American System, each one of the Contracting Parties may determine the immediate measures which it may individually take in fulfillment of the obligation contained in the preceding paragraph and in accordance with the principle of continental solidarity. The Organ of Consultation shall meet without delay for the purpose of examining those measures and agreeing upon the measures of a collective character that should be taken.

3.) The provisions of this ARTICLE shall be applied in case of any armed attack which takes place within the region described in ARTICLE 4 or within the territory of an American State. When the attack takes place outside of the said areas, the provisions of ARTICLE 6 shall be applied.

4.) Measures of self-defense provided for under this ARTICLE may be taken until the Security Council of the United Nations has taken the measures necessary to maintain international peace and security.

ARTICLE 4

The region to which this Treaty refers is bounded as follows: beginning at the North Pole; thence due south to a point 74 degrees north latitude, 10 degrees west longitude; thence by a rhumb line to a point 47 degrees 30 minutes north latitude, 50 degrees west longitude; thence by a rhumb line to a point 35 degrees north latitude, 60 degrees west longitude; thence due south to a point in 20 degrees north latitude; thence by a rhumb line to a point 5 degrees north latitude, 24 degrees west longitude; thence due south to the South Pole; thence due north to a point 30 degrees south latitude, 90 degrees west longitude; thence by a rhumb line to a point on the Equator at 97 degrees west longitude; thence by a rhumb line to a point 15 degrees north latitude, 120 degrees west longitude; thence by a rhumb line to a point 50 degrees north latitude, 170 degrees east longitude; thence due north to a point in 54 degrees north latitude; thence by a rhumb line to a point 65 degrees 30 minutes north latitude, 168 degrees 58 minutes 5 seconds west longitude; thence due north to the North Pole.

ARTICLE 5

The High Contracting Parties shall immediately send to the Security Council of the United Nations, in conformity with ARTICLES 51 and 54 of the Charter of the United Nations, complete information concerning the activities undertaken or in contemplation in the exercise of the right of self-defense or for the purpose of maintaining inter-American peace and security.

ARTICLE 6

If the inviolability or the integrity of the territory or the sovereignty or political independence of any American State should be affected by an aggression which is not an armed attack or by an extra-continental or intra-continental conflict, or by any other fact or situation that might endanger the peace of America, the Organ of Consultation shall meet immediately in order to agree on the measures which must be taken in case of aggression to assist the victim of the aggression, or, in any case, the measures which should be taken for the common defense and for the maintenance of the peace and security of the Continent.

ARTICLE 7

In the case of a conflict between two or more American States, without prejudice to the right of self-defense in conformity with ARTICLE 51 of the Charter of the

United Nations, the High Contracting Parties, meeting in consultation shall call upon the contending States to suspend hostilities and restore matters to the *statu quo ante bellum,* and shall take in addition all other necessary measures to re-establish or maintain inter-American peace and security and for the solution of the conflict by peaceful means. The rejection of the pacifying action will be considered in the determination of the aggressor and in the application of the measures which the consultative meeting may agree upon.

ARTICLE 8

For the purposes of this Treaty, the measures on which the Organ of Consultation may agree will comprise one or more of the following: recall of chiefs of diplomatic missions; breaking of diplomatic relations; breaking of consular relations; partial or complete interruption of economic relations or of rail, sea, air, postal, telegraphic, telephonic, and radio-telephonic communications; and use of armed force.

ARTICLE 9

In addition to other acts which the Organ of Consultation may characterize as aggression, the following shall be considered as such:

a.) Unprovoked armed attack by a State against the territory, the people, or the land, sea or air forces of another State;

b.) Invasion, by the armed forces of a State, of the territory of an American State, through the trespassing of boundaries demarcated in accordance with a treaty, judicial decision, or arbitral award, or, in the absence of frontiers thus demarcated, invasion affecting a region which is under the effective jurisdiction of another State.

ARTICLE 10

None of the provisions of this Treaty shall be construed as impairing the rights and obligations of the High Contracting Parties under the Charter of the United Nations.

ARTICLE 11

The consultations to which this Treaty refers shall be carried out by means of the Meetings of Ministers of Foreign Affairs of the American Republics which have ratified the Treaty, or in the manner or by the organ which in the future may be agreed upon.

ARTICLE 12

The Governing Board of the Pan American Union may act provisionally as an organ of consultation until the meeting of the Organ of Consultation referred to in the preceding ARTICLE takes place.

ARTICLE 13

The consultations shall be initiated at the request addressed to the Governing Board of the Pan American Union by any of the Signatory States which has ratified the Treaty.

ARTICLE 14

In the voting referred to in this Treaty only the representatives of the Signatory States which have ratified the Treaty may take part.

ARTICLE 15

The Governing Board of the Pan American Union shall act in all matters concerning this Treaty as an organ of liaison among the Signatory States which have ratified this Treaty and between these States and the United Nations.

ARTICLE 16

The decisions of the Governing Board of the Pan American Union referred to in ARTICLES 13 and 15 above shall be taken by an absolute majority of the Members entitled to vote.

ARTICLE 17

The Organ of Consultation shall take its decisions by a vote of two-thirds of the Signatory States which have ratified the Treaty.

ARTICLE 18

In the case of a situation or dispute between American States, the parties directly interested shall be excluded from the voting referred to in the two preceding ARTICLES.

ARTICLE 19

To constitute a quorum in all the meetings referred to in the previous ARTICLES, it shall be necessary that the number of States represented shall be at least equal to the number of votes necessary for the taking of the decision.

ARTICLE 20

Decisions which require the application of the measures specified in ARTICLE 8 shall be binding upon all the Signatory States which have ratified this Treaty, with the sole exception that no State shall be required to use armed force without its consent.

ARTICLE 21

The measures agreed upon by the Organ of Consultation shall be executed through the procedures and agencies now existing or those which may in the future be established.

ARTICLE 22

This Treaty shall come into effect between the States which ratify it as soon as the ratifications of two-thirds of the Signatory States have been deposited.

ARTICLE 23

This Treaty is open for signature by the American States at the city of Rio de Janeiro, and shall be ratified by the Signatory States as soon as possible in accordance with their respective constitutional processes. The ratifications shall be deposited with the Pan American Union, which shall notify the Signatory States of each deposit. Such notification shall be considered as an exchange of ratifications.

ARTICLE 24

The present Treaty shall be registered with the Secretariat of the United Nations through the Pan American Union, when two-thirds of the Signatory States have deposited their ratifications.

ARTICLE 25

This Treaty shall remain in force indefinitely, but may be denounced by any High Contracting Party by a notification in writing to the Pan American Union, which shall inform all the other High Contracting Parties of each notification of denunciation received. After the expiration of two years from the date of the receipt by the Pan American Union of a notification of denunciation by any High Contracting Party, the present Treaty shall cease to be in force and effect with respect to all the other High Contracting Parties.

ARTICLE 26

The principles and fundamental provisions of this Treaty shall be incorporated in the Organic Pact of the Inter-American System.

IN WITNESS WHEREOF, the undersigned Plenipotentiaries, having deposited their full powers found to be in due and proper form, sign this Treaty on behalf of their respective Governments, on the dates appearing opposite their signatures.

Done in the city of Rio de Janeiro, in four texts respectively in the English, French, Portuguese and Spanish languages, on the second of September nineteen hundred forty-seven.

EXCERPTS FROM THE AMERICAN TREATY OF PACIFIC SETTLEMENT (PACT OF BOGOTÁ, 1948)

ARTICLE I

The High Contracting Parties, solemnly reaffirming their commitments made in earlier international conventions and declarations as well as in the Charter of the United Nations, agree to refrain from the threat or the use of force, or from any other means of coercion for the settlement of their controversies, and to have recourse at all times to pacific procedures.

ARTICLE II

The High Contracting Parties recognize the obligation to settle international controversies by regional procedures before referring them to the Security Council of the United Nations.

Consequently, in the event that a controversy arises between two or more signatory states which, in the opinion of the parties, cannot be settled by direct negotiations through the usual diplomatic channels, the parties bind themselves to use the procedures established in the present Treaty, in the manner and under the conditions provided for in the following ARTICLES, or, alternatively, such special procedures as, in their opinion, will permit them to arrive at a solution.

. . .

ARTICLE V

The aforesaid procedures may not be applied to matters which, by their nature, are within the domestic jurisdiction of the state. If the parties are not in agreement as to whether the controversy concerns a matter of domestic jurisdiction, this preliminary question shall be submitted to decision by the International Court of Justice, at the request of any of the parties.

. . .

ARTICLE VII

The High Contracting Parties bind themselves not to make diplomatic representations in order to protect their nationals, or to refer a controversy to a court of international jurisdiction for that purpose, when the said nationals have had available the means to place their case before competent domestic courts of the respective state.

ARTICLE VIII

Neither recourse to pacific means for the solution of controversies, nor the recommendation of their use, shall, in the case of an armed attack, be ground for delaying the exercise of the right of individual or collective self-defense, as provided for in the Charter of the United Nations.

. . .

CHAPTER SIX
FULFILLMENT OF DECISIONS
ARTICLE L

If one of the High Contracting Parties should fail to carry out the obligations imposed upon it by a decision of the International Court of Justice or by an arbitral award, the other party or parties concerned shall, before resorting to the Security Council of the United Nations, propose a Meeting of Consultation of Ministers of Foreign Affairs to agree upon appropriate measures to ensure the fulfillment of the judicial decision or arbitral award.

CHAPTER SEVEN
ADVISORY OPINIONS
ARTICLE LI

The parties concerned in the solution of a controversy may, by agreement, petition the General Assembly or the Security Council of the United Nations to request an advisory opinion of the International Court of Justice on any juridical question.

The petition shall be made through the Council of the Organization of American States.

. . .

CHAPTER EIGHT
FINAL PROVISIONS
ARTICLE LIV

Any American State which is not a signatory to the present Treaty, or which has made reservations thereto, may adhere to it, or may withdraw its reservations in whole or in part, by transmitting an official instrument to the Pan American Union, which shall notify the other High Contracting Parties in the manner herein established.

. . .

ARTICLE LVIII

As this Treaty comes into effect through the successive ratifications of the High Contracting Parties, the following treaties, conventions and protocols shall cease to be in force with respect to such parties:

Treaty to Avoid or Prevent Conflicts Between the American States, of May 3, 1923;

General Convention of Inter-American Conciliation, of January 5, 1929;

General Treaty of Inter-American Arbitration and Additional Protocol of Progressive Arbitration, of January 5, 1929;

Additional Protocol to the General Convention of Inter-American Conciliation, of December 26, 1933;

Anti-War Treaty of Non-Aggression and Conciliation, of October 10, 1933;

Convention to Coordinate, Extend and Assure the Fulfillment of the Existing Treaties between the American States, of December 23, 1936;

Inter-American Treaty on Good Offices and Mediation, of December 23, 1936;

Treaty on the Prevention of Controversies, of December 23, 1936.

. . .

ARTICLE LX

The present Treaty shall be called the "Pact of Bogotá."

DECLARATION OF SOLIDARITY FOR THE PRESERVATION OF THE
POLITICAL INTEGRITY OF THE AMERICAN STATES AGAINST
THE INTERVENTION OF INTERNATIONAL COMMUNISM
(DECLARATION OF CARACAS, 1954)

WHEREAS:

The American republics at the Ninth International Conference of American States declared that international communism, by its anti-democratic nature and its interventionist tendency, is incompatible with the concept of American freedom, and resolved to adopt within their respective territories the measures necessary to eradicate and prevent subversive activities.

The Fourth Meeting of Consultation of Ministers of Foreign Affairs recognized that, in addition to adequate internal measures in each state, a high degree of international cooperation is required to eradicate the danger which the subversive activities of international communism pose for the American States; and

The aggressive character of the international communist movement continues to constitute, in the context of world affairs, a special and immediate threat to the national institutions and the peace and security of the American States, and to the right of each state to develop its cultural, political, and economic life freely and naturally without intervention in its internal or external affairs by other states,

The Tenth Inter-American Conference

I

CONDEMNS:

The activities of the international communist movement as constituting intervention in American affairs;

EXPRESSES:

The determination of the American States to take the necessary measures to protect their political independence against the intervention of international communism, acting in the interests of an alien despotism;

REITERATES:

The faith of the peoples of America in the effective exercise of representative democracy as the best means to promote their social and political progress; and

DECLARES:

That the domination or control of the political institutions of any American state by the international communist movement, extending to this Hemisphere the political system of an extra-continental power, would constitute a threat to the sovereignty and political independence of the American States, endangering the peace of America, and would call for a Meeting of Consultation to consider the adoption of appropriate action in accordance with existing treaties.

II

RECOMMENDS:

That, without prejudice to such other measures as they may consider desirable, special attention be given by each of the American governments to the following steps for the purpose of counteracting the subversive activities of the international communist movement within their respective jurisdictions;

1. Measures to require disclosure of the identity, activities, and sources of funds to those who are spreading propaganda of the international communist

movement or who travel in the interests of that movement, and of those who act as its agents or in its behalf; and

2. The exchange of information among governments to assist in fulfilling the purpose of the resolutions adopted by the Inter-American Conferences and Meetings of Ministers of Foreign Affairs regarding international communism.

III

This declaration of foreign policy made by the American Republics in relation to dangers originating outside this Hemisphere is designed to protect and not to impair the inalienable right of each American State freely to choose its own form of government and economic system and to live its own social and cultural life.

ACT OF BOGOTÁ (1960)

The Special Committee for the study of new measures of economic cooperation,

Recognizing that the preservation and strengthening of free and democratic institutions in the American republics requires the acceleration of social and economic progress in Latin America adequate to meet the legitimate aspirations of the individual citizen of Latin America for a better life and to provide him the fullest opportunity to improve his status;

Recognizing that the interests of the American republics are so inter-related that sound social and economic progress in each is of importance to all and that lack of it in any American republic may have serious repercussions in others;

Cognizant of the steps already taken by many American republics to cope with the serious economic and social problems that affect them, but convinced that the magnitude of these problems calls for redoubled efforts by governments and for a new and vigorous program of inter-American cooperation;

Recognizing that economic development programs, which should be urgently strengthened and expanded, may have a delayed effect on social welfare, and that accordingly early measures are needed to cope with initial needs;

Recognizing that the success of a cooperative program of social progress will require maximum self-help efforts on the part of the American republics, and in many cases, the improvement of existing institutions and practices, particularly in the fields of taxation, the ownership and use of land, education and training, health and housing;

Believing it opportune to give further practical expression to the spirit of Operation Pan-America by immediately enlarging the opportunities of the people of Latin America for social progress, thus strengthening their hopes for the future;

Considering it advisable to launch a program for social development, in which emphasis should be given to those measures that meet social needs and also promote increases in productivity and strengthen economic development;

Recommends to the Council of the Organization of American States:

I. MEASURES FOR SOCIAL IMPROVEMENT

An inter-American program for social development should be established which should be directed to the carrying-out of the following measures of social improvement in Latin America, as considered appropriate in each country:

1. *Measures for the improvement of rural living and land use.*
   1.1. The examination of existing legal and institutional systems with respect to:
   (a) Land tenure legislation and facilities with a view to insuring a wider and more equitable distribution of the ownership of land, in a manner consistent with the objectives of employment, productivity and economic growth.
   (b) Agricultural credit institutions with a view to providing adequate financing to individual farmers or groups of farmers.
   (c) Tax systems and procedures and fiscal policies with a view to assuring equity of taxation and encouraging improved use of land, especially of privately owned land which is idle.
   1.2. The initiation or acceleration of appropriate programs to modernize and improve the existing legal and institutional framework to insure better conditions of land tenure, extend more adequate credit facilities and provide increased incentives in the land tax structure.

1.3. The acceleration of the preparation of projects and programs for:

(a) Land reclamation and land settlement, with a view to promoting more widespread ownership and efficient use of land, particularly of unutilized or under-utilized land.

(b) The increase of the productivity of land already in use.

(c) The construction of farm-to-market and access roads.

1.4. The adoption or acceleration of other government service programs designed particularly to assist the small farmer, such as new or improved marketing organizations; extension services; research and basic surveys; and demonstration, education and training facilities.

2. *Measures for the improvement of housing and community facilities.*

2.1. The examination of existing policies in the field of housing and community facilities, including urban and regional planning, with a view to improving such policies, strengthening public institutions and promoting private initiative and participation in programs in these fields. Special consideration should be given to encouraging financial institutions to invest in low-cost housing on a long-term basis and in building and construction industries.

2.2. The strengthening of the existing legal and institutional framework for mobilizing financial resources to provide better housing and related facilities for the people, and to create new institutions for this purpose when necessary. Special consideration should be given to legislation and measures which would encourage the establishment and growth of:

(a) Private financing institutions, such as building and loan associations.

(b) Institutions to insure sound housing loans against loss.

(c) Institutions to serve as a secondary market for home mortgages.

(d) Institutions to provide financial assistance to local communities for the development of facilities such as water supply, sanitation and other public works.

Existing national institutions should be utilized wherever practical in the application of external resources to further the development of housing and community facilities.

2.3. The expansion of home building industries through such measures as the training of craftsmen and other personnel, research and the introduction of new techniques, and the development of construction standards for low- and medium-cost housing.

2.4. The lending of encouragement and assistance to programs, on a pilot basis, for aided self-help housing, for the acquisition and subdivision of land for low-cost housing developments, and for industrial housing projects.

3. *Measures for the improvement of educational systems and training facilities.*

3.1. The re-examination of educational systems, giving particular attention to:

3.1.1. The development of modern methods of mass education for the eradication of illiteracy.

3.1.2. The adequacy of training in the industrial arts and sciences with due emphasis on laboratory and work experience and on the practical application of knowledge for the solution of social and economic problems.

3.1.3. The need to provide instruction in rural schools not only in basic subjects but also in agriculture, health, sanitation, nutrition and the methods of home and community improvement.

3.1.4. The broadening of courses of study in secondary schools to provide the training necessary for clerical and executive personnel in industry, commerce, public administration and community service.

3.1.5. Specialized trade and industrial education related to the commercial and industrial needs of the community.

3.1.6. Vocational agricultural instruction.

3.1.7. Advanced education of administrators, engineers, economists and other professional personnel of key importance to economic development.

4. *Measures for the improvement of public health.*

4.1. Re-examination of programs and policies of public health giving particular attention to:

4.1.1. Strengthening the expansion of national and local health services, especially those directed to the reduction of infant mortality.

4.1.2. The progressive development of health insurance systems, including those providing for maternity, accident and disability insurance in urban and rural areas.

4.1.3. The provision of hospital and health service in areas located away from main centers of population.

4.1.4. The extension of public medical services to areas of exceptional need.

4.1.5. The strengthening of campaigns for the control or elimination of communicable diseases with special attention to the eradication of malaria.

4.1.6. The provision of water-supply facilities for purposes of health and economic development.

4.1.7. The training of public health officials and technicians.

4.1.8. The strengthening of programs of nutrition for low-income groups.

5. *Measures for the mobilization of domestic resources.*

5.1. This program shall be carried out within the framework of the maximum creation of domestic savings and the improvement of national fiscal and financial practices.

5.2. The allocation of tax revenues shall be reviewed, having in mind an adequate provision of such revenues to the areas of social development mentioned in the foregoing paragraphs.

II. CREATION OF A SPECIAL FUND FOR SOCIAL DEVELOPMENT

1. The delegations of the governments of the Latin-American republics welcome the decisions of the Government of the United States to establish a special inter-American fund for social development with the Inter-American Development Bank to become the primary mechanism for the administration of the fund.

2. It is understood that the purpose of the special fund would be to contribute capital resources and technical assistance on flexible terms and conditions, including repayment in local currencies and the relending of repaid funds, in accordance with appropriate and collective criteria in the light of the resources available, to support the efforts of the Latin-American countries which are prepared to initiate or expand effective improvements and to adopt measures to employ efficiently their own resources with a view to achieving greater social progress and more balanced economic growth.

III. MEASURES FOR ECONOMIC DEVELOPMENT

The special committee, having in view Resolution VII adopted at the Seventh Meeting of Consultation of Ministers of Foreign Affairs expressing the need for the maximum contribution of member countries in continental cooperation in the fight against under-development, in pursuance of the objectives of Operation Pan-America recommends:

1. That as soon as possible additional resources, domestic and external, be made available for the financing plans and projects of basic economic and industrial development in Latin America, with special attention to:

(a) The need for loans on flexible terms and conditions, including, whenever advisable in the light of the balance-of-payments situation of individual countries, the possibility of repayment in local currency.

(b) The desirability of the adequate preparation and implementation of development projects and plans, within the framework of the monetary, fiscal and exchange policies necessary for their effectiveness, utilizing as appropriate the technical assistance of inter-American and/or international agencies.

(c) The advisability, in special cases, of extending foreign financing for the coverage of local expenditures.

(d) The necessity for developing and strengthening credit facilities for small and medium private business, agriculture and industry.

2. That special attention be given to an expansion of long-term lending, particularly in view of the instability of exchange earnings of countries exporting primary products and of the unfavorable effect of the excessive accumulation of short- and medium-term debt and orderly economic development.

3. That urgent attention be given to the search for effective and practical ways, appropriate to each commodity, to deal with the problem of the instability of exchange earnings of countries heavily dependent upon the exportation of primary products.

IV. MULTILATERAL COOPERATION FOR SOCIAL AND ECONOMIC PROGRESS

The special committee considering the need for providing instruments and mechanisms for the implementation of the program of inter-American economic and social cooperation which would periodically review the progress made and propose measures for further mobilization of resources, recommends:

1. That the Inter-American Economic and Social Council undertakes to organize annual consultative meetings to review the social and economic progress of member countries, to analyze and discuss the progress achieved, and the problems encountered in each country, to exchange opinions on possible measures that might be adopted to intensify further social and economic progress, in pursuance of Operation Pan-America, and to prepare reports on the outlook for the future. Such annual meetings would begin with an examination by experts and terminate with a session at the ministerial level.

2. That the Council of the Organization of American States convene within sixty days of the date of this Act a special meeting of senior government representatives to find ways of strengthening and improving the ability of the Inter-American Economic and Social Council to render effective assistance to governments with a view to achieving the objectives enumerated below taking into account the proposal submitted by the delegation of Argentina in Document CECE/III—13:

(a) To further the economic and social development of Latin American countries.

(b) To promote aid between the countries of the Western Hemisphere as well as between them and extra-continental countries.

(c) To facilitate the flow of capital and the extension of credits to the countries of Latin America, both from the Western Hemisphere and from extra-continental sources.

3. The special meeting shall:

(a) Examine the existing structure of the Inter-American Economic and Social Council, and of the Secretariat of the Organization of American States working in the economic and social fields, for the purpose of formulating recommendations to the Council of the Organization of American States designed to strengthen and improve the Inter-American Economic and Social Council.

(b) Determine the needs of strengthening inter-American economic and social cooperation by an administrative reform of the Secretariat, which should be given sufficient technical, administrative and financial flexibility for the adequate fulfillment of its tasks.

(c) Formulate recommendations designed to assure effective coordination between the Inter-American Economic and Social Council, the Economic Commission for Latin America, the Inter-American Development Bank, the United Nations and its specialized agencies and other agencies offering technical advice and services in the Western Hemisphere.

(d) Propose procedures designed to establish effective liaison of the Inter-American Economic and Social Council and other regional American organizations with other international organizations for the purpose of study, discussion and consultation in the fields of international trade and financial and technical assistance.

In approving the Act of Bogotá, the delegations to the special committee, convinced that the people of the Americas can achieve a good life only within the democratic system, renew their faith in the essential values which lie at the base of Western civilization, and reaffirm their determination to assure the fullest measure of well-being to the people of the Americas under conditions of freedom and respect for the supreme dignity of the individual.

THE CHARTER OF PUNTA DEL ESTE ESTABLISHING AN ALLIANCE FOR PROGRESS WITHIN THE FRAMEWORK OF OPERATION PAN AMERICA
(1961)

PREAMBLE

We, the American Republics, hereby proclaim our decision to unite in a common effort to bring our people accelerated economic progress and broader social justice within the framework of personal dignity and political liberty.

Almost two hundred years ago we began in this Hemisphere the long struggle for freedom which now inspires people in all parts of the world. Today, in ancient lands, men moved to hope by the revolutions of our young nations search for liberty. Now we must give a new meaning to that revolutionary heritage. For America stands at a turning point in history. The men and women of our Hemisphere are reaching for the better life which today's skills have placed within their grasp. They are determined for themselves and their children to have decent and ever more abundant lives, to gain access to knowledge and equal opportunity for all, to end those conditions which benefit the few at the expense of the needs and dignity of the many. It is our inescapable task to fulfill these just desires—to demonstrate to the poor and forsaken of our countries, and of all lands, that the creative powers of free men hold the key to their progress and to the progress of future generations. And our certainty of ultimate success rests not alone on our faith in ourselves and in our nations but on the indomitable spirit of free man which has been the heritage of American civilization.

Inspired by these principles, and by the principles of Operation Pan America and the Act of Bogotá, the American Republics hereby resolve to adopt the following program of action to establish and carry forward an Alliance for Progress.

TITLE I
OBJECTIVES OF THE ALLIANCE FOR PROGRESS

It is the purpose of the Alliance for Progress to enlist the full energies of the peoples and governments of the American Republics in a great cooperative effort to accelerate the economic and social development of the participating countries of Latin America, so that they may achieve maximum levels of well-being, with equal opportunities for all, in democratic societies adapted to their own needs and desires.

The American republics hereby agree to work toward the achievement of the following fundamental goals in the present decade:

1. To achieve in the participating Latin American countries a substantial and sustained growth of per capita income at a rate designed to attain, at the earliest possible date, levels of income capable of assuring self-sustaining development, and sufficient to make Latin American income levels constantly larger in relation to the levels of the more industrialized nations. In this way the gap between the living standards of Latin America and those of the more developed countries can be narrowed. Similarly, presently existing dfferences in income levels among the Latin American countries will be reduced by accelerating the development of the relatively less developed countries and granting them maximum priority in the distribution of resources and in international cooperation in general. In evaluating the degree of relative development, account will be taken not only of average levels of real income and gross product per capita, but also of indices of infant mortality, illiteracy, and per capita daily caloric intake.

It is recognized that, in order to reach these objectives within a reasonable time, the rate of economic growth in any country of Latin America should be not less than 2.5 per cent per capita per year, and that each participating country should determine its own growth target in the light of its stage of social and economic evolution, resource endowment, and ability to mobilize national efforts for development.

2. To make the benefits of economic progress available to all citizens of all economic and social groups through a more equitable distribution of national income, raising more rapidly the income and standard of living of the needier sectors of the population, at the same time that a higher proportion of the national product is devoted to investment.

3. To achieve balanced diversification in national economic structures, both regional and functional, making them increasingly free from dependence on the export of a limited number of primary products and the importation of capital goods while attaining stability in the prices of exports or in income derived from exports.

4. To accelerate the process of national industrialization so as to increase the productivity of the economy as a whole, taking full advantage of the talents and energies of both the private and public sectors, utilizing the natural resources of the country and providing productive and remunerative employment for unemployed or part-time workers. Within this process of industrialization, special attention should be given to the establishment and development of capital-goods industries.

5. To raise greatly the level of agricultural productivity and output and to improve related storage, transportation, and marketing services.

6. To encourage, in accordance with the characteristics of each country, programs of comprehensive agrarian reform leading to the effective transformation, where required, of unjust structures and systems of land tenure and use, with a view to replacing latifundia and dwarf holdings by an equitable system of land tenure so that, with the help of timely and adequate credit, technical assistance and facilities for the marketing and distribution of products, the land will become for the man who works it the basis of his economic stability, the foundation of his increasing welfare, and the guarantee of his freedom and dignity.

7. To eliminate adult illiteracy and by 1970 to assure, as a minimum, access to six years of primary education for each school-age child in Latin America; to modernize and expand vocational, technical, secondary and higher educational and training facilities, to strengthen the capacity for basic and applied research; and to provide the competent personnel required in rapidly growing societies.

8. To increase life expectancy at birth by a minimum of five years, and to increase the ability to learn and produce, by improving individual and public health. To attain this goal it will be necessary, among other measures, to provide adequate potable water supply, and sewage disposal, to not less than 70 per cent of the urban and 50 per cent of the rural population; to reduce the present mortality rate of children less than five years of age by at least one-half; to control the more serious communicable diseases, according to their importance as a cause of sickness, disability, and death; to eradicate those illnesses, especially malaria, for which effective techniques are known; to improve nutrition; to train medical and health personnel to meet at least minimum requirements; to improve basic health services at national and local levels; and to intensify scientific research and apply its results more fully and effectively to the prevention and cure of illness.

9. To increase the construction of low-cost houses for low-income families in order to replace inadequate and deficient housing and to reduce housing shortages; and to provide necessary public services to both urban and rural centers of population.

10. To maintain stable price levels, avoiding inflation or deflation and the consequent social hardships and maldistribution of resources, always bearing in mind the necessity of maintaining an adequate rate of economic growth.

11. To strengthen existing agreements on economic integration, with a view to the ultimate fulfillment of aspirations for a Latin American common market that will expand and diversify trade among the Latin American countries and thus contribute to the economic growth of the region.

12. To develop cooperative programs designed to prevent the harmful

effects of excessive fluctuations in the foreign exchange earnings derived from exports of primary products, which are of vital importance to economic and social development; and to adopt the measures necessary to facilitate the access of Latin American exports to international markets.

TITLE II

ECONOMIC AND SOCIAL DEVELOPMENT

Chapter I. Basic Requirements for Economic and Social Development

The American Republics recognize that to achieve the foregoing goals it will be necessary:

1. That comprehensive and well-conceived national programs of economic and social development, aimed at the achievement of self-sustaining growth, be carried out in accordance with democratic principles.

2. That national programs of economic and social development be based on the principle of self-help—as established in the Act of Bogotá—and on the maximum use of domestic resources, taking into account the special conditions of each country.

3. That in the preparation and execution of plans for economic and social development, women should be placed on an equal footing with men.

4. That the Latin American countries obtain sufficient external financial assistance, a substantial portion of which should be extended on flexible conditions with respect to periods and terms of repayment and forms of utilization, in order to supplement domestic capital formation and reinforce their import capacity; and that, in support of well-conceived programs, which include the necessary structural reforms and measures for the mobilization of internal resources, a supply of capital from all external sources during the coming ten years of at least twenty billion dollars be made available to the Latin American countries, with priority to the relatively less-developed countries. The greater part of this sum should be in public funds.

5. That institutions in both the public and private sectors, including labor organizations, cooperatives, and commercial, industrial, and financial institutions, be strengthened and improved for the increasing and effective use of domestic resources, and that the social reforms necessary to permit a fair distribution of the fruits of economic and social progress be carried out.

Chapter II. National Development Programs

1. Participating Latin American countries agree to introduce or strengthen systems for the preparation, execution, and periodic revision of national programs for economic and social development consistent with the principles, objectives, and requirements contained in this document. Participating Latin American countries should formulate, if possible within the next eighteen months, long-term development programs. Such programs should embrace, according to the characteristics of each country, the elements outlined in the Appendix.

2. National development programs should incorporate self-help efforts directed toward:

a. Improvement of human resources and widening of opportunities by raising general standards of education and health; improving and extending technical education and professional training with emphasis on science and technology; providing adequate remuneration for work performed; encouraging the talents of managers, entrepreneurs, and wage earners; providing more productive employment for under-employed manpower; establishing effective systems of labor relations and procedures for consultation and collaboration among public authorities, employer associations, and labor organizations; promoting the establishment and expansion of local institutions for basic and applied research; and improving the standards of public administration.

b. Wider development and more efficient use of natural resources, especially those which are now idle or under-utilized, including measures for the processing of raw materials.

c. The strengthening of the agricultural base, progressively extending the benefits of the land to those who work it, and ensuring in countries with Indian populations the integration of these populations into the economic, social, and cultural processes of modern life. To carry out these aims, measures should be adopted, among others, to establish or improve, as the case may be, the following services: extension, credit, technical assistance, agricultural research and mechanization; health and education; storage and distribution; cooperatives and farmers' associations; and community development.

d. More effective, rational and equitable mobilization and use of financial resources through the reform of tax structures, including fair and adequate taxation of large incomes and real estate, and the strict application of measures to improve fiscal administration. Development programs should include the adaptation of budget expenditures to development needs, measures for the maintenance of price stability, the creation of essential credit facilities at reasonable rates of interest, and the encouragement of private savings.

e. Promotion through appropriate measures, including the signing of agreements for the purpose of reducing or eliminating double taxation, of conditions that will encourage the flow of foreign investments and help to increase the capital resources of participating countries in need of capital.

f. Improvement of systems of distribution and sales in order to make markets more competitive and prevent monopolistic practices.

Chapter III. Immediate and Short-Term Action Measures

1. Recognizing that a number of Latin American countries, despite their best efforts, may require emergency financial assistance, the United States will provide assistance from the funds which are or may be established for such purposes. The United States stands ready to take prompt action on applications for such assistance. Applications relating to existing situations should be submitted within the next sixty days.

2. Participating Latin American countries should, in addition to creating or strengthening machinery for long-term development programming, immediately increase their efforts to accelerate their development by giving special emphasis to the following objectives:

a. The completion of projects already under way and the initiation of projects for which the basic studies have been made, in order to accelerate their financing and execution.

b. The implementation of new projects which are designed:

(1) To meet the most pressing economic and social needs and benefit directly the greatest number of people;

(2) To concentrate efforts within each country in the less-developed or more-depressed areas in which particularly serious social problems exist;

(3) To utilize idle capacity or resources, particularly under-employed manpower; and

(4) To survey and assess natural resources.

c. The facilitation of the preparation and execution of long-term programs through measures designed:

(1) To train teachers, technicians, and specialists;

(2) To provide accelerated training to workers and farmers;

(3) To improve basic statistics;

(4) To establish needed credit and marketing facilities; and

(5) To improve services and administration.

3. The United States will assist in carrying out these short-term measures with a view to achieving concrete results from the Alliance for Progress at the earliest possible moment. In connection with the measures set forth above, and in accordance with the statement of President Kennedy, the United States will provide

assistance under the Alliance, including assistance for the financing of short-term measures, totalling more than one billion dollars in the year ending March 1962.

Chapter IV. External Assistance in Support of National Development Programs

1. The economic and social development of Latin America will require a large amount of additional and private financial assistance on the part of capital-exporting countries, including the members of the Development Assistance Group and international lending agencies. The measures provided for in the Act of Bogotá and the new measures provided for in this Charter, are designed to create a framework within which such additional assistance can be provided and effectively utilized.

2. The United States will assist those participating countries whose development programs establish self-help measures and economic and social policies and programs consistent with the goals and principles of this Charter. To supplement the domestic efforts of such countries, the United States is prepared to allocate resources which, along with those anticipated from other external sources, will be of a scope and magnitude adequate to realize the goals envisaged in this Charter. Such assistance will be allocated to both social and economic development and, where appropriate, will take the form of grants or loans on flexible terms and conditions. The participating countries will request the support of other capital-exporting countries and appropriate institutions so that they may provide assistance for the attainment of these objectives.

3. The United States will help in the financing of technical assistance projects proposed by a participating country or by the General Secretariat of the Organization of American States for the purpose of:

a. Providing experts contracted in agreement with the governments to work under their direction and to assist them in the preparation of specific investment projects and the strengthening of national mechanisms for preparing projects, using specialized engineering firms where appropriate;

b. Carrying out, pursuant to existing agreements for cooperation among the General Secretariat of the Organization of American States, the Economic Commission for Latin America, and the Inter-American Development Bank, field investigations and studies, including those relating to development problems, the organization of national agencies for the preparation of development programs, agrarian reform and rural development, health, cooperatives, housing, education and professional training, and taxation and tax administration; and

c. Convening meetings of experts and officials on development and related problems.

The governments or above-mentioned organizations should, when appropriate, seek the cooperation of the United Nations and its specialized agencies in the execution of these activities.

4. The participating Latin American countries recognize that each has in varying degree a capacity to assist fellow republics by providing technical and financial assistance. They recognize that this capacity will increase as their economies grow. They therefore affirm their intention to assist fellow republics increasingly as their individual circumstances permit.

Chapter V. Organization and Procedures

1. In order to provide technical assistance for the formulation of development programs, as may be requested by participating nations, the Organization of American States, the Economic Commission for Latin America, and the Inter-American Development Bank will continue and strengthen their agreements for coordination in this field, in order to have available a group of programming experts whose service can be used to facilitate the implementation of this Charter. The participating countries will also seek an intensification of technical assistance from the specialized agencies of the United Nations for the same purpose.

2. The Inter-American Economic and Social Council, on the joint nomination

of the Secretary General of the Organization of American States, the President of the Inter-American Development Bank, and the Executive Secretary of the United Nations Economic Commission for Latin America, will appoint a panel of nine high-level experts, exclusively on the basis of their experience, technical ability, and competence in the various aspects of economic and social development. The experts may be of any nationality, though if of Latin American origin an appropriate geographical distribution will be sought. They will be attached to the Inter-American Economic and Social Council, but will nevertheless enjoy complete autonomy in the performance of their duties. They may not hold any other remunerative position. The appointment of these experts will be for a period of three years, and may be renewed.

3. Each government, if it so wishes, may present its program for economic and social development for consideration by an *ad hoc* committee, composed of no more than three members drawn from the panel of experts referred to in the preceding paragraph together with an equal number of experts not on the panel. The experts who compose the *ad hoc* committee will be appointed by the Secretary General of the Organization of American States at the request of the interested government and with its consent.

4. The committee will study the development program, exchange opinions with the interested government as to possible modifications, and, with the consent of the government, report its conclusions to the Inter-American Development Bank and to other governments and institutions that may be prepared to extend external financial and technical assistance in connection with the execution of the program.

5. In considering a development program presented to it, the *ad hoc* committee will examine the consistency of the program with the principles of the Act of Bogotá and of this Charter, taking into account the elements in the Appendix.

6. The General Secretariat of the Organization of American States will provide the personnel needed by the experts referred to in Paragraphs 2 and 3 of this Chapter in order to fulfill their tasks. Such personnel may be employed specifically for this purpose or may be made available from the permanent staffs of the Organization of American States, the Economic Commission for Latin America, and the Inter-American Development Bank, in accordance with the present liaison arrangements between the three organizations. The General Secretariat of the Organization of American States may seek arrangements with the United Nations Secretariat, its specialized agencies and the Inter-American Specialized Organizations, for the temporary assignment of necessary personnel.

7. A government whose development program has been the object of recommendations made by the *ad hoc* committee with respect to external financing requirements may submit the program to the Inter-American Development Bank so that the Bank may undertake the negotiations required to obtain such financing, including the organization of a consortium of credit institutions and governments disposed to contribute to the continuing and systematic financing, on appropriate terms, of the development program. However, the government will have full freedom to resort through any other channels to all sources of financing, for the purpose of obtaining, in full or in part, the required resources.

The *ad hoc* committee shall not interfere with the right of each government to formulate its own goals, priorities, and reforms in its national development programs.

The recommendations of the *ad hoc* committee will be of great importance in determining the distribution of public funds under the Alliance for Progress which contribute to the external financing of such programs. These recommendations shall give special consideration to Title I.1.

The participating governments will also use their good offices to the end that these recommendations may be accepted as a factor of great importance in the decisions taken, for the same purpose, by inter-American credit institutions, other international credit agencies, and other friendly governments which may be potential sources of capital.

8. The Inter-American Economic and Social Council will review annually the progress achieved in the formulation, national implementation, and international

financing of development programs; and will submit to the Council of the Organization of American States such recommendations as it deems pertinent.

APPENDIX
ELEMENTS OF NATIONAL DEVELOPMENT PROGRAMS

1. The establishment of mutually consistent targets to be aimed at over the program period in expanding productive capacity in industry, agriculture, mining, transport, power and communications, and in improving conditions of urban and rural life, including better housing, education, and health.

2. The assignment of priorities and the description of methods to achieve the targets, including specific measures and major projects. Specific development projects should be justified in terms of their relative costs and benefits, including their contribution to social productivity.

3. The measures which will be adopted to direct the operations of the public sector and to encourage private action in support of the development program.

4. The estimated cost, in national and foreign currency, of major projects and of the development program as a whole, year by year over the program period.

5. The internal resources, public and private, estimated to become available for the execution of the programs.

6. The direct and indirect effects of the program on the balance of payments, and the external financing, public and private, estimated to be acquired for the execution of the program.

7. The basic fiscal and monetary policies to be followed in order to permit implementation of the program within a framework of price stability.

8. The machinery of public administration—including relationships with local governments, decentralized agencies and non-governmental organizations, such as labor organizations, cooperatives, business and industrial organizations—to be used in carrying out the program, adapting it to changing circumstances and evaluating the progress made.

TITLE III
ECONOMIC INTEGRATION OF LATIN AMERICA

The American republics consider that the broadening of present national markets in Latin America is essential to accelerate the process of economic development in the Hemisphere. It is also an appropriate means for obtaining greater productivity through specialized and complementary industrial production which will, in turn, facilitate the attainment of greater social benefits for the inhabitants of the various regions of Latin America. The broadening of markets will also make possible the better use of resources under the Alliance for Progress. Consequently, the American republics recognize that:

1. The Montevideo Treaty (because of its flexibility and because it is open to the adherence of all the Latin American nations) and the Central American Treaty on Economic Integration are appropriate instruments for the attainment of these objectives, as was recognized in Resolution No. 11 (III) of the Ninth Session of the Economic Commission for Latin America.

2. The integration process can be intensified and accelerated not only by the specialization resulting from the broadening of markets through the liberalization of trade but also through the use of such instruments as the agreements for complementary production within economic sectors provided for in the Montevideo Treaty.

3. In order to insure the balanced and complementary economic expansion of all of the countries involved, the integration process should take into account, on a flexible basis, the condition of countries at a relatively less advanced stage of economic development, permitting them to be granted special, fair, and equitable treatment.

4. In order to facilitate economic integration in Latin America, it is advisable to establish effective relationships between the Latin American Free Trade Association and the group of countries adhering to the Central American Economic Integration Treaty, as well as between either of these groups and other Latin American countries. These arrangements should be established within the limits determined by these instruments.

5. The Latin American countries should coordinate their actions to meet the unfavorable treatment accorded to their foreign trade in world markets, particularly that resulting from certain restrictive and discriminatory policies of extra-continental countries and economic groups.

6. In the application of resources under the Alliance for Progress, special attention should be given not only to investments for multi-national projects that will contribute to strengthening the integration process in all its aspects, but also to the necessary financing of industrial products within Latin America.

7. In order to facilitate the participation of countries at a relatively low stage of economic development in multi-national Latin American economic cooperation programs, and in order to promote the balanced and harmonious development of the Latin American integration process, special attention should be given to the needs of these countries in the administration of financial resources provided under the Alliance for Progress, particularly in connection with infra-structure programs and the promotion of new lines of production.

8. The economic integration process implies a need for additional investment in various fields of economic activity and funds provided under the Alliance for Progress should cover these needs as well as those required for the financing of national development programs.

9. When groups of Latin American countries have their own institutions for financing economic integration, the financing referred to in the preceding paragraph should preferably be channeled through these institutions. With respect to regional financing designed to further the purposes of existing regional integration instruments, the cooperation of the Inter-American Development Bank should be sought in channeling extra-regional contributions which may be granted for these purposes.

10. One of the possible means for making effective a policy for the financing of Latin American integration would be to approach the International Monetary Fund and other financial sources with a view to providing a means for solving temporary balance-of-payments problems that may occur in countries participating in economic integration arrangements.

11. The promotion and coordination of transportation and communications systems are an effective way to accelerate the integration process. In order to counteract abusive practices in relation to freight rates and tariffs, it is advisable to encourage the establishment of multi-national transport and communication enterprises in the Latin American countries, or to find other appropriate solutions.

12. In working toward economic integration and complementary economies, efforts should be made to achieve an appropriate coordination of national plans, or to engage in joint planning for various economies through the existing regional integration organizations. Efforts should also be made to promote an investment policy directed to the progressive elimination of unequal growth rates in the different geographic areas, particularly in the case of countries which are relatively less developed.

13. It is necessary to promote the development of national Latin American enterprises, in order that they may compete on an equal footing with foreign enterprises.

14. The active participation of the private sector is essential to economic integration and development, and except in those countries in which free enterprise does not exist, development planning by the pertinent national public agencies, far from hindering such participation, can facilitate and guide it, thus opening new perspectives for the benefit of the community.

15. As the countries of the Hemisphere still under colonial domination achieve their independence, they should be invited to participate in Latin American economic integration programs.

TITLE IV
BASIC EXPORT COMMODITIES

The American republics recognize that the economic development of Latin America requires expansion of its trade, a simultaneous and corresponding increase in foreign exchange incomes received from exports, a lessening of cyclical or seasonal fluctuations in the incomes of those countries that still depend heavily on the export of raw materials, and the correction of the secular deterioration in their terms of trade.

They therefore agree that the following measures should be taken:

Chapter I. National Measures

National measures affecting commerce in primary products should be directed and applied in order to:

1. Avoid undue obstacles to the expansion of trade in these products;

2. Avoid market instability;

3. Improve the efficiency of international plans and mechanisms for stabilization; and

4. Increase their present markets and expand their area of trade at a rate compatible with rapid development.

Therefore:

A. Importing member countries should reduce and if possible eliminate, as soon as feasible, all restrictions and discriminatory practices affecting the consumption and importation of primary products, including those with the highest possible degree of processing in the country of origin, except when these restrictions are imposed temporarily for purposes of economic diversification, to hasten the economic development of less-developed nations, or to establish basic national reserves. Importing countries should also be ready to support, by adequate regulations, stabilization programs for primary products that may be agreed upon with producing countries.

B. Industrialized countries should give special attention to the need for hastening economic development of less-developed countries. Therefore, they should make maximum efforts to create conditions, compatible with their international obligations, through which they may extend advantages to less-developed countries so as to permit the rapid expansion of their markets. In view of the great need for this rapid development, industrialized countries should also study ways in which to modify, wherever possible, international commitments which prevent the achievement of this objective.

C. Producing member countries should formulate their plans for production and export, taking account of their effect on world markets and of the necessity of supporting and improving the effectiveness of international stabilization programs and mechanisms. Similarly they should try to avoid increasing the uneconomic production of goods which can be obtained under better conditions in the less-developed countries of the Continent, in which the production of these goods is an important source of employment.

D. Member countries should adopt all necessary measures to direct technological studies toward finding new uses and by-products of those primary commodities that are most important to their economies.

E. Member countries should try to reduce, and, if possible, eliminate within a reasonable time export subsidies and other measures which cause instability in the markets for basic commodities and excessive fluctuations in prices and income.

Chapter II. International Cooperation Measures

1. Member countries should make coordinated, and if possible, joint efforts designed:

   a. To eliminate as soon as possible undue protection of the production of basic products;

   b. To eliminate taxes and reduce excessive domestic prices which discourage the consumption of imported basic products;

   c. To seek to end preferential agreements and other measures which limit world consumption of Latin American basic products and their access to international markets, especially the markets of Western European countries in process of economic integration, and of countries with centrally planned economies; and

   d. To adopt the necessary consultation mechanisms so that their marketing policies will not have damaging effects on the stability of the markets for basic commodities.

2. Industrialized countries should give maximum cooperation to less-developed countries so that their raw material exports will have undergone the greatest degree of processing that is economic.

3. Through their representation in international financial organizations, member countries should suggest that these organizations, when considering loans for the promotion of production for export, take into account the effect of such loans on products which are in surplus in world markets.

4. Member countries should support the efforts being made by international commodity study groups and by the Commission on International Commodity Trade of the United Nations. In this connection, it should be considered that producing and consuming nations bear a joint responsibility for taking national and international steps to reduce market instability.

5. The Secretary General of the Organization of American States shall convene a group of experts appointed by their respective governments to meet before November 30, 1961 and to report, not later than March 31, 1962 on measures to provide an adequate and effective means of offsetting the effects of fluctuations in the volume and prices of exports of basic products. The experts shall:

   a. Consider the questions regarding compensatory financing raised during the present meeting;

   b. Analyze the proposal for establishing an international fund for the stabilization of export receipts contained in the Report of the Group of Experts to the Special Meeting of the Inter-American Economic and Social Council, as well as any other alternative proposals;

   c. Prepare a draft plan for the creation of mechanisms for compensatory financing. This draft plan should be circulated among the member governments and their opinions obtained well in advance of the next meeting of the Commission on International Commodity Trade.

6. Member countries should support the efforts under way to improve and strengthen international commodity agreements and should be prepared to cooperate in the solution of specific commodity problems. Furthermore, they should endeavor to adopt adequate solutions for the short- and long-term problems affecting markets for such commodities so that the economic interests of producers and consumers are equally safeguarded.

7. Member countries should request other producer and consumer countries to cooperate in stabilization programs, bearing in mind that the raw materials of the Western Hemisphere are also produced and consumed in other parts of the world.

8. Member countries recognize that the disposal of accumulated reserves and surpluses can be a means of achieving the goals outlined in the first chapter of this

Title, provided that, along with the generation of local resources, the consumption of essential products in the receiving countries is immediately increased. The disposal of surpluses and reserves should be carried out in an orderly manner, in order to:

a. Avoid disturbing existing commercial markets in member countries, and

b. Encourage expansion of the sale of their products to other markets.

However, it is recognized that:

a. The disposal of surpluses should not displace commercial sales of identical products traditionally carried out by other countries; and

b. Such disposal cannot substitute for large-scale financial and technical assistance programs.

IN WITNESS WHEREOF this Charter is signed, in Punta del Este, Uruguay, on the seventeenth day of August, nineteen hundred sixty-one.

EXCERPTS FROM THE CHARTER OF THE UNITED NATIONS (1945)

. . .

ARTICLE 24
1. In order to insure prompt and effective action by the United Nations, its Members confer on the Security Council primary responsibility for the maintenance of international peace and security, and agree that in carrying out its duties under this responsibility the Security Council acts on their behalf.

. . .

ARTICLE 32
Any Member of the United Nations which is not a member of the Security Council or any state which is not a Member of the United Nations, if it is a party to a dispute under consideration by the Security Council, shall be invited to participate, without vote, in the discussion relating to the dispute. The Security Council shall lay down such conditions as it deems just for the participation of a state which is not a Member of the United Nations.

ARTICLE 33
1. The parties to any dispute, the continuance of which is likely to endanger the maintenance of international peace and security, shall, first of all, seek a solution by negotiation, inquiry, mediation, conciliation, arbitration, judicial settlement, resort to regional agencies or arrangements, or other peaceful means of their own choice.
2. The Security Council shall, when it deems necessary, call upon the parties to settle their dispute by such means.

ARTICLE 34
The Security Council may investigate any dispute, or any situation which might lead to international friction or give rise to a dispute, in order to determine whether the continuance of the dispute or situation is likely to endanger the maintenance of international peace and security.

ARTICLE 35
1. Any Member of the United Nations may bring any dispute or any situation of the nature referred to in ARTICLE 34, to the attention of the Security Council or of the General Assembly.
. . .

ARTICLE 36
. . .
2. The Security Council should take into consideration any procedures for the settlement of the dispute which have already been adopted by the parties.

. . .

ARTICLE 51
Nothing in the present Charter shall impair the inherent right of individual or collective self-defense if an armed attack occurs against a Member of the United Nations, until the Security Council has taken the measures necessary to maintain international peace and security. Measures taken by Members in the exercise of this

right of self-defense shall be immediately reported to the Security Council and shall not in any way affect the authority and responsibility of the Security Council under the present Charter to take at any time such action as it deems necessary in order to maintain or restore international peace and security.

ARTICLE 52

1. Nothing in the present Charter precludes the existence of regional arrangements or agencies for dealing with such matters relating to the maintenance of international peace and security as are appropriate for regional action, provided that such arrangements or agencies and their activities are consistent with the Purposes and Principles of the United Nations.

2. The Members of the United Nations entering into such arrangements or constituting such agencies shall make every effort to achieve pacific settlement of local disputes through such regional arrangements or by such regional agencies before referring them to the Security Council.

3. The Security Council shall encourage the development of pacific settlement of local disputes through such regional arrangements or by such regional agencies either on the initiative of the states concerned or by reference from the Security Council.

4. This ARTICLE in no way impairs the application of ARTICLES 34 and 35.

ARTICLE 53

1. The Security Council shall, where appropriate, utilize such regional arrangements or agencies for enforcement action under its authority. But no enforcement action shall be taken under regional arrangements or by regional agencies without the authorization of the Security Council, ...

ARTICLE 54

The Security Council shall at all times be kept informed of activities undertaken or in contemplation under regional arrangements or by regional agencies for the maintenance of international peace and security.

. . .

ARTICLE 103

In the event of a conflict between the obligations of the Members of the United Nations under the present Charter and their obligations under any other international agreement, their obligations under the present Charter shall prevail.

TREATY ESTABLISHING A FREE-TRADE AREA AND INSTITUTING THE LATIN AMERICAN FREE-TRADE ASSOCIATION (MONTEVIDEO TREATY, (1960)

The Governments represented at the Inter-Governmental Conference for the Establishment of a Free-Trade Area among Latin American countries,

Persuaded that the expansion of present national markets, through the gradual elimination of barriers to intra-regional trade, is a prerequisite if the Latin American countries are to accelerate their economic development process in such a way as to ensure a higher level of living for their peoples,

Aware that economic development should be attained through the maximum utilization of available production factors and the more effective coordination of the development programmes of the different production sectors in accordance with norms which take due account of the interests of each and all and which make proper compensation, by means of appropriate measures, for the special situation of countries which are at a relatively less advanced stage of economic development,

Convinced that the strengthening of national economies will contribute to the expansion of trade within Latin America and with the rest of the world,

Sure that, by the adoption of suitable formulas, conditions can be created that will be conducive to the gradual and smooth adaptation of existing productive activities to new patterns of reciprocal trade, and that further incentives will thereby be provided for the improvement and expansion of such trade,

Certain that any action to achieve such ends must take into account the commitments arising out of the international instruments which govern their trade,

Determined to persevere in their efforts to establish, gradually and progressively, a Latin American common market and, hence, to continue collaborating with the Latin American Governments as a whole in the work already initiated for this purpose, and

Motivated by the desire to pool their efforts to achieve the progressive complementarity and integration of their national economies on the basis of an effective reciprocity of benefits, decide to establish a Free-Trade Area and, to that end, to conclude a Treaty instituting the Latin American Free-Trade Association; and have, for this purpose, appointed their plenipotentiaries who have agreed as follows:

Chapter I
NAME AND PURPOSE
ARTICLE 1

By this Treaty the Contracting Parties establish a Free-Trade Area and institute the Latin American Free-Trade Association (hereinafter referred to as "the Association"), with headquarters in the city of Montevideo (Eastern Republic of Uruguay).

The term "Area," when used in this Treaty, means the combined territories of the Contracting Parties.

Chapter II
PROGRAMME FOR TRADE LIBERALIZATION
ARTICLE 2

The Free-Trade Area, established under the terms of the present Treaty, shall be brought into full operation within not more than twelve (12) years from the date of the Treaty's entry into force.

ARTICLE 3

During the period indicated in ARTICLE 2, the Contracting Parties shall gradually eliminate, in respect of substantially all their reciprocal trade, such duties, charges and restrictions as may be applied to imports of goods originating in the territory of any Contracting Party.

For the purposes of the present Treaty the term "duties and charges" means customs duties and any other charges of equivalent effect—whether fiscal, monetary or exchange—that are levied on imports.

The provisions of the present ARTICLE do not apply to fees and similar charges in respect of services rendered.

ARTICLE 4

The purpose set forth in ARTICLE 3 shall be achieved through negotiations to be held from time to time among the Contracting Parties with a view to drawing up:

(a) National Schedules specifying the annual reductions in duties, charges and other restrictions which each Contracting Party grants to the other Contracting Parties in accordance with the provisions of ARTICLE 5; and

(b) a Common Schedule listing the products on which the Contracting Parties collectively agree to eliminate duties, charges and other restrictions completely, so far as intra-Area trade is concerned, within the period mentioned in ARTICLE 2, by complying with the minimum percentages set out in ARTICLE 7 and through the gradual reduction provided for in ARTICLE 5.

ARTICLE 5

With a view to the preparation of the National Schedules referred to in ARTICLE 4, sub-paragraph (a), each Contracting Party shall annually grant to the other Contracting Parties reductions in duties and charges equivalent to not less than eight (8) per cent of the weighted average applicable to third countries, until they are eliminated in respect of substantially all of its imports from the Area, in accordance with the definitions, methods of calculation, rules and procedures laid down in the Protocol appended to the present Treaty.

For this purpose, duties and charges for third parties shall be deemed to be those in force on 31 December prior to each negotiation.

When the import régime of a Contracting Party contains restrictions of such a kind that the requisite equivalence with the reductions in duties and charges granted by another Contracting Party or other Contracting Parties is unobtainable, the counterpart of these reductions shall be complemented by means of the elimination or relaxation of those restrictions.

ARTICLE 6

The National Schedules shall enter into force on 1 January of each year, except that those deriving from the initial negotiations shall enter into force on the date fixed by the Contracting Parties.

ARTICLE 7

The Common Schedule shall consist of products which, in terms of the aggregate value of the trade among the Contracting Parties, shall constitute not less than the following percentages, calculated in accordance with the provisions of the Protocol:

Twenty-five (25) per cent during the first three-year period;
Fifty (50) per cent during the second three-year period;
Seventy-five (75) per cent during the third three-year period;
Substantially all of such trade during the fourth three-year period.

ARTICLE 8

The inclusion of products in the Common Schedule shall be final and the concessions granted in respect thereof irrevocable.

Concessions granted in respect of products which appear only in the National Schedules may be withdrawn by negotiation among the Contracting Parties and on a basis of adequate compensation.

ARTICLE 9
The percentages referred to in ARTICLES 5 and 7 shall be calculated on the basis of the average annual value of trade during the three years preceding the year in which each negotiation is effected.

ARTICLE 10
The purpose of the negotiations—based on reciprocity of concessions—referred to in ARTICLE 4 shall be to expand and diversify trade and to promote the progressive complementarity of the economies of the countries in the Area.

In these negotiations the situation of those Contracting Parties whose levels of duties, charges and restrictions differ substantially from those of the other Contracting Parties shall be considered with due fairness.

ARTICLE 11
If, as a result of the concessions granted, significant and persistent disadvantages are created in respect of trade between one Contracting Party and the others as a whole in the products included in the liberalization programme, the Contracting Parties shall, at the request of the Contracting Party affected, consider steps to remedy these disadvantages with a view to the adoption of suitable, non-restrictive measures designed to promote trade at the highest possible levels.

ARTICLE 12
If, as a result of circumstances other than those referred to in ARTICLE 11, significant and persistent disadvantages are created in respect of trade in the products included in the liberalization programme, the Contracting Parties shall, at the request of the Contracting Party concerned, make every effort within their power to remedy these disadvantages.

ARTICLE 13
The reciprocity mentioned in ARTICLE 10 refers to the expected growth in the flow of trade between each Contracting Party and the others as a whole, in the products included in the liberalization programme and those which may subsequently be added.

Chapter III
EXPANSION OF TRADE AND ECONOMIC COMPLEMENTARITY
ARTICLE 14
In order to ensure the continued expansion and diversification of reciprocal trade, the Contracting Parties shall take steps:

(a) to grant one another, while observing the principle of reciprocity, concessions which will ensure that, in the first negotiation, treatment not less favourable than that which existed before the date of entry into force of the present Treaty is accorded to imports from within the Area;

(b) to include in the National Schedules the largest possible number of products in which trade is carried on among the Contracting Parties; and

(c) to add to these Schedules an increasing number of products which are not yet included in reciprocal trade.

ARTICLE 15
In order to ensure fair competitive conditions among the Contracting Parties and to facilitate the increasing integration and complementarity of their economies,

particularly with regard to industrial production, the Contracting Parties shall make every effort—in keeping with the liberalization objectives of the present Treaty—to reconcile their import and export régimes, as well as the treatment they accord to capital, goods and services from outside the Area.

ARTICLE 16
With a view to expediting the process of integration and complementarity referred to in ARTICLE 15, the Contracting Parties:

(a) shall endeavour to promote progressively closer co-ordination of the corresponding industrialization policies, and shall sponsor for this purpose agreements among representatives of the economic sectors concerned; and

(b) may negotiate mutual agreements on complementarity by industrial sectors.

ARTICLE 17
The complementarity agreements referred to in ARTICLE 16, sub-paragraph (b), shall set forth the liberalization programme to be applied to products of the sector concerned and may contain, *inter alia,* clauses designed to reconcile the treatment accorded to raw materials and other components used in the manufacture of these products.

Any Contracting Party concerned with the complementarity programmes shall be free to participate in the negotiation of these agreements.

The results of these negotiations shall, in every case, be embodied in protocols which shall enter into force after the Contracting Parties have decided that they are consistent with the general principles and purposes of the present Treaty.

Chapter IV
MOST-FAVOURED-NATION TREATMENT
ARTICLE 18
Any advantage, benefit, franchise, immunity or privilege applied by a Contracting Party in respect of a product originating in or intended for consignment to any other country shall be immediately and unconditionally extended to the similar product originating in or intended for consignment to the territory of the other Contracting Parties.

ARTICLE 19
The most-favoured-nation treatment referred to in ARTICLE 18 shall not be applicable to the advantages, benefits, franchises, immunities and privileges already granted or which may be granted by virtue of agreements among Contracting Parties or between Contracting Parties and third countries with a view to facilitating border trade.

ARTICLE 20
Capital originating in the Area shall enjoy, in the territory of each Contracting Party, treatment not less favourable than that granted to capital originating in any other country.

Chapter V
TREATMENT IN RESPECT OF INTERNAL TAXATION
ARTICLE 21
With respect to taxes, rates and other internal duties and charges, products originating in the territory of a Contracting Party shall enjoy, in the territory of another Contracting Party, treatment no less favourable than that accorded to similar national products.

ARTICLE 22

Each Contracting Party shall endeavour to ensure that the charges or other domestic measures applied to products included in the liberalization programme which are not produced, or are produced only in small quantities, in its territory, do not nullify or reduce any concession or advantage obtained by any Contracting Party during the negotiations.

If a Contracting Party considers itself injured by virtue of the measures mentioned in the previous paragraph, it may appeal to the competent organs of the Association with a view to having the matter examined and appropriate recommendations made.

Chapter VI
SAVING CLAUSES
ARTICLE 23

The Contracting Parties may, as a provisional measure and providing that the customary level of consumption in the importer country is not thereby lowered, authorize a Contracting Party to impose non-discriminatory restrictions upon imports of products included in the liberalization programme which originate in the Area, if these products are imported in such quantities or under such conditions that they have, or are liable to have, serious repercussions on specific productive activities of vital importance to the national economy.

ARTICLE 24

The Contracting Parties may likewise authorize a Contracting Party which has adopted measures to correct its unfavourable over-all balance of payments to extend these measures, provisionally and without discrimination, to intra-Area trade in the products included in the liberalization programme.

The Contracting Parties shall endeavour to ensure that the imposition of restrictions deriving from the balance-of-payments situation does not affect trade, within the Area, in the products included in the liberalization programme.

ARTICLE 25

If the situations referred to in ARTICLES 23 and 24 call for immediate action, the Contracting Party concerned may, as an emergency arrangement to be referred to the Contracting Parties, apply the measures provided for in the said ARTICLES. The measures adopted must immediately be communicated to the Committee mentioned in ARTICLE 33, which, if it deems necessary, shall convene a special session of the Conference.

ARTICLE 26

Should the measures envisaged in this chapter be prolonged for more than one year, the Committee shall propose to the Conference, referred to in ARTICLE 33, either *ex officio* or at the request of any of the Contracting Parties, the immediate initiation of negotiations with a view to eliminating the restrictions adopted.

The present ARTICLE does not affect the provisions of ARTICLE 8.

Chapter VII
SPECIAL PROVISIONS CONCERNING AGRICULTURE
ARTICLE 27

The Contracting Parties shall seek to co-ordinate their agricultural development and agricultural commodity trade policies, with a view to securing the most efficient utilization of their natural resources, raising the standard of living of the rural population, and guaranteeing normal supplies to consumers, without disorganizing the regular productive activities of each Contracting Party.

ARTICLE 28

Providing that no lowering of its customary consumption or increase in anti-economic production is involved, a Contracting Party may apply, within the period mentioned in ARTICLE 2, and in respect of trade in agricultural commodities of substantial importance to its economy that are included in the liberalization programme, appropriate non-discriminatory measures designed to:

(a) limit imports to the amount required to meet the deficit in internal production; and

(b) equalize the prices of the imported and domestic product.

The Contracting Party which decides to apply these measures shall inform the other Contracting Parties before it puts them into effect.

ARTICLE 29

During the period prescribed in ARTICLE 2 an attempt shall be made to expand intra-Area trade in agricultural commodities by such means as agreements among the Contracting Parties designed to cover deficits in domestic production.

For this purpose, the Contracting Parties shall give priority, under normal competitive conditions, to products originating in the territories of the other Contracting Parties, due consideration being given to the traditional flows of intra-Area trade.

Should such agreements be concluded among two or more Contracting Parties, the other Contracting Parties shall be notified before the agreements enter into force.

ARTICLE 30

The measures provided for in this Chapter shall not be applied for the purpose of incorporating, in the production of agricultural commodities, resources which imply a reduction in the average level of productivity existing on the date on which the present Treaty enters into force.

ARTICLE 31

If a Contracting Party considers itself injured by a reduction of its exports attributable to the lowering of the usual consumption level of the importer country as a result of the measures referred in ARTICLE 28 and/or an anti-economic increase in the production referred in the previous ARTICLE, it may appeal to the competent organs of the Association to study the situation and, if necessary, to make recommendations for the adoption of appropriate measures to be applied in accordance with ARTICLE 12.

Chapter VIII
MEASURES IN FAVOUR OF COUNTRIES AT A RELATIVELY LESS ADVANCED STAGE OF ECONOMIC DEVELOPMENT
ARTICLE 32

The Contracting Parties, recognizing that fulfillment of the purposes of the present Treaty will be facilitated by the economic growth of the countries in the Area that are at a relatively less advanced stage of economic development, shall take steps to create conditions conducive to such growth.

To this end, the Contracting Parties may:

(a) Authorize a Contracting Party to grant to another Contracting Party which is at a relatively less advanced stage of economic development within the Area, as long as necessary and as a temporary measure, for the purposes set out in the present ARTICLE, advantages not extended to the other Contracting Parties, in order to encourage the introduction or expansion of specific productive activities;

(b) Authorize a Contracting Party at a relatively less advanced stage of economic development within the Area to implement the programme for the reduction of duties, charges and other restrictions under more favourable conditions, specially agreed upon;

(c) Authorize a Contracting Party at a relatively less advanced stage of economic development within the Area to adopt appropriate measures to correct an unfavourable balance of payments, if the case arises;

(d) Authorize a Contracting Party at a relatively less advanced stage of economic development within the Area to apply, if necessary and as a temporary measure, and providing that this does not entail a decrease in its customary consumption, appropriate non-discriminatory measures designed to protect the domestic output of products included in the liberalization programme which are of vital importance to its economic development;

(e) Make collective arrangements in favour of a Contracting Party at a relatively less advanced stage of economic development within the Area with respect to the support and promotion, both inside and outside the Area, of financial or technical measures designed to bring about the expansion of existing productive activities or to encourage new activities, particularly those intended for the industrialization of its raw materials; and

(f) Promote or support, as the case may be, special technical assistance programmes for one or more Contracting Parties, intended to raise, in countries at a relatively less advanced stage of economic development within the Area, productivity levels in specific production sectors.

Chapter IX
ORGANS OF THE ASSOCIATION
ARTICLE 33

The organs of the Association are the Conference of the Contracting Parties (referred to in this Treaty as "the Conference") and the Standing Executive Committee (referred to in this Treaty as "the Committee").

ARTICLE 34

The Conference is the supreme organ of the Association. It shall adopt all decisions in matters requiring joint action on the part of the Contracting Parties, and it shall be empowered, *inter alia:*

(a) To take the necessary steps to carry out the present Treaty and to study the results of its implementation;

(b) To promote the negotiations provided for in ARTICLE 4 and to assess the results thereof;

(c) To approve the Committee's annual budget and to fix the contributions of each Contracting Party;

(d) To lay down its own rules of procedure and to approve the Committee's rules of procedure;

(e) To elect a Chairman and two Vice-Chairmen for each session;

(f) To appoint the Executive Secretary of the Committee; and

(g) To deal with other business of common interest.

ARTICLE 35

The Conference shall be composed of duly accredited representatives of the Contracting Parties. Each delegation shall have one vote.

ARTICLE 36

The Conference shall hold: (a) a regular session once a year; and (b) special sessions when convened by the Committee.

At each session the Conference shall decide the place and date of the following regular session.

ARTICLE 37

The Conference may not take decisions unless at least two-thirds (2/3) of the Contracting Parties are present.

ARTICLE 38

During the first two years in which the present Treaty is in force, decisions of the Conference shall be adopted when affirmative votes are cast by at least two-thirds (2/3) of the Contracting Parties and providing that no negative vote is cast.

The Contracting Parties shall likewise determine the voting system to be adopted after this two-year period.

The affirmative vote of two-thirds (2/3) of the Contracting Parties shall be required:

(a) To approve the Committee's annual budget;

(b) To elect the Chairman and Vice-Chairmen of the Conference, as well as the Executive Secretary; and

(c) To fix the time and place of the sessions of the Conference.

ARTICLE 39

The Committee is the permanent organ of the Association responsible for supervising the implementation of the provisions of the present Treaty. Its duties and responsibilities shall be, *inter alia:*

(a) To convene the Conference;

(b) To submit for the approval of the Conference an annual work programme and the Committee's annual budget estimates;

(c) To represent the Association in dealings with third countries and international organs and entities for the purpose of considering matters of common interest. It shall also represent the Association in contracts and other instruments of public and private law;

(d) To undertake studies, to suggest measures and to submit to the Conference such recommendations as it deems appropriate for the effective implementation of the Treaty;

(e) To submit to the Conference at its regular sessions an annual report on its activities and on the results of the implementation of the present Treaty;

(f) To request the technical advice and the co-operation of individuals and of national and international organizations;

(g) To take such decisions as may be delegated to it by the Conference; and

(h) To undertake the work assigned to it by the Conference.

ARTICLE 40

The Committee shall consist of a Permanent Representative of each Contracting Party, who shall have a single vote.

Each Representative shall have an Alternate.

ARTICLE 41

The Committee shall have a Secretariat headed by an Executive Secretary and comprising technical and administrative personnel.

The Executive Secretary, elected by the Conference for a three-year term and re-eligible for similar periods, shall attend the plenary meetings of the Committee without the right to vote.

The Executive Secretary shall be the General Secretary of the Conference. His duties shall be, *inter alia:*

(a) To organize the work of the Conference and of the Committee;

(b) To prepare the Committee's annual budget estimates; and

(c) To recruit and engage the technical and administrative staff in accordance with the Committee's rules of procedure.

ARTICLE 42

In the performance of their duties, the Executive Secretary and the Secretariat staff shall not seek or receive instructions from any Government or from any other national or international entity. They shall refrain from any action which might reflect on their position as international civil servants.

The Contracting Parties undertake to respect the international character of the responsibilities of the Executive Secretary and of the Secretariat staff and shall refrain from influencing them in any way in the discharge of their responsibilities.

ARTICLE 43

In order to facilitate the study of specific problems, the Committee may set up Advisory Commissions composed of representatives of the various sectors of economic activity of each of the Contracting Parties.

ARTICLE 44

The Committee shall request, for the organs of the Association, the technical advice of the Secretariat of the United Nations Economic Commission for Latin America (ECLA) and of the Inter-American Economic and Social Council (IA-ECOSOC) of the Organization of American States.

ARTICLE 45

The Committee shall be constituted sixty days from the entry into force of the present Treaty and shall have its headquarters in the city of Montevideo.

Chapter X
JURIDICAL PERSONALITY—IMMUNITIES AND PRIVILEGES
ARTICLE 46

The Latin American Free-Trade Association shall possess complete juridical personality and shall, in particular, have the power:

(a) To contract;

(b) To acquire and dispose of the movable and immovable property it needs for the achievement of its objectives;

(c) To institute legal proceedings; and

(d) To hold funds in any currency and to transfer them as necessary.

ARTICLE 47

The representatives of the Contracting Parties and the international staff and advisers of the Association shall enjoy in the Area such diplomatic and other immunities and privileges as are necessary for the exercise of their functions.

The Contracting Parties undertake to conclude, as soon as possible, an Agreement regulating the provisions of the previous paragraph in which the aforesaid privileges and immunities shall be defined.

The Association shall conclude with the Government of the Eastern Republic of Uruguay an Agreement for the purpose of specifying the privileges and immunities which the Association, its organs and its international staff and advisers shall enjoy.

Chapter XI
MISCELLANEOUS PROVISIONS
ARTICLE 48

No change introduced by a Contracting Party in its régime of import duties and charges shall imply a level of duties and charges less favourable than that in force before the change for any commodity in respect of which concessions are granted to the other Contracting Parties.

The requirement set out in the previous paragraph shall not apply to the conversion to present worth of the official base value (*aforo*) in respect of customs duties and charges, providing that such conversion corresponds exclusively to the real value of the goods. In such cases, the value shall not include the customs duties and charges levied on the goods.

ARTICLE 49

In order to facilitate the implementation of the provisions of the present Treaty, the Contracting Parties shall, as soon as possible:

(a) Determine the criteria to be adopted for the purpose of determining the origin of goods and for classifying them as raw materials, semi-manufactured goods or finished products;

(b) Simplify and standardize procedures and formalities relating to reciprocal trade;

(c) Prepare a tariff nomenclature to serve as a common basis for the presentation of statistics and for carrying out the negotiations provided for in the present Treaty;

(d) Determine what shall be deemed to constitute border trade within the meaning of ARTICLE 19;

(e) Determine the criteria for the purpose of defining "dumping" and other unfair trade practices and the procedures relating thereto.

ARTICLE 50

The products imported from the Area by a Contracting Party may not be re-exported save by agreement between the Contracting Parties concerned.

A product shall not be deemed to be a re-export if it has been subjected in the importer country to industrial processing or manufacture, the degree of which shall be determined by the Committee.

ARTICLE 51

Products imported or exported by a Contracting Party shall enjoy freedom of transit within the Area and shall only be subject to the payment of the normal rates for services rendered.

ARTICLE 52

No Contracting Party shall promote its exports by means of subsidies or other measures likely to disrupt normal competitive conditions in the Area.

An export shall not be deemed to have been subsidized if it is exempted from duties and charges levied on the product or its components when destined for internal consumption, or if it is subject to drawback.

ARTICLE 53

No provision of the present Treaty shall be so construed as to constitute an impediment to the adoption and execution of measures relating to:

(a) The protection of public morality;

(b) The application of security laws and regulations;

(c) The control of imports or exports of arms, ammunitions and other war equipment and, in exceptional circumstances, of all other military items, in so far as this is compatible with the terms of ARTICLE 51 and of the treaties on the unrestricted freedom of transit in force among the Contracting Parties;

(d) The protection of human, animal and plant life and health;

(e) Imports and exports of gold and silver bullion;

(f) The protection of the nation's heritage of artistic, historical and archaeological value; and

(g) The export, use and consumption of nuclear materials, radio-active products or any other material that may be used in the development or exploitation of nuclear energy.

ARTICLE 54

The Contracting Parties shall make every effort to direct their policies with a view to creating conditions favourable to the establishment of a Latin American common market. To that end, the Committee shall undertake studies and consider projects and plans designed to achieve this purpose, and shall endeavour to co-ordinate its work with that of other international organizations.

Chapter XII
FINAL CLAUSES
ARTICLE 55

The present Treaty may not be signed with reservations nor shall reservations be admitted at the time of ratification or accession.

ARTICLE 56

The present Treaty shall be ratified by the signatory States at the earliest opportunity.

The instruments of ratification shall be deposited with the Government of the Eastern Republic of Uruguay, which shall communicate the date of deposit to the Governments of the signatory and successively acceding States.

ARTICLE 57

The present Treaty shall enter into force for the first three ratifying States thirty days after the third instrument of ratification has been deposited; and, for the other signatories, thirty days after the respective instrument of ratification has been deposited, and in the order in which the ratifications are deposited.

The Government of the Eastern Republic of Uruguay shall communicate the date of the entry into force of the present Treaty to the Government of each of the signatory States.

ARTICLE 58

Following its entry into force, the present Treaty shall remain open to accession by the other Latin American States, which for this purpose shall deposit the relevant instrument of accession with the Government of the Eastern Republic of Uruguay. The Treaty shall enter into force for the acceding State thirty days after the deposit of the corresponding instrument.

Acceding States shall enter into the negotiations referred to in ARTICLE 4 at the session of the Conference immediately following the date of deposit of the instrument of accession.

ARTICLE 59

Each Contracting Party shall begin to benefit from the concessions already granted to one another by the other Contracting Parties as from the date of entry into force of the reductions in duties and charges and other restrictions negotiated by them on a basis of reciprocity, and after the minimum obligations referred to in ARTICLE 5, accumulated during the period which has elapsed since the entry into force of the present Treaty, have been carried out.

ARTICLE 60

The Contracting Parties may present amendments to the present Treaty, which shall be set out in protocols that shall enter into force upon their ratification by all the Contracting Parties and after the corresponding instruments have been deposited.

ARTICLE 61

On the expiry of the twelve-year term starting on the date of entry into force of the present Treaty, the Contracting Parties shall proceed to study the results of the

Treaty's implementation and shall initiate the necessary collective negotiations with a view to fulfilling more effectively the purposes of the Treaty and, if desirable, to adapting it to a new stage of economic integration.

ARTICLE 62
The provisions of the present Treaty shall not affect the rights and obligations deriving from agreements signed by any of the Contracting Parties prior to the entry into force of the present Treaty.

However, each Contracting Party shall take the necessary steps to reconcile the provisions of existing agreements with the provisions of the present Treaty.

ARTICLE 63
The present Treaty shall be of unlimited duration.

ARTICLE 64
A Contracting Party wishing to withdraw from the present Treaty shall inform the other Contracting Parties of its intention at a regular session of the Conference, and shall formally submit the instrument of denunciation at the following regular session.

When the formalities of denunciation have been completed, those rights and obligations of the denouncing Government which derive from its status as a Contracting Party shall cease automatically, with the exception of those relating to reductions in duties and charges and other restrictions, received or granted under the liberalization programme, which shall remain in force for a period of five years from the date on which the denunciation becomes formally effective.

The period specified in the preceding paragraph may be shortened if there is sufficient jusification, with the consent of the Conference and at the request of the Contracting Party concerned.

ARTICLE 65
The present Treaty shall be called the Montevideo Treaty.

INDEX

245